THE PENGUIN POETS

D50

FRENCH VERSE

I: TO THE FIFTEENTH CENTURY

THE PENGUIN BOOK OF

FRENCH VERSE

I

TO THE FIFTEENTH CENTURY

*

INTRODUCED AND EDITED BY

BRIAN WOLEDGE

*

WITH PLAIN PROSE TRANSLATIONS
OF EACH POEM

PENGUIN BOOKS

Penguin Books Ltd, Harmondsworth, Middlesex, England
Penguin Books Inc., 7110 Ambassador Court, Baltimore, Maryland 21207, U.S.A.
Penguin Books Australia Ltd, Ringwood, Victoria, Australia

—

First published 1961
Reprinted 1966, 1968

—

Copyright © Brian Woledge, 1966

—

Made and printed in Great Britain
by Richard Clay (The Chaucer Press) Ltd,
Bungay, Suffolk
Set in Monotype Fournier

GENERAL EDITOR'S FOREWORD

THE purpose of these Penguin books of verse in the chief European languages is to make a fair selection of the world's finest poetry available to readers who could not, but for the translations at the foot of each page, approach it without dictionaries and a slow plodding from line to line. They offer even to those with fair linguistic knowledge the readiest introduction to each country's lyrical inheritance, and a sound base from which to make further explorations. The anthologist, too, gains a considerable advantage from this method, since he can choose much more freely among medieval, dialect, and difficult modern poems when he knows that all the reader's problems can be solved by a glance at the bottom of the page.

But these anthologies are not intended only for those with a command of languages. They should appeal also to the adventurous who, for sheer love of poetry, will attack a poem in a tongue almost unknown to them guided only by their previous reading and some Latin or French. In this way, if they are willing to start with a careful word-for-word comparison, they will soon dispense with the English, and read a poem by Petrarch, Campanella, or Montale, by Garcilaso, Góngora, or Lorca, straight through. Even German poetry can be approached in this unorthodox way. Something will, of course, always be lost, but not so much as will be gained.

The selections in each book have been made by the anthologist alone. But all alike reflect contemporary trends in taste, and include only poetry that can be read for pleasure. No specimens have been included for their historical interest, or to represent some particular school or phase of literary history.

J. M. COHEN

TABLE OF CONTENTS

*

BENOÎT DE SAINTE-MAURE (second half of the twelfth
century). Nothing is known for certain about his life; the town
of Sainte-Maure, from which he took his name, is near Chinon.
He is chiefly famous as the author of the *Roman de Troie*, and is
probably identical with the Benoît who succeeded Wace as
chronicler of the Dukes of Normandy. *Le Roman de Troie* is a
very free adaptation of Latin accounts of the Trojan War,
suited to contemporary aristocratic taste by the introduction of
love interest, as in the two extracts given. In the first, the poet
pictures the state of mind of the amorous Medea; in the second
he anatomizes the faithless Briseida (her change of heart is an
incident of his own invention later told by Boccaccio, Chaucer,
and Shakespeare, with the name changed to Cressida).

CHRÉTIEN DE TROYES (fl. 1160–90). One of the most
famous Old French poets, the author of the earliest extant
romances dealing with King Arthur and his knights. Five of
his Arthurian romances have survived.

BEROUL, a Norman of the second half of the twelfth century.
Nothing else of his survives but less than five thousand lines of
his *Tristran*, which must have been a romance of much greater
length.

MARIE DE FRANCE (second half of the twelfth century)
probably wrote for the Court of Henry II of England. Her lays
and fables seem to have been much appreciated in her own day.
The shortest of her twelve lays is given here complete.

CONTENTS

ix

CONTENTS

CONTENTS

xii

CONTENTS

CONTENTS

CONTENTS

CHRISTINE DE PISAN (1365–1431?). Her father was an Italian doctor in the service of the French king, and she was brought up at Court. Left a widow with three children at the age of twenty-five, she became to some extent a professional writer. Her works in prose and verse are extremely varied and reveal an unusually vigorous and intelligent personality. She was a delicate lyric poet, sometimes capable of expressing deep personal feelings.

ALAIN CHARTIER (1385–1429) spent much of his life in the service of King Charles VII, writing prose works on politics in both French and Latin. As a poet he is mainly famous for *La Belle Dame sans Merci*, a story in which a lady's refusal causes her suitor to die of love.

CONTENTS

CHARLES D'ORLÉANS (1394–1465), a member of the French royal family who was captured at Agincourt (1415) and kept a prisoner in England till 1440. His last years were spent peacefully at Blois, where he gathered round him a circle of poets. His works consist mostly of ballades and rondeaux, which he wrote with unrivalled mastery.

VAILLANT, a minor poet who belonged to the circle of Charles d'Orléans.

CONTENTS

ANONYMOUS RONDEAUX. Three of the large number of anonymous rondeaux which have come down to us from the fifteenth century.

FRANÇOIS VILLON (1431–63 or later). Took the degree of Master of Arts in Paris; concerned in various crimes; he was condemned to be hanged in 1463, but the sentence was changed to one of ten years' banishment from Paris. His most important work is his *Testament*, a half-serious, half-comic will, which includes most of his famous short poems. Though much of the *Testament* is of only ephemeral interest, it contains some great poetry.

CHANSONS POPULAIRES. These songs are taken from a collection made in the second half of the fifteenth century.

INTRODUCTION

THANKS to François Villon, English readers have long been familiar with the idea that great poetry was written in medieval France; yet many people are slow to venture beyond Villon, and some do not realize that Villon had behind him a tradition of French poetry stretching back for centuries. Others, who recognize that this vast literature exists, imagine that its artistic value is slight or that it is the preserve of the philologist. The truth is that Old French poetry, besides being of capital interest to the historian of civilization because of the influence it exerted in medieval Europe, is worth reading today for the simple reason that it offers us an immense amount of pleasure. This fact would be more widely recognized if the reader with an appetite for medieval poetry were better catered for; but anthologists tend to neglect the first six hundred years of French literature, and editors of single works generally write for the specialist and often pay more attention to literary history than to aesthetics. In the present series French medieval poetry takes its natural place beside the later and better-known poetry of France. What is offered to the reader in this first volume is a selection from the vast store of poetry written before 1500, chosen simply on the grounds of artistic merit.

*

From the ninth, tenth, and eleventh centuries only a handful of works in French verse have survived; doubtless other works existed, but we do not know how much literary activity there was in France at this stage. It is during the twelfth century that French poetry emerges as an immensely rich and varied literature, admired and imitated all over Western Europe. France was then, in many ways, the cultural and intellectual centre of Europe, the source not only of literary movements like the one that launched the romances of King Arthur and the Round Table but also of such new ideas and attitudes as those conveyed by the Old French words *courtesy* and *chivalry*.

Thanks to the Norman Conquest, England was closely associated with the great period of French literature. French was the language of the English Court and most of the nobility; many French works were written in England, and many copies of continental French works were made for English readers. In fact, Old French poetry of the twelfth century is a part of the literature of England.

By the fourteenth century the cultural leadership of Europe was passing to Italy, but literary output in French continued undiminished; there was perhaps less exciting experiment than in the twelfth and thirteenth centuries, and a larger output of inferior works, but there was also a continuous tradition of genuine poetry, at least until the disappearance of Villon in 1463.

The earliest surviving French poetry deals with Christian subjects, and the continuing importance of religion and the Church over the whole 600 years of medieval French literature may come as a surprise to the modern reader. It is not only that there is a steady stream of saints' lives, prayers, and sermons in verse, and that canons, monks, and bishops write some of the best poetry: for nearly 200 years the emotions aroused by the Crusades appear again and again in songs and epics, and indeed, throughout the Middle Ages, deep religious feeling may well up in almost any work, however much we label it 'secular'.

If the oldest poems can be seen as the natural product of a society so largely dominated by the Church, feudalism, the other face of medieval society, appears as the background against which we see the earliest secular literature. The oldest works of secular literature that have come down to us are the epic or heroic poems known as the *chansons de geste*. Nearly a hundred of these have survived, dating from about 1100 onwards. Though some of the authors seem to be concerned almost entirely with military prowess, the best of them are more interested in the moral questions of the knight's loyalty to his lord, to his companions, to his family, to God. Though the subjects are mostly taken from French history, the historical element is small: thus in the *Chanson de Roland*, the earliest epic we possess,

and the most famous as well as the greatest, the nucleus of the
story is an event that happened in 778, but it has been completely
transformed and re-created in the imagination of a man living
300 years later and taking his own feudal society and its values as
a matter of course. The best of these epic authors handle their
characters with superb understanding; they have considerable
narrative skill, and achieve great dramatic intensity. Not all the
poems are as tragic as the *Chanson de Roland*; some of them show
an attractive blend of humour and seriousness, as in the *Moniage
Guillaume*, where the author sees both the incongruity and the
pathos of the warrior who turns monk in his old age.

It was probably towards the middle of the twelfth century
that, side by side with these epics, the first romances appeared.
The contrast between the two genres is striking. In the romances
the love element comes to the fore, and the heroine takes her
place beside the hero. This raises a host of new questions about
the nature of love, its symptoms, its course, its place in life,
questions which seem to have had an inexhaustible fascination
for the French upper classes of the second half of the twelfth
century. It is in these romances that the knight errant first enters
literature, bringing with him new ideals of conduct and almost
a new way of looking at life. He is a Christian, of course, but he
is undeniably more secular than the epic warrior. He has felt the
touch of Virgil and Ovid, though he does not know their names
and their influence has reached him at second hand.

For this new matter a new style was evolved. The authors
of the early epics used assonanced * groups of ten-syllable lines,
with a slight pause at the end of each line, a style with a certain
stiffness, though capable of great nobility. In the romances verse
becomes elegant and supple, the new metre being the rhymed
octosyllabic couplet, which writers soon learned to break up and
twist into any shape that suited their fancy.

It is impossible to discuss this new literature without some
reference to Provençal (the language not only of Provence but

* The final words of the lines do not rhyme, but the final *vowel* is
similar for all the lines of each group or 'laisse'.

of all the southern half of France). It produced a sudden flowering of lyrical poetry in the first half of the twelfth century, and it was probably here that the new ideas were first expressed. The Provençal lyricists – the Troubadours – had well-established literary conventions; their matter was love, their manner closely prescribed: a new stanza form for each poem, five to seven stanzas metrically identical, and a tune composed by the poet.

Provençal differs so much from the Old French that none of these poems has been included in this book, but the Provençal conventions had spread to Northern France by the last third of the twelfth century, if not sooner, and can be seen in the songs of the Châtelain de Coucy, Gace Brulé, and Conon de Béthune, who achieved triumphs of metrical skill, and devoted their songs almost exclusively to the theme of love and the glorification of woman.

It is not surprising that such great changes in literature should have been described as a revolution – the 'courtly revolution'. It was not merely a literary movement, it was part of a profound and complex change in the outlook of the upper classes in Europe, a change shown by a more elegant and cultured life at the courts of the nobility, a higher standard of living, more leisure, more travel. The new and important place given to women in courtly literature no doubt reflects the change in their position in twelfth-century society, where they had become an important element in the poet's public.

The courtly revolution gave rise to the preoccupation with romantic love which was to be for so long the dominant idea of Western European literature, and many of the great and recurrent themes that have haunted that literature here first take literary shape. Benoît de Sainte-Maure, in his *Romance of Troy*, though drawing much of his material from the Ancients, greatly expanded episodes which gave him a chance of applying the new-found skill in the analysis of love, and completely invented others, for instance the story of Troilus and Cressida. It was French romance writers, drawing on Celtic legends, who gave to the world the story of Tristram and Iseult; others exploited the vast new field of Arthurian legend (we need not ask ourselves here how far their sources were Celtic, though this has long been a matter of dispute). It was Chrétien de Troyes who gave to Western Europe the stories of Lancelot and of the Grail: they doubtless existed in some form or other before he took them up, but they owed their success to his narrative skill and to his artistry in combining a realistic treatment of character with a setting full of magic and mystery. No doubt some of his public appreciated the realism more than the mystery, and they were soon catered for by other authors. Jean Renart is perhaps the best of a number of poets who gave their romances a realistic setting. His tales are full of lively wit and amused observation of his contemporaries. Altogether about sixty or seventy verse romances survive and most of them contain passages well worth quoting, but in a book of this kind it is obviously quite impossible to do them justice.

It must not be thought that all the literature of the time shared the courtly tone of the romances. A flourishing satirical vein was being developed at the same time in the *Roman de Renart* and the fabliaux and beginning to colour lyrical poetry. Meanwhile such social changes as the growth of town life were a potential threat to courtly ideas, though these were still powerful throughout the thirteenth century and persisted long after. In Arras, which in the thirteenth century was one of the most flourishing towns in France, there was great literary activity, and the most important poet of Arras, Adam de la Halle, still wrote the old courtly type of song and excelled at it. But in Paris, Rutebeuf, even when writing for aristocratic patrons, speaks of his own poverty in a direct, realistic, and personal style that is new to French literature, while Colin Muset in Lorraine is celebrating the pleasures of good food and an easy life.

The biggest change in the thirteenth-century outlook, however, came with the *Roman de la Rose*, the most famous of all Old French poems. Guillaume de Lorris, who started the work about 1240, set out to analyse the course of a love-affair. He cast his story in the form of a dream, narrated by the lover; the heroine never appears as a woman; she is symbolized by a rose-bud, which the lover finds in the enchanted garden of the God of Love. His efforts to reach and pluck the rose represent the course of his love. He is helped and hindered by a crowd of allegorical characters, some standing for the characteristics and moods of his lady (Chastity, Shame, Fear, Pity, Fair Welcome), some for his own state of mind (Hope, Sweet Thought, and so on), and some for the society that surrounds the lovers (Slander, Riches, Reason, and many more). This was a subject very much to the taste of the courtly public, and the allegorical treatment was to set a fashion all over Europe; besides this, Guillaume de Lorris wrote brilliantly, so that the poem had all the ingredients of success; but it was left unfinished, presumably because of Guillaume's death.

About forty years later the story was taken up again by Jean de Meung, equally brilliant as a writer, but a man of a completely different turn of mind. Before he allowed the lover to pluck the Rose, he added no less than eighteen thousand lines to the poem, pouring into it his ideas on every subject that interested him: social relations and morals, religion, philosophy, and science. In dealing with the love theme, he completely rejected the courtly tradition and dealt with love as Nature's device for the propagation of the species, while he made women the target for some of his most biting satire: the advice given to the lover about the treatment of women is full of the implications of the sex war. But in spite of their cynicism, his references to women are packed with instances of humorous observation and some-times of sympathetic understanding; they were to prove a rich quarry for subsequent writers: here Chaucer found very much of the *Wife of Bath* and Villon almost all of *La Belle Hëaumiere*. The complete poem enjoyed a tremendous and lasting success, probably owing more to the challenging ideas of Jean de Meung than to the charming fancies of Guillaume de Lorris. It must certainly have been by far the most widely read of all medieval French poems: the number of surviving manuscripts runs into hundreds.

When we reach the fourteenth and fifteenth centuries, poetry gradually assumes a look that is more familiar to the modern reader. Prose fiction gains new territory, so that there is less narrative poetry, and lyrical work forms a larger and larger proportion of the total output. There is less anonymous work and a keener sense of literary property; the greatest writers are less shadowy figures; we know about their lives and possess something like their complete works in something very near the form they intended them to have. The outline of literary history tends to become a procession of great names in lyrical poetry: Guillaume de Machaut, Eustache Deschamps, Christine de Pisan, Charles d'Orléans, Villon. There are plenty of lesser figures, certainly, and in the background a swarm of minor writers who turn out ballades and rondeaux because it is the fashionable amusement.

In fact, it had never before been so easy to write French poetry of a sort, and perhaps it has never been so easy since. The recipe was simple: take one or more allegorical figures, preferably from the *Roman de la Rose*, mix with the leftovers of courtly love (dying for love, inaccessible lady, etc.), and pour into the ready-made mould of rondeau or ballade. If done neatly, the result can be quite palatable, but the modern reader at least looks for some added ingredient. This can be found in Machaut's polished urbanity and technical perfection (it was he who created the moulds, perhaps a doubtful gain for French poetry) or in Deschamps's realism and his wide choice of unexpected subjects. Christine de Pisan, trying to turn the tide of anti-feminism and revive the courtly spirit, shows in her best work great delicacy and sincerity in portraying the woman in love. It is Charles d'Orléans who most successfully exploits the allegorical inheritance of the *Roman de la Rose*. Every mood, every sentiment, every season is personified, and he creates a whole world of his own with its own atmosphere of enchantment, a world in which we can feel immediately at home even today.

The latest poet represented in this book is François Villon, who has long been by far the best-known of French medieval

poets, at least in England. If he has perhaps sometimes been re-
garded too much as an innovator, he still stands out above all
his contemporaries for intensity of feeling and force and direct-
ness of expression: he can convey to us the full poignancy of the
situation of the Outsider, the failure in society.

*

The fact that so many of the best Old French poems are long
narrative works creates a difficulty for the anthologist, which I
have solved by including a good many extracts (wherever the
complete poem is not given, omissions are shown by ...). But in
a book of this size it is not possible to give more than a taste of
Old French narrative poetry, which is far too vast to be properly represented; moreover, some of the best works, too long
to be given in full, defy quotation, and it has seemed best to ex-
clude them altogether: the reader will find nothing here from
Aucassin et Nicolette or the *Châtelaine de Vergy*, nor has it been
possible to find room for examples of the drama, the fabliaux, or
the *Roman de Renart*.

   In this book, as in the others of the series, the English translations are intended merely as a help in understanding the original;
it is hoped that the reader will submit them to no severer test.

LANGUAGE AND VERSIFICATION

For anyone who can read Modern French, it is not difficult to
get used to reading Old French, but a few hints about the language may be useful.

   An *s* at the end of a noun is nowadays almost always a sign
of the plural; it is often not so in Old French, and for a number
of poems in this book it is helpful to know the old system of
declension, which can be summarized thus:

   'The king' as subject of sentence: *li rois*
   'The king' otherwise: *le roi*
   'The kings' as subject of sentence: *li roi*
   'The kings' otherwise: *les rois*

This system was at one time in use for most masculine nouns and
adjectives, but our poems cover the period when it was gradually

dying out, so that while some of them show declension used consistently, others show it spasmodically, and the later poets, such as Charles d'Orléans and Villon, do not use it at all. With so much variety, it is sometimes the verb that is the best guide to whether the subject is singular or plural: 'cling to the verb' is useful advice to anyone in difficulties with an Old French sentence.

Words such as *je*, *tu*, *il* are often not present in Old French sentences, so that, for example, *voit* by itself means *he sees* (this and many other peculiarities will give no trouble to the reader who can think of Old French as a stage on the way from Latin to Modern French).

In some ways the English reader has an advantage over the French reader who tackles the medieval language: the constructions tend to be free and easy, more like those of English than the very formalized grammar of French as it has been since the classical period. English, too, which was so mixed up with French after 1066, has preserved some medieval words and meanings that have been given up on the Continent: *fail, remain, despise* all occur in the poems below, used much as we still use them.

Old French contains many more contractions than the modern language: *si les* becomes *ses*, *en le* becomes *el*, later *ou*, and so on. Fortunately, these forms gradually become rarer as we reach modern times (the only survivors today are *du*, *des*, *au*, and *aux*).

One of the commonest Old French words is *si*; its meaning is not 'if', but something more like 'and'; the Old French for 'if' is *se*. Other common words that are liable to be misunderstood are:

a, 'there is, there are'
aïe, 'help'
ainc ... ne, 'never'
ainz, 'before; but' (not to be confused with *ainsi*)
baillier, 'to give' and also 'to touch'
ça, 'here'

car is used to strengthen the imperative, as well as having its modern use

cheoir, 'to fall'

choisir, 'to notice'

ci, 'here'

ço, 'that'

corage, 'feeling, desire'

crient, 'he fears'

cuens, 'count, lord'

cui, 'whom, to whom'

cuider, 'to think'

dont, 'hence, so that' (also modern use)

el, (i) 'en le', (ii) 'otherwise', (iii) 'she'

ert, 'he was', 'he will be'

estuet, 'it is necessary'

ferir, 'to strike'

garir, 'to be saved', 'to recover' (modern *guérir*)

gesir, 'to lie'

hui, 'today'

i- can be prefixed to any demonstrative with no effect on the meaning, thus *ice* = *ce*. Also added to *donc*, *tant*, and *tel*

illuec, 'there'

issir, 'to go out'

ja, 'soon'; its meaning is often a rather vague 'indeed'

jus, 'down'

lé, 'wide'

lès, 'beside'

li, (i) definite article, (ii) pronoun corresponding to certain modern uses of *lui* and *elle*

lié, 'glad'

mais has its modern meaning, but also others, of which the most important is 'henceforth'

mar, 'unfortunately'

ne, 'not'; 'and, or' (with a negative idea in the background); also has its modern uses.

nen, 'not'

o, 'with'
onc, 'ever'
or, 'now'
ot, (i) 'he had', (ii) 'there was', (iii) 'he hears'
paor, 'fear'
pieça, 'some time ago'
que has most of its modern uses, and also corresponds to modern
    'car' and 'pourquoi'
querre, 'to seek'
rien, 'thing'; *ne ... rien*, 'not a thing, nothing'
talent, 'desire, wish, feelings'
tolir, 'to take away'
traire, 'to pull, draw, shoot'
trop, (i) 'very', (ii) 'too much'
truis, 'I find'
tuit, 'all' (masculine plural subject)
uis, 'door'
veuil, (i) 'I wish', (ii) 'wish' (noun)
vis, 'face'; *estre vis*, 'to seem'
voir, 'true, truly' ('to see' is *veoir*)
vois, 'I go' ('I see' is *voi*)

French spelling in the Middle Ages was not a matter of rules, and each scribe spelt as he liked, swayed by such influences as the sound of the word as he heard it, the look of the word as he was used to seeing it, and mere force of habit. The immense variety and inconsistency of Old French spelling has been considerably lessened in this book, though the spelling has been kept medieval. The main principle has been to spell in the most modern way that is consistent with medieval habits. Thus the line which appears in the MS. of Charles d'Orléans' poem as

Alez vous ant allez ales

I have printed as

Allez vous en, allez, allez

(taking the most modern of the three spellings of *allez* used by the scribe, and rejecting *ant*, which was rare even in the fifteenth century, in favour of *en*, which was already almost universal). I have not attempted complete uniformity of spelling: it would have been impossible to achieve without giving an entirely false picture, since the language was changing rapidly and the spelling suitable for the eleventh-century Western poem on the life of St Alexis would have been quite unsuitable for Villon, a fifteenth-century Parisian.

As for accents, medieval scribes hardly used any; modern scholars usually add a few when printing Old French, and I have added rather more than is usual. All those used here have the function of distinguishing words which might otherwise be confused.

Old French versification is fundamentally like that of Modern French, the main elements being rhyme (superseding the old system of assonance during the twelfth century) and the number of syllables in the line. To make the lines scan, it is necessary to pronounce a great many *e*'s which have since become silent, and to be prepared for adjacent vowels to form sometimes a single syllable, sometimes two. It is impossible to give all the rules here, but the following lines will show the system:

> Se je i fuss(e) à tens venue
>
> Vie vous eüsse rendue,
>
> Et parlé doucement à vous
>
> De l'amour qui fu entre nous.
>
> Plaint(e) eüsse nostr(e) aventure,
>
> Nostre joie, nostr(e) envoisure.

(Note that weak *e* at the end of a line is not counted; and that at the end of a word weak *e* disappears if the next word begins with a vowel.) Every length of line from two to thirteen syllables occurs in this book, but the most common are seven syllables (frequent in lyric verse), eight (normal in romances), and ten (normal in epics). It is useful to remember the so-called epic cesura, which allows an extra weak *e* at the pause in lines of ten or twelve syllables.

Apart from the rule about weak *e*, it is difficult to give much advice about pronunciation because of the immense changes that took place during the 450 years covered by this book. At the beginning of the period there were very few silent letters and spelling was largely phonetic (for example, the *s*'s in words like *escoles* could be heard as well as seen and in groups like *oi*, *au*, *eau* each vowel kept its own value). Changes came quickly, and by Villon's time French sounded much as it does today, although spelling was by then often archaic (we still show twelfth-century pronunciation when we write *rois*, which once rhymed with voice, and *faute* the first two vowels of which were once pronounced like *ou* in *about*, and so on).

A few modern rules that will be familiar to the reader are valid for the Middle Ages. *U* already had its typical French sound; *c* and *g* were hard before *a*, *o*, *u* and soft before *i* and *e*; *ch* and soft *g* (both found in words like *charge*) took their modern sounds about the thirteenth century (in earlier poems the reader who wants accuracy should pronounce the consonants as in English 'charge'); the letter *j* has the same values as soft *g*.

*

I should like to thank Mr J. M. Cohen for his advice on many aspects of this book, Miss G. E. Brereton, Dr D. J. A. Ross, and Professor T. B. W. Reid, who have helped me with difficult points of translation, and especially my wife, whose constant collaboration has been essential.

from LA VIE DE SAINT ALEXIS

... D E la dolor qu'en demena li pere
Grant fut la noise, si l'entendit la mere:
La vint corant com femme forsenee,
Batant ses palmes, criant, eschevelee;
Vit mort son fils, à terre chet pasmee.

Qui donc li vit son grant duel demener,
Son piz debatre et son cors dejeter,
Ses crins derompre et son vis maiseler,
Son mort enfant detraire et acoler,
Moult fust il dur qui n'estoüst plorer.

Trait ses chevels et debat sa poitrine,
A grant duel met la soe carn meïsme:
«E! fils, dist ele, com m'eüs enhaïe!
Et jo, dolent, com par fui avoglie!
Net conoisseie plus qu'onques net veïsse.»

from THE LIFE OF ST ALEXIS

... G REAT was the noise of the lament that his father made for
him, and his mother heard it. She came running like a mad woman,
beating her hands together, wailing, dishevelled; she saw her dead
son and fell fainting to the ground.

Anyone who saw her then, giving way to her great grief, beating
her breast and throwing herself to the ground, tearing her hair and
clawing her face, clasping her dead son to her and embracing him,
would have been hard-hearted indeed if he had not felt obliged to
weep.

She tears her hair and beats her breast; she puts her own flesh to
great torment. 'Oh! my son,' she says,' how cruel you were to me,
and I alas! how utterly I was blinded. I knew you no more than if
I had never seen you.'

I

Plorent si oil et si jete granz criz;
Sempres regrete: «Mar te portai, bels fils!
Et de ta mere que n'aveies merci?
Pur teim veeies desirer à morir,
Ço'st grant merveille que pieté ne t'en prist.

«A! lasse, mezre, com oi fort aventure!
Or vei je morte tote ma porteüre.
Ma longe atente à grant duel est venue.
Por queit portai, dolente, malfeüe?
C'est grant merveille que li miens cuers tant dure.

«Fils Alexis, moult eüs dur corage,
Com avilas tot ton gentil lignage!
Se à mei sole vels une feis parlasses,
Ta lasse mere, si la reconfortasses,
Qui si'st dolente. Cher fils, bor i alasses.

«Fils Alexis, de la toue carn tendre!
A quel dolor deduit as ta jovente!
Por quèim fuïs? Jat portai en mon ventre,
Et Dieus le set que tote sui dolente;
Ja mais n'er liee pour homme ne por femme. ...

Her eyes weep, and she cries out aloud; often she laments: 'Alas! that I ever bore you, my fair son! Oh! why did you not have mercy on your son? You saw me longing for death for your sake; it is a great marvel that you did not take pity on me.

'Alas! poor woman, what dreadful news I hear. Now I see all my offspring dead. My long waiting has ended in great grief. Why did I bear you, wretched ill-fated woman? It is a great wonder that my heart has not yet broken.

'Alexis, my son! how hard a heart you had when you scorned all your noble family. If you had only been willing to speak even once to me, your poor mother, then you would have consoled her who is so full of sorrow. It would have been well if you had gone to her.

'Alexis, my son! alas for your tender flesh! In what hardship you have spent your youth. Why did you flee from me? I bore you in my body, and God knows that now I am full of grief and never more shall be glad for any man or woman. ...

«Ainz quet veïsse, sin fui moult desirose;
Ainz que né fusses, sin fui moult angossose;
Quant jot vi né, sin fui liee et joiose.
Or te vei mort, tote en sui dolerose.
Ço peise mei que ma fin tant demore.

«Seignors de Rome, por amor Dieu, merci!
Aidiez m'à plaindre le duel de mon ami.
Grans est li duels qui sor mei est vertis,
Ne puis tant faire que mes cuers s'en sazit:
N'est pas merveille: n'ai mais fille ne fils.» ...

from LA CHANSON DE ROLAND

... Paien s'adobent des osbercs sarazineis,
Tuit li plusor en sont doblés en treis;
Lacent lor helmes molt bons sarragozeis,
Ceignent espees de l'acier vianeis;
Escus ont genz, espiez valentineis
Et gonfanons blancs et blois et vermeils;

'Before I saw you, then I longed for you; before you were born,
then was I full of anguish; when I saw you born, then was I glad
and joyful. Now I see you dead, and I am filled with sorrow. It
grieves me that my death is so long delayed.

'Lords of Rome, for the love of God, take pity on me. Help me
to bewail the loss of my beloved. Great is the sadness that is come
upon me; I cannot grieve enough to sate my heart with sorrow; it
is no wonder: I have no longer daughter or son.'

from THE SONG OF ROLAND

... The Paynims arm themselves with Saracen hauberks, almost
all of them with triple thickness of chain mail, they lace their excellent Saragossan helmets, and gird on their swords of Viana steel;
they have noble shields and lances from Valence, and pennons
white and blue and red; they have left the mules and palfreys and

Laissent les muls et tos les palefreis,
Es destriers montent, si chevalchent estreis.
Clers fut li jors et bels fut li soleilz,
N'ont garnement que tot ne reflambeit;
Sonent mil grailes por ce que plus bel seit;
Grans est la noise, si l'oïrent Franceis.
Dist Oliver: «Sire compains, ce crei,
De Sarrazins porrons bataille aveir.»
Respont Rollant: «Et Dieus la nos otreit!
Bien devons ci estre por nostre rei:
Por son seignor deit hom sofrir destreis
Et endurer et granz chalz et granz freiz,
Sin deit hom perdre et del cuir et del peil.
Or gart chascuns que granz colps i empleit,
Que malvaise chançon de nos chanté ne seit!
Paien ont tort et chrestiens ont dreit;
Malvaise essample n'en sera ja de mei.» A O I

Oliver est desur un pui halçor,
Garde sur destre parmi un val herbos,
Si veit venir cele gent paienor,

are mounted on chargers and ride in serried ranks. Clear was the day and bright was the sun; not a piece of armour that did not sparkle; they sound a thousand bugles so that [their array] may be more splendid. The noise is great; the French heard it. Said Oliver: 'Sir comrade, I believe we may come to battle with the Saracens.' Roland replied: 'May God grant that to us! We must hold out here for our king: for his lord, a man must suffer distress and endure both great heat and great cold, and for his sake a man should be prepared to lose both skin and hair. Now let every man see that he deals mighty blows, so that a bad song may not be sung about us. The Pagans are in the wrong and the Christians in the right; my deeds shall never be told as a bad example.' A O I*

Oliver is on a lofty hill. He looks to the right through a grassy valley and sees the people of the Pagans coming; and he calls to

---

* These letters are repeated at intervals throughout the *Chanson de Roland*; their meaning is unknown.

Sin apela Rollant son compaignon:
«Devers Espaigne vei venir tel brunor,
Tanz blancs osbercs, tanz helmes flambios;
Icil feront nos Franceis grant iror.
Guenes le sout, li fel, li traïtor, .
Qui nos jugea devant l'empereor.»
«Tais, Oliver, li cuens Rollant respont,
Mis parrastre est, ne voeil que mot en sons.»

Oliver est desur un pui monté;
Or veit il bien d'Espaigne le regné
Et Sarrazins qui tant sont assemblé.
Luisent cil helme qui à or sont gemmé
Et cil escu et cil osbercs safré,
Et cil espié, cil gonfanon fermé;
Sol les escheles ne poet il aconter:
Tant en i a que mesure n'en set.
En lui meïsme en est moult esgaré;
Com il ainz pout, del pui est avalé,
Vint as Franceis, tot lor a aconté.

Dist Oliver: «Jo ai paiens veüs,
Onc mais nuls hom en terre n'en vit plus.

Roland, to his companion: 'From Spain I see such a tumult coming, so many white hauberks, so many shining helmets. These will do great damage to our Frenchmen. Ganelon knew it, the coward, the traitor, when he proposed us before the emperor [for the rearguard].' 'Be silent, Oliver,' Count Roland replies, 'he is my stepfather, I do not want you to say a word against him.'

Oliver has climbed a height; now he can see the kingdom of Spain, and the Saracens who are assembled in such numbers, the helmets shining with gems set in gold, and the shields and the yellow-burnished hauberks, and the lances with pennons fixed. He cannot even count the battalions; there are so many that he does not know the sum of them. Within his heart he is greatly distressed. As fast as he could, he came down from the height, came to the French and told them all.

Said Oliver: 'I have seen the Pagans; never before did any man on earth see more of them. There before us are a hundred thousand

Cil devant sont cent mile à escus,
Helmes laciés et blancs osbercs vestus,
Dreites ces hanstes, luisent cil espié brun.
Bataille avrez, onques mais tel ne fut.
Seignors Franceis, de Dieu aiez vertu;
El champ estez, que ne seions vencus.»
Dient Franceis: «Dehet ait qui s'en fuit.
Ja por morir ne vos en faldra uns.» A O I

Dist Oliver: «Paien ont grant esforz;
De nos Franceis m'i semble aveir moult poi.
Compaign Rollant, car sonez vostre corn,
Si l'orra Charles, si retornera l'ost.»
Respont Rollant: «Je fereie que fols;
En dolce France en perdreie mon los.
Sempres ferrai de Durendal grans colps,
Sanglant en ert li branz entresqu'à l'or.
Felon paien mar i vindrent as porz.
Je vos plevis, tos sont jugés à mort.» A O I

«Compaign Rollant, l'olifan car sonez!
Si l'orra Charles, fera l'ost retorner.

bearing their shields, helmets laced, wearing white hauberks, their lances shining brown with shafts upraised. You will have a battle such as never before was seen. French lords! may God give you His strength. Hold your ground that we may not be defeated.' The French say: 'Curse the man who flees. Not one will fail you, even in the face of death.' A O I

Said Oliver: 'The Pagans are in great strength, and of our French it seems to me there are but few. Roland, my comrade, now sound your horn, and Charles will hear it and the army will come back.' Roland replies: 'I should behave like a madman [if I did]; I should lose my renown in sweet France. I shall straightway strike great blows with Durendal, his blade shall be bloody to the gold of the hilt. In an ill hour for them the Pagans have come to the pass: I swear to you they are all doomed to death.' A O I

'Comrade Roland, now sound the horn, and Charles will hear it

Soccorra nos li reis o son barné.»
Respont Rollant: «Ne place Damnedeu
Que mi parent por mei seient blasmé,
Ne France dolce ja chee en vilté.
Ainz i ferrai de Durendal assez,
Ma bone espee que ai ceint al costé:
Tot en verrez le brant ensanglanté.
Felon paien mar i sont assemblés.
Je vos plevis, tos sont à mort livrés.» A O I

«Compaign Rollant, sonez vostre olifan,
Si l'orra Charles, qui est as porz passant.
Je vos plevis, ja retorneront Franc.»
«Ne place Dieu, ce li respont Rollant,
Que ce seit dit de nul home vivant
Ne por paien que je seie cornant!
Ja n'en avront reproece mi parent.
Quant je serai en la bataille grant
Et je ferrai et mil colps et set cenz,
De Durendal verrez l'acer sanglent.
Franceis sont bon, si ferront vassalment;
Ja cil d'Espaigne n'avront de mort garant.»

and will make the host turn back. The king with his barons will
come to our help.' Roland replies: 'May it never please God that
my kin should be reproached for my sake, nor that sweet France
should fall into contempt! Rather will I strike hard with Durendal,
my good sword which I have girded at my side; you shall see the
blade all stained with blood. In an ill hour for them the wicked
Pagans have assembled. I swear to you they are all delivered to
death.' A O I

'Comrade Roland, sound your horn, and Charles will hear it as
he goes through the pass; I swear to you the French will come back
at once.' 'May it not please God,' Roland replies, 'that it should be
said by any living man that I had sounded my horn for the Pagans.
My kindred shall never be reproached for that. When I am in the
great fight and I strike a thousand blows and seven hundred, you
will see Durendal's blade all bloody. The French are brave and will
strike boldly; the men of Spain will never escape death.'

Dist Oliver: «D'iço ne sai je blasme;
Je ai veü les Sarrazins d'Espaigne:
Covert en sont li val et les montaignes
Et li lariz et trestotes les plaignes.
Grans sont les os de cele gent estrange,
Nos i avons moult petite conpaigne.»
Respont Rollant: «Mis talenz en engraigne!
Ne place Damnedeu ne ses angles
Que ja por mei perde sa valor France!
Mielz voeil morir que hontage me vegne;
Por bien ferir l'emperere plus nos aime.» ...

... Li cuens Rollant des soens i veit grant perte,
Son compaignon Oliver en apele:
«Bel sire, chers compainz, por Dieu, que vos en haite?
Tanz bons vassals veez gesir par terre!
Plaindre poons France douce, la bele:
De tels barons com or remaint deserte!
E! reis, amis, que vos ici nen estes!
Oliver, frere, com le porrons nos faire?
Comfaitement li manderons noveles?»

Said Oliver: 'In this I know no blame. I have seen the Saracens of Spain; the valleys and the mountains are covered with them, and the hillsides and all the plains. Great are the hosts of these foreign people, and we have but a small company.' Roland replies: 'My eagerness is the greater because of that. May it never please God or his angels that through me France should lose her good name. I would rather die than that shame should come to me. For our hard blows the emperor loves us better.' ...

... Count Roland sees the great losses of his men. He calls his companion Oliver: 'Fair sir, dear companion, for God's sake, what seems right to you? So many brave knights you see lying on the ground! Well may we pity fair sweet France: how deeply she will feel the loss of these noble men! Ah! king, friend, if only you were here! Oliver, my brother, how can we do it? how can we send news

Dist Oliver: «Jo nel sai coment querre.
Mielz voeil morir que honte nos seit retraite.» AOI

Ço dist Rollant: «Cornerai l'olifant,
Si l'orra Charles, qui est as porz passant.
Je vos plevis, ja retorneront Franc.»
Dist Oliver: «Vergoigne sereit grant
Et reprover à trestoz vos parenz;
Iceste honte dureit al lor vivant.
Quant jel vos dis, n'en feïstes nient;
Mais nel ferez par le mien loement.
Se vos cornez, n'ert mie hardement:
Ja avez vos ambsdous les braz sanglanz.»
Respont li cuens: «Colps i ai fait molt genz.» AOI

Ço dit Rollant: «Forz est nostre bataille:
Je cornerai, si l'orra li reis Charles.»
Dist Oliver: «Ne sereit vasselage.
Quant jel vos dis, compainz, vos ne deignastes.
S'i fust li reis, n'i eüssons damage.
Cil qui là sont n'en deivent aveir blasme.»

to him?' Said Oliver: 'I do not know how to send for him; I would rather die than that a shameful tale should be told of us.' AOI

Said Roland: 'I will sound my horn, and Charles will hear it as he goes through the pass; I swear to you, the French will come back.' Said Oliver: 'It would be a great shame and reproach to all your kin, and this disgrace would last to the end of their lives. When I asked you to do it, you would not; you shall not do it now by my counsel. If you blow your horn [now], it will look like cowardice; by now your arms are both covered with blood.' The count replies: 'I have been striking mighty blows.' AOI

Says Roland: 'Our battle is hard: I shall blow my horn, and Charles the king will hear it.' Said Oliver: 'It would not be a knightly deed. When I asked you, companion, you did not deign to do it. If the king had been here, we should not have suffered these losses. Those who lie dead here must not have shame brought

Dist Oliver: «Par ceste meie barbe,
Se puis veeir ma gente soror Alde,
Ne gerreiez jamais entre sa brace.» A O I

Ço dist Rollant: «Por quei me portez ire?»
Et il respont: «Compainz, vos le feïstes,
Car vasselage par sens nen est folie;
Mielz valt mesure que ne fait estoltie.
Franceis sont mort par vostre legerie.
Jamais Charlon de nos n'avra servise.
Sem creïssez, venuz i fust mi sire;
Ceste bataille eüssons faite ou prise,
Ou pris ou mort i fust li reis Marsille.
Vostre proece, Rollant, mar la veïmes!
Charles li Magnes de nos n'avra aïe.
N'ert mais tel home dès qu'à Dieu juïse.
Vos i morrez et France en ert honie.
Hui nos defalt la leial compaignie:
Ainz le vespre molt ert grief la departie.» A O I

Li arcevesque les ot contrarier;
Le cheval broche des esperons d'or mier,

upon them.' Said Oliver: 'By this beard of mine, if ever I see my
sweet sister Alde again, you shall never lie in her arms.' A O I
    Then spoke Roland: 'Why are you angry with me?' and he re-
plied: 'Companion, the fault is yours, for valour tempered with
prudence is a different thing from folly, and discretion is better
than recklessness. The French lie dead for your foolhardiness. If
you had taken my advice, my lord would have come, we should
have [won] this battle, and King Marsille would have been killed or
captured. Little good has your bravery done us, Roland. Charlemagne will never again have our help – there will never again be
such a man as he until the Day of Judgement. You will die here and
France will be shamed for it. Today is the end of our loyal companionship: before evening will come our heavy parting.' A O I
    The Archbishop heard them disputing. He pricked his horse
with his spurs of pure gold, came up to them, and began to reprove

Vint tresqu'à els, sis prist à chastier:
«Sire Rollant, et vos, sire Oliver,
Por Dieu vos pri, ne vos contrariez.
Ja li corners ne nos avreit mestier,
Mais neporquant si est il assez mielz:
Vegne li reis, si nos porra venger.
Ja cil d'Espagne ne s'en deivent torner liez.
Nostre Franceis i descendront à pied,
Troveront nos et morz et detrenchés,
Leveront nos en bieres sur somers,
Si nos plorront de duel et de pitié;
Enfueront nos en aitres de mostiers,
N'en mengeront ne lu ne porc ne chien.»
Respont Rollant: «Sire, molt dites bien.» ...

from LA CHANSON DE GUILLAUME

... CLERS fu li jors et bels fu li matins,
Li soleil raie, si est li jors esclariz.
Paien devalent par un broillet antif;
Par ont qu'il passent tote la terre fremist.

---

them: 'Sir Roland, and you, Sir Oliver, for God's sake, I beseech you, do not quarrel. It would not help us now to blow the horn, but nevertheless it is better to do so: let the king come, and he will be able to avenge us. These Spaniards must not go home rejoicing. Our French knights will dismount here, they will find us dead, cut to pieces. They will raise us on biers, on packhorses, and will mourn for us in grief and sorrow. They will bury us in the holy ground of churches; we shall not be eaten by wolves or pigs or dogs.' Roland replies: 'Sir, you have spoken well.'

from THE SONG OF WILLIAM

... CLEAR was the day and fair was the morning, the sun was shining and the daylight bright. The pagans come down through an ancient thicket; wherever they pass, the whole earth trembles.

Des durs healmes qu'il ont à or sartiz,
Triés lor espaules, li bois en reflambist.
Qui donc les veist eslaissier et saillir,
De durs vassals li peüst sovenir.
Idonc les mostre Vivien à Esturmi.

«Esturmi, frere, je voi paiens venant;
Les lor chevals par sont si coranz,
Por quinze lieues tozjorz aler brochant,
Ne por plus corre, ja ne lor batra flanc.
Aincui morront li couart en l'Archamp.
Or apresment li foëor de devant.
Ja ne garra li petit por le grant;
N'i peut garir le pere son enfant.
Fions nos ent en Dieu le totpoant,
Car il est mieldre que tuit li mescreant.
Combatons nous, si veintrons bien le champ.»

Donc dist Tiedbalt: «Qu'en loez, Vivien,
De la bataille?» — «Ore ja vient bien.»

With the strong helmets set with gold and jewels that are slung across their shoulders, the wood is all aflame. Any man who saw them then, galloping and leaping onwards, could remember the sight of mighty warriors. Thereupon Vivien points them out to Esturmi.

'Esturmi, comrade, I see the pagans coming; their horses are so swift that even if they were spurred on for fifteen leagues, or more than that, they would not be winded. Before the day is out the cowards will die in Archamp. Already their vanguard draws near. Now the weak cannot be protected by the strong, nor can the father save his child. Let us put our trust in God the Almighty, for he is stronger than all the Infidels. Let us fight, and we shall surely win the battle.'

Then said Tibald, 'What is your counsel, Vivien, about the battle?' 'It is already upon us.'

Aprof demande: «Qu'en loez, Esturmi?»
– «Que chascuns penst de sa vie garir:
Qui or ne fuit, tost i peut mort gesir.
Alons nous en por nos vies garir.»
Dist Vivien: «Or oi parler mastin.»
Respont Tiedbalt: «Ainc pres de mon lin
Ne volt enquerre dont mes cors soit honi,
Ne enginié, ne malement bailli.

«Esturmi, niés, deromp cest gonfanon,
Que en fuiant ne nous conoisse l'on;
Car à l'enseigne trairont paien felon.»
Dist Esturmi: «A la Dieu beneiçon!»

Encontre mont li glot presenta s'anste,
Sur son arçon devant mist la lance,
A ses deus poinz deront l'enseigne blanche,
Puis la fola à ses piez en la fange.

Tiedbalt le conte teneit un grant espié;
L'arestuel torne contremont vers le ciel,
Mist en le fer sur l'arçon de triés;
Deront l'enseigne de l'anste de pomier,
Puis la fola enz el fanc à ses piez.

Then he asks, 'What do you counsel, Esturmi?' 'Let every man think of saving his own life: he who does not flee now may soon be lying there dead. Let us flee to save our lives.' Said Vivien, 'You speak like a cur.' Tibald rejoins, 'Never has any kinsman of mine sought to bring on me shame, betrayal, or injury.

'Esturmi my nephew, tear up that standard, so that none may know us as we flee, for the cruel pagans would shoot at our standard.' Said Esturmi, 'With the blessing of God.'

The villain turned his lance shaft upwards, rested the point before him on his saddle-bow; with his two hands he tears off the white standard, then tramples it with his feet in the mud.

Tibald the count was holding a great lance; he turns the hand-hold upwards to the sky, places the iron point on the saddle-bow behind him; he tears off the standard from the shaft of apple-wood,

«Mielz vueil, enseigne, flambe t'arde del ciel
Que en bataille me conoissent paien.»
– «Graimes noveles, dist li quens Viviens:
En champ nous faillent nostre gonfanonier.»

«Franche maisniee, que porrons devenir?
En champ nous sont nostre gonfanon failli,
Laissié nous ont Tiedbalt et Esturmi.
Veez paiens qui molt sont pres d'ici.
Quant li nostre home i sont ou cinc ou dis,
Et li paien i sont ou cent ou mil;
Donc n'avrons nous qui nous puisse tenir,
Ne tel enseigne où puissons revertir.
Genz sans seignor sont malement bailli:
Alez vos en, francs chevaliers gentilz,
Car je ne puis endurer ne souffrir
Tant gentil home soient à tort bailli.
Je me rendrai el dolorous peril,
N'en tornerai, car à Dieu l'ai promis
Que ne fuirai por paor de morir.»
Franceis respondent; oez qu'il li ont dit:

then tramples it in the mud with his feet. 'I would rather, banner, that a flame from Heaven should consume you than that the pagans should recognize me in battle.' – 'Bitter news!' said Count Vivien. 'On the field of battle our standard-bearers fail us.'

'My noble followers, what is to become of us? On the field of battle our standards have failed us, Tibald and Esturmi have abandoned us. See, the Infidels are close upon us. Where our men are but five or ten, the pagans number a hundred or a thousand; now we shall have no one who can hold us together, nor any standard we can rally to. Men without a lord are lost indeed; leave me, noble, valiant knights, for I cannot bear or endure that so many noble men should be betrayed. I shall go forward into this grievous peril; I shall not leave this place, for I have sworn to God that I will never flee because of the fear of death.' The French reply; hear

«Vivien, sire, ja es tu d'icel lin
En grant bataille nous dois bien maintenir.
Ja fustes filz Boeve Cornebut, au marchis,
Nés de la fille au bon conte Aimeri,
Et niés Guillelme au corb nés le marchis.
En grant bataille nous dois bien maintenir.»
– «Voire, seignors, de Dieu cinc cenz merciz.
Mais d'une chose i a grant contredit:
Vous n'estes miens, ne je vostre sire ne devinc;
Sans toz parjures me porriez guerpir.»
Et cil respondent tous ensemble à un cri:
«Tais! ber, nel dire! ja t'averons plevi
En cele loi que Dieus en terre mist
A ses apostles quant entre eus descendit,
Ne te faldrons tant com tu seras vifs.»

– «Et je rafi vous de Dieu le roi fort,
Et cel esprit que il ot en son cors,
Por pecheors quant il souffri la mort:
Ne vos faldrai por destrece de cors.»
A icest mot donc mist s'enseigne fors.

what they have said to him: 'Vivien, lord, you are of a lineage well worthy to uphold us in a great battle. You are the son of Bevis Cornebut the marquis, born of the daughter of brave Count Aimeri, and you are the nephew of the marquis William of the crooked nose. In a great battle, you should uphold us well.' 'Indeed, my lords, I thank you five hundred times in God's name. But in one thing there is a great obstacle: you are not my vassals, and I was never made your lord. Without any perjury you could leave me.' And they answer all together with one voice: 'Be silent, lord, do not say it; we will swear to you now, by that law that God brought down to earth to his apostles when he came among them, we will never fail you as long as you live.'

'And I on my side swear to you, by God the mighty king, and by the spirit which he had in his body when he suffered death for sinners, I will not fail you whatever I may suffer.' Then at this word he brought out his standard.

Donc met sa main en sa vermeille chauce,
Et si traist fors une enseigne de paile;
A treis clous d'or la ferma en sa lance,
Od le braz destre en a brandi la hanste
Desi qu'as poinz l'en batirent les langes;
Point le cheval, ne peut muer ne saille,
Et fiert un paien sur sa doble targe,
Tote li fent de l'un our jusqu'à l'autre,
Trencha le bras qui li sist en l'enarme,
Coupe le piz et trencha la coraille,
Par mi l'eschine son grant espié li passe,
Tot estendu l'abat mort en la place.
Crie «Monjoie»: ce fu l'enseigne Charle. ...

from LE MONIAGE GUILLAUME

... TANT va li cuens et arriere et avant,
Qu'en un val entre moult soutil et moult grant.
Dessous un arbre foillu et verdoiant
Une riviere i ot bele et corant;
Sour la riviere troeve un habitoment:

Then he puts his hand into his scarlet hose and drew out a pennon of silk; with three golden nails he fastened it to his lance; with his right arm he has brandished the shaft; the streamers reach down to his fists. He spurs on his horse, so that it cannot but leap forward, and strikes a pagan on his double shield; he splits it across from one edge to the other, he cuts through the arm in the shield-strap, he cuts open his chest, and strikes right through his heart; he thrusts his great lance through his spine, and strikes him down full-length dead on the ground. He shouts 'Monjoie'; that was the battle-cry of Charlemagne. ...

from HOW WILLIAM BECAME A MONK

...THE count wanders here and there until he comes into a deep and lonely valley. Beneath a green and leafy tree there was a fair, swift-flowing river; on the bank of the river he finds a dwelling: a holy

Uns sains hermites i prist herbergement,
Iluec sert Dieu moult enterinement.
De set grans lieues n'ot ne vile ne gent
De quoi il ait nesun confortement,
S'hermites non, ainsi com je l'entent,
Qui ens el bois ont lor estorement.
Et lor bestailles avoient voirement,
Lor cortisiaus, lor edefiement;
Là se garissent et vivent saintement.
Mais li larron (se l'estoire ne ment)
Lor font maint mal et menu et souvent:
Prendent lor bestes et vendent à argent,
Lor maisons brisent, sachiés certainement,
Lor dras lor tolent et meinent malement,
Ses enkembelent et loient moult forment.
Douze en i ot de tel afaitement;
Mais je cuit bien que grans deus lor atent,
Car dans Guillaumes, qui moult a fier talent,
Ainz demain vespres les fera tous dolens:
Trestous li mieudres, sachiés certainement,
N'i voudroit estre pour plein un val d'argent.

hermit had settled in it and there served God with his whole heart.
For seven good leagues around there was neither town nor people
from whom he could have any help, except for hermits, as I understand, who find all they need in the wood; they have their cattle
there, indeed, their little kitchen-gardens, their buildings; there
they provide for themselves and live a holy life. But the robbers, if
the story does not lie, are always doing them some injury, over and
over again. They take their cattle and sell them for money, break
down their houses, you may be sure, steal their clothes, and ill-
treat them, and tie them up and bind them very tightly. There are
twelve of these robbers who did these things, but I think that there
is great trouble in store for them, for Lord William, who is very
stout-hearted, before tomorrow evening will make them all sorry.
The very best of them, you may be sure, would not wish to be
there for a valley full of silver.

Va s'en Guillaumes, si com Dieus li aprent;
De ses pechiés a grant repentement.
A l'ermitage s'en vient delivrement,
Le maillot troeve qui droit au postis pent;
Li cuens i fiert trois cous menuement.
La maisoncele est bien close en tous sens
De bone soif espinee forment,
Et un fossé i ot fait voirement;
Li sains hermites qui prie Dieu souvent
S'estoit hourdés ensifaitierement.
Le maillot ot, cele part vient errant,
Le postis oevre tost et isnelement:
«Qui'st la? fait il, por Dieu omnipotent.»
Li cuens respont moult debonairement:
«Pechieres sui, ainc hom ne vit plus grant.
Herbergiez moi, pour Dieu le vous demant!
Parmi ce bois ai alé traversant,
Plus de set jours, sachiés certainement;
Ainc n'i trovai maison n'habitement,
Au champ ai jut, à la pluie et au vent;
Or me herberge, se toi vient à talent.»
Li sains hermites l'esgarda durement;

William goes his way as God leads him; he deeply repents of his sins. He soon comes to the hermitage and finds the knocker which hangs on the gate. The count gives three rapid knocks. The little house is well fenced in on every side, with a good hedge bristling with thorns – and in fact there was a ditch dug too. The holy hermit, who often prays to God, had fortified his dwelling in this way. He hears the knocker and comes that way at once, and immediately he quickly opens the gate. 'Who's there?' he says, 'in the name of Almighty God.' The count replies very meekly, 'I am a sinner, never man saw a greater. Give me shelter, for God's sake I ask it of you. I have been wandering through the midst of this wood for more than seven days, I assure you, and never found a house or a dwelling. I have slept in the open, in the wind, and the rain; now give me lodging if it pleases you.' The holy hermit

Quant il le vit vestu si povrement,
Si malaisieu, si grant et si parant,
Au saint hermite si grant paor en prent,
N'i vousist estre pour plein un val d'argent.
La porte clot, si s'en fuit durement;
Pour cent mars d'or n'i fust plus longuement.
«Dieus, dist l'hermites, par ton commandement,
De cel maufé, se toi plaist, me defent,
Car je sui mors se il as poins me prent;
Tout mon hostel et tout mon mandement
Ferroit il jus à un pié seulement:
Sainte Marie, dont vient si grande gent?»
Li cuens Guillaumes à la porte l'atent,
Iluec s'asiet, si pleure tendrement
Pour ses pechiés, dont se repent forment.
Lors en apele l'hermite doucement.

Li cuens Guillaumes a apelé l'hermite,
Mout doucement et par amour li prie:
«Oevre la porte, frere, Dieus le te mire,
Herberge moi, pour Dieu le fil Marie;
De moi n'as garde, se Dieus me beneïe:

looked hard at him. When he saw him so poorly dressed and so evil-looking, so tall and so imposing, such great dread seized the holy hermit that he would not willingly have been there for a valley full of silver. He shuts the door and makes off as fast as he can; he would not have stayed longer for a hundred gold marks. 'God,' said the hermit, 'by Thy commandment, defend me, if it please Thee, from this devil, for I am as good as dead if he gets his hands on me. All my house and all my dwelling he could knock down with one foot only. St Mary! where do such tall people come from?' Count William waits at the door; he sits down there and weeps bitterly for his sins, which he deeply repents; then he calls gently to the hermit.

Count William has called the hermit; very gently he begs him, and for charity's sake, 'Open the door, brother, God reward you. Give me lodging for the sake of God the son of Mary; you have nothing to fear from me, as God may bless me; I am a penitent, do

Penëans sui, si ne le mescroi mie,
Tant ai fait mal, n'est hom qui le puist dire.»
L'hermite l'ot, li cuers li atendrie,
Vient à la porte, le postis à lui tire,
Le conte apele à la chiere hardie:
«Venez avant, de par Jesu, beaus sire,
De ce que j'ai vous ferai departie.»
Et dist Guillaumes: «Frere, Dieus le vous mire.»

Li cuens entra en la herbergerie,
Et li hermites la porte a veroillie
Pour les larrons, que Jesus maleïe.
Guillaumes a la chapele choisie;
Li cuens i va qui ne s'atarge mie,
Mais à l'entrer li dut estre petite,
Car li marquis se hurta à la liste.
«Abaissiez vous, sire» dist li hermite.
Et dist Guillaumes: «J'en ai ja une prise;
Trop par fesistes petite manandie.»
«Ele m'est grans, sire, dist li hermite,
El ne fu pas à vostre point taillie.»
Lors comencierent li doi preudome à rire.

not disbelieve me. I have done so much evil that no man could tell it all.' The hermit hears him and his heart is softened. He comes to the gateway and pulls the gate towards him. He calls to the count with the bold face: 'Come in, for Jesu's sake, fair sir; what I have I will share with you.' And William said: 'Brother, may God reward you.'

The count entered into the dwelling, and the hermit bolted the door because of the robbers, Jesu's curse upon them! William saw the chapel; the count went straight there without lingering, but as he went in, it must have been too low for him, for the marquis knocked his head on the beam. 'Keep your head down, sir,' said the hermit. And William said, 'I've got a bump already. You built your house far too small.' 'It is big enough for me, sir,' said the hermit; 'it was not cut to your measure.' Then the two good men

Li cuens Guillaumes a ses orisons dites,
Puis si s'en vont andoi à la cuisine.
Li sains hermites, cui Dieus soit en aïe,
Dona Guillaume de ce qu'il ot à vivre
A grant plenté, ainc n'i fist avarice:
Eaue boulie à un poi de farine,
Et pain de soile: et si burent du cidre,
Et puis mengierent de pomes, de faïnes,
Les melles bletes n'i oublierent mie.
Quant mangié ont, Damedieu en mercient.
«Dieus, dist Guillaumes, com ci a bone vie!
Mieus aim ce mès que je ne fais un cisne,
Paon ne grue ne capon ne geline,
Ne cerf de lande, ours ne chevreul ne biche.»
L'hermites l'ot, s'a la teste baissie,
Un petit pense, si dist à soi meïsme:
«Je cuit cist hom a forment esté riches
Qui ci parole de si fiere devise.»
Li cuens l'apele, si li a pris à dire:
«Dites moi, frere, pour Dieu, où vous naquistes,
Com avez nom, ne le me celez mie.»

began to laugh. Count William has said his prayers, then they both
go to the kitchen. The holy hermit, may God be his help, gave
William a generous share of what he had to live on (he did not
treat him meanly!): water boiled with a little flour, and rye bread,
and they drank some cider, and then they ate apples and beech nuts
and did not forget the ripe medlars. When they had eaten, they
gave thanks to the Lord. 'God,' said William, 'what a good life
this is! I would rather have this food than a swan, peacock, or crane,
or capon or fowl, stag from the moor or bear or roebuck or doe.'
The hermit hears him and has bent his head. He thinks a moment,
then says to himself: 'I think this man has been extremely rich, to
talk here in this grand manner.' The count addresses him and has
begun to say to him: 'Tell me, brother, for God's sake, where you
were born and what your name is: do not hide it from me.' The

L'hermites l'ot, tous li sans li formie,
Pleure des ieus, la face en a mouillie.
Voit le li cuens, li cuers l'en atendrie:
«Frere, fait il, vous faites vilenie;
Dites vo nom, que il n'i ait detrie.»
E cil respont: «Volentiers, beaus dous sire.»

Or fu Guillaumes laiens en l'hermitage,
Dist à l'hermite: «Dites moi vo parage,
Dites vo nom, se Dieus grant bien vous face.»
Dist li hermites: «Volentiers, par saint Jaque!
Nés sui de France, del païs honorable,
Gaidons ai nom, niés sui dame Anestasse,
Feme Garin d'Anseüne le large.
Fils fui d'un duc qui fu de grant parage,
Gerars ot nom et si tint quite Blaives.
Ma mere fu estraite d'un lignage
Qui ainc ne vout nule traïson faire:
Cuens Aimeris de Narbone le large
Fu ses cousins, ce me disoit mes maistre.
Je le servi moult grant piece pour armes,
Et si li fis mainte ruiste bataille.

hermit hears him and all his blood trembles. Tears fall from his eyes, his face is wet with them. The count sees it and his heart aches for him. 'Brother,' he says, 'you do wrong [to hesitate]. Tell your name, let there be no holding back.' And he replies, 'Willingly, fair sweet sir.'

Now was William inside the hermitage. He said to the hermit: 'Tell me your lineage, tell your name, as God may be good to you.' Said the hermit: 'Willingly, by St James. I was born in France, that famous land. My name is Gaidon, I am the nephew of the lady Anastasia, wife of Garin of Anseüne the generous. I was the son of a duke who was of noble birth: Gerard was his name and he held Blaie freely. My mother came from a line that was never capable of treachery; the generous count Aimeri of Narbonne was her cousin, so my tutor used to tell me. I served him long to earn my arms, and fought many a fierce battle for him. He dubbed me

Il m'adouba à Narbone en la sale;
Là fu Guillaumes, li marchis Fierebrace,
Hernaus li rous, Aïmers et li autre,
De Commarchis dus Bueves à la barbe:
Avec iceus fui norris en la sale.
Ne sai qu'en mente ne pour quoi le celasse:
Je ai tant fait de pechiés mortuables,
Tant home mort et tante cité arse,
Terres destruites et chasteaus fait abatre,
Que li pechié moult durement m'esmaient
Que je ne voise en enfer parmanable.
Vint et quatre ans avra à ceste Paque
Que je laissai mes viles et mes marches
Et que m'en ving çaiens en ce boscage;
En ceste terre qui tant par est sauvage
Deving hermites et pris cest herbergage.
Ainc puis du siecle, certes, ne me fu gaires.
Moult a d'hermites en icestui boscage,
Qui par ce bois lor viande porchacent,
Lor besteletes i nourrissent et paissent,
De quoi l'hiver et la saison trespassent.
Moult a bon tens, par Dieu l'esperitable,

knight at Narbonne in the hall. William the marquis Fierebrace was
there, Hernaut the Red, Aimer and the others; Duke Bevis of Commarchis with the beard; with these men was I brought up in the hall.
I know not why I should lie, or why I should conceal it. I have
committed so many mortal sins, I have killed so many men and
burnt so many cities, laid waste lands and destroyed castles, until
my sins make me very much dread lest I should go to everlasting
Hell. It will be twenty-four years this Easter since I left my towns
and my lands and came away here into this wood. In this land which
is so wild I became a hermit and took this dwelling, and since then,
indeed, the world has meant little to me. There are many hermits
in this forest who find their living in the woodland. They feed and
nourish their few cattle here in order to get through the winter and
the sowing season. He who serves God with a whole heart has a

Qui Damedieu sert de tres fin courage:
En Dieu servir a moult tres bon usage.
Or vous ai, sire, tout conté mon afaire.
Mais li larron me font souvent contraire,
Ma maison brisent, si me font grant damage.
Mais par cel Dieu qui me fist à s'image,
Se vous voulez, ja lairai l'hermitage,
O vous irai, sire, mais qu'il vous place.
Bien vous connois as poins et au visage,
Au fier courage et as lees espaules:
Mes cousins estes, s'avez à nom Guillaume,
D'Orange fustes sires et connestables,
Et si presistes à moullier dame Orable.»
A icest mot li cousin s'entrebaisent;
Chascuns d'eux deus a pleins les ieus de larmes.

Quant li baron se sont entr'acointié,
Ambedoi furent moult joiant et moult lié.
Dist Gaidons: «Sire, or ne me soit noié:
Dont venez vous si povrement à pié?
Avez perdu vos honeurs et vos fiés?»
Et dist li cuens: «Naie, certes, beaus niés!
Morte est Guibours, ma cortoise moullier,

good life, by the Heavenly Lord. The service of God is a very good way of life. Now I have told you, sir, all my story; but the robbers often do me injury and destroy my house and do me great wrong. But by that God who made me in his image, if you wish it, I will leave the hermitage and go with you, sir, if only it is pleasing to you. I know you well by your hands and your face, your proud bearing and your broad shoulders: you are my cousin, and your name is William; you were lord and constable of Orange and you took to wife the Lady Orable.' At these words, the cousins kissed each other, and each of the two had his eyes full of tears.

When the barons had made themselves known to one another they were both very joyful and glad. Said Gaidon: 'Sir, now do not let it be hidden from me: whence do you come so ill-clad and on foot? Have you lost your lands and your estates?' And the count said: 'No, indeed, fair nephew. Guibourg is dead, my noble

Et mes lignages, dont je sui moult iriés.
Or ai pour Dieu tout mon païs laissié.»
Trestout li conte li marchis au vis fier:
Comment il fu moines saint Gratien,
Tout son affaire li dist de chief en chief,
Et des larrons qu'il ot mors el ramier,
Le prieus mort, les moines laidengiés;
«Mais or me doi envers Dieu amaisnier,
Hermites ere, se Dieus m'en veut aidier.»
Dist Gaidons: «Sire, Dieus en soit graciés!
O moi manrez, s'il à plaisir vous vient.»
«Naie, cousins, dist Guillaumes li fiers,
En autre lieu voudrai estre ostagiés.» ...

WACE

Le Roman de Brut

[Julius Caesar demands tribute from the Britons]

... Donc fist ses briefs faire et porter
A Cassibelan outre mer,
Si manda que de lui tenist

wife, and all my kin, which grieves me deeply. Now I have left all my lands for God's sake.' The marquis with the proud face tells him all: how he was a monk of St Gratien, and all his story he told him, and about the robbers he had killed in the forest, the prior he killed and the monks he wounded. 'But now I must make my peace with God: I shall be a hermit, if God will help me to do so.' Said Gaidon: 'God be thanked for that. You shall stay with me, if that will please you.' 'No, cousin,' says the proud William, 'in some other place I wish to make my dwelling.' ...

The History of Brutus

... So [Caesar] caused letters to be written and carried to Cassive-launus across the sea, ordering him to do homage for his lands and

Et as Romains treü rendist.

Cassibelan, quil tint à grief,

Brief refist faire contre brief;

Onques salut n'i volt escrire,

Ainz li manda comme par ire:

«Cesar, moult par nous merveillons,

Et merveillant nous desdeignons

Des Romains et de lor sorfait

Qui tant durë et tant loin vait.

Ne peut soufrir lor couvoitise

Que nuls hom ait, fors eus, franchise.

Tout l'or du monde et tout l'argent,

Les rois, les contes, l'autre gent,

Veulent mettre sous lor empire;

Nule rien ne lor peut souffire;

Tout l'avoir veulent à eus traire:

Que doivent il de tout ço faire?

Nous, qui el chief du mond manons,

En une isle que nous tenons,

Ne veulent Romain trespasser,

Ainz nous font treü demander.

Sire Cesar, tu nous essaies,

Treü requiers que de nous aies,

Et faire nous veus tributaires;

to pay tribute to the Romans. Cassivelaunus, who thought it an outrage, had this letter answered by another. Never a greeting would he write in it, but addressed him as in anger: 'Caesar, we marvel greatly, and marvelling, we scorn the Romans and their arrogance that lasts so long and goes so far. Their greed cannot suffer any man but themselves to enjoy freedom. All the gold in the world, and all the silver, the kings, the counts, the common people, they must subdue beneath their rule; nothing will satisfy them; all wealth must come into their hands: what can they do with it all? We live at the end of the world, on an island of our own, yet the Romans will not pass us over, but make demands on us for tribute. Lord Caesar, you are making trial of us; you demand to have tribute from us, you want to turn us into payers of tribute, but you

Mais tu nen esploiteras guaires.
Nous avons tous tens franc vescu
Et franchement avons tenu,
Et vivre devons franchement
Come li Romain droitement;
Car nous sommes d'une racine
Et d'une gent et d'une orine.
Cesar, se tu te pourpensoies
Et se tu raison esgardoies,
Merveillouse honte feïs
Quant de treü nous requeïs
Et mettre nous vols en servage
Qui sommes de vostre parage;
Per as Romains estre devons
Qui d'un lignage descendons.
Si sages hom, si gentil sire
Come tu es, com osas dire
Que nous doions sers devenir
Qui n'avons apris à servir?
Ne ja, se Dieu plaist, n'aprendrons,
Ço saces tu, que nous puissons!
Tout tens avons si franc esté
Onc hom de nostre parenté
Ne sot encor, ne ja ne sache

will have little success. We have always lived free and held our lands as free men, and we have the right to live in freedom exactly as the Romans do; for we are of the same kindred, and of one race, of one origin. Caesar, if you would consider carefully and look at the rights of the matter, it was a very shameful thing you did when you demanded tribute from us, and desired to make slaves of us, who are of your own kindred. Peers of the Romans we should be who descend from the same lineage. So wise a man, so noble a lord as you are, how dared you say we ought to become slaves, we who have never learnt to serve and who, if it please God, never shall, mark this well, if we can help it? We have always been so free that never a man of our kindred has known, or knows now, what it

Come l'on doit vivre en servage:
Ne savons, s'il ne nous est dit,
Come sers en servage vit.
Franc somes et franc voulons estre;
Se meïsmes li Dieu celestre
Nous en vouloient abaissier,
Si nous voulons nous efforcier
Que nous par home ne perdons
Ce que nous tant tenu avons.
Or peus savoir, nel celons mie,
Que, tant com nous serons en vie,
Et nous maintenir nous pourrons,
Nostre franchise defendrons.
Franc voulons vivre et à honour,
Si com firent nostre ancessour.» ...

[Famine and plague in Britain during the reign of
Cadwalader]

... EN son tens fu falte de blé,
Et de la falte vint chierté,
Et de la chierté vint famine.
Chier fu en bourc, chier fu en ville;
Bien peüssiez trois jours errer
Ne trovissiez à achater

is to live in slavery. We do not even know, unless it is explained to us, how the slave lives in servitude. Free we are and free we mean to be. If the heavenly Gods themselves wanted to cast us down, we would still strive not to lose to any man what we have held so long. Now you may know – we do not hide it – that as long as we are alive and can defend ourselves we shall fight for our freedom. We mean to live in freedom and honour just as our ancestors did.' ...

... IN his time the corn failed, and from this failure came high prices, and from the high prices came famine. Corn was dear in the town and dear in the village. You could have travelled for three

Ne pain ne blé n'autre vitaille,
Tant par ert grant partout la faille.
De poissons et de sauvagines,
De venoisons et de racines,
De feuilles et d'erbes vivoient:
Autre viande nen avoient.
Avec cele mesaventure
Revint une autre autresi dure:
Mortalité fu grant de gent
Par air corrompu et par vent;
Es maisons, es champs et es rues
Et es marchiés et as charrues,
Manjant, alant, parlant cheoient,
Soudement sans langour mouroient.
Meurent pere, meurent enfant,
Meurent seignour, meurent serjant;
Meurt li sire, meurt la moillier,
Meurent vilain et chevalier;
N'estuet au filz son pere plaindre.
Moult veïssiez poi gent remaindre
Es voies soutives et guastes;
Onques tel duel nen esgardastes.
Ne pooient pas foisoner
Tuit li vif as morz enterrer;

days without finding for sale either bread or corn or any food, so very great was the shortage everywhere. They lived on fish and wild game, venison and roots, and leaves and grass, they had no other food; and with this disaster came another just as hard: there was a great mortality among the people because of corruption carried on the air and in the wind. In houses, in fields, and in the streets, in the markets and at the plough, eating, walking, or talking they fell, and suddenly, without languishing, they died. Fathers die and children die, lords die and servants die; the husband dies and the wife dies, peasants die, and knights; the son does not live to mourn his father; very few were those who could be found alive, and those by hidden ways and in waste places. Never was such mourning seen. All that were left alive were not enough to bury the dead. He who

Cil qui le mort enterrer dut
O le mort enterrer estut.
Cil qui porent fuïr fuïrent,
Lor fieus et lor maisons guerpirent,
Tant pour la grant chierté de blé,
Tant pour la grant mortalité.
En sa maison a mal espoir
Qui la son voisin voit ardoir. ...

Le Roman de Rou

(*Prologue*)

Pour remembrer des ancessours
Les faiz et les diz et les mours,
Doit l'on les livres et les gestes
Et les estoires lire as festes,
Les felonies des felons
Et les barnages des barons.
Pour ce firent bien et savoir
Et grant pris durent cil avoir
Qui escristrent premierement,
Et li autour plenierement
Qui firent livres et escriz

should have buried a dead man had to be buried with him. Those who could flee fled away, they left their lands and their houses, as much because of the great dearth of corn as for the fearful pestilence: a man has little hope for his own house when he sees his neighbour's on fire.

The History of Rollo

To keep in mind the deeds and words and ways of our ancestors, records and chronicles and histories ought to be read out at festivals: the crimes of the wicked and the good deeds of the noble. Therefore those men worked well and wisely, and should be greatly honoured, who first invented writing, and those authors should be fully esteemed who made books and writings about the

Des nobles faiz et des bons diz .
Que li baron et li seignour
Firent de tens ancianour.
Tourné fussent en oubliance,
Se ne fust tant de remembrance
Que li escriture nous fait
Qui les estoires nous retrait.

Mainte cité a ja esté,
Et mainte riche poesté,
Dont nous or rien ne seüssons
Se les escriz n'en eüssons.
De Thebes est grant reparlance,
Et Babiloine ot grant puissance,
Et Troie fu de grant podnee,
Et Ninive fu grant et lee:
Qui or ireit querant les places,
A peine trouvereit les traces.
Rois fu Nabugodonosor,
Une image fist faire d'or,
Soissante coutes de hautour
Et sis coutes ot de laour;
Qui or voudreit son cors veoir,
Ne trouvereit, al mien espoir,
Qui moustrer ne dire seüst

noble feats and the good words of lords and barons in ancient days.
These would have all sunk into oblivion were it not for the
measure of remembrance brought to us by the written word which
tells their stories.

There has been many a city in the past, and many a wealthy empire, of which we should now know nothing if its chronicles had
not come down to us. Thebes is famous in story, and great was the
might of Babylon and great the power of Troy, and Nineveh was
great and wide; but now, if you were to seek the places where they
stood, you would hardly find a trace of them. Nebuchadnezzar was
a king; he caused a golden image to be made sixty cubits high and
six cubits wide; but now, if you were to try to find his body, I do

Ou os de lui ne poudre eüst.
Mais par les bons clers qui l'escristrent,
Qui les gestes es livres mistrent,
Savons nous du vieil tens parler
Et des oevres plusours conter.

Alixandre fu rois puissanz,
Douze regnes prist en douze anz,
Moult ot terres, moult ot avoir,
Et rois fu de moult grant pooir;
Mais cil conquez poi li valut:
Envenimez fu, si mourut.

Cesar, qui tant fist et tant pot,
Qui tout le mont conquist et ot,
Onques nuls hom, puis ne avant,
Mien escient ne conquist tant,
Puis fu ocis en traïson
El Capitoile, ce savom.
Cil dui vassal qui tant conquistrent,
Tant orent terres et tant pristrent,
Après la mort, de lor honour
N'ot chascun fors que sa longour.

not believe you would find anybody able to show or tell you where
bone or ash of him is laid. But because of the worthy clerks who
wrote and set down the chronicles in their books we can still speak
of ancient times and tell of many of their works.

Alexander was a mighty king; twelve kingdoms he conquered in
twelve years, many lands he had and great possessions, and was
ruler of a vast empire; but all these conquests availed him little:
he was poisoned and he died.

Caesar, who did so much and wielded such power, conquered
and held the whole world; never any man before or after him, as I
believe, was such a conqueror. Then, as we know, he was treacher-
ously killed in the Capitol. These two great men, who conquered
so much, who had so many lands and seized so much territory,
after their death, of all the lands they held, neither had more than

Quel bien lor fait, que mieuz lor est
De lor pris et de lor conquest,
Ne mais tant que l'on va disant,
Si com l'on le treuve lisant,
Qu'Alixandre et Cesar furent?
Tant i a d'eus que lor nons durent,
Et si refussent oublié
S'il escrit n'eüssent esté.

Toute rien se tourne en declin,
Tout chiet, tout meurt, tout vait à fin;
Hom meurt, fer use, fust pourrist,
Tour font, mur chiet, rose flaistrist,
Cheval trebuche, drap vieillist,
Toute oevre faite o mains perist.
Bien entent et conois et sai
Que tuit mourront, et clerc et lai,
Et moult avra lor renomee
Apres lor mort courte duree,
Se par clerc nen est mise en livre:
Ne puet par el durer ne vivre.

his own length of earth. What good to them is all their honour and their conquest, and what better are they for it, except in so far as men still say of them – what they have learnt by reading – that they were Alexander and Caesar? So much is left of them that their names endure, and even these would have been forgotten if they had not been put into writing.

Everything tends towards decay; all falls, all dies, all draws towards its end; man dies, iron wears away, wood rots, towers come to ruin, walls fall down, the rose withers, the horse stumbles, cloth grows threadbare, and every work of man's hand perishes. Well do I understand and realize and know that all men will die, both clerks and laymen, and short-lived indeed will be their fame after their death if no clerk sets it down in writing, for by no other means can it endure or live.

[King Louis of France tries to kidnap Richard, the
young Duke of Normandy]

... Lı rois vint à Rouem, en la cité entra;
Riches fu li ostels où il se herberga.
Demander fist Richart, Osmont li amena;
Li enfes vint au roi, et li rois le baisa.
Dieus! pourquoi l'a baisié quant foi ne li porta?
Salua le de bouche, mais li cuers el pensa.
Moult se loa du pere et moult le regreta.
Cele nuit tint Richart qu'aler ne l'en laissa,
Si fist il l'endemain, et au tiers le garda.
Quant Osmont l'aperçut, moult s'en espoenta,
A Bernart le Danois tout souef le conta,
Et Bernart as borgeois ce qu'il volt conseilla,
Et as chevaliers tous qu'en la vile trouva.
Puis vint devant le roi, d'un et d'autre parla;
Diversement penserent, mais chascun se cela.

Moult s'ala par la vile la nouvele espeissant
Que li rois tint Richart si l'aloit demuçant.
Moult en sont tuit dolent et Breton et Normant,

... THE king came to Rouen, he went into the city; rich was the
dwelling where he was lodged. He sent for Richard; Osmund
brought him to him. The boy came to the king, and the king kissed
him; God! why did he kiss him when he did not keep faith with
him? His mouth welcomed him, but his heart had other thoughts;
he gave great praise to [the boy's] father and lamented his death.
That night he kept Richard with him, for he would not let him go,
and he did the same the next day, and on the third day he still held
him. When Osmund saw this, he was much alarmed; to Bernard the
Dane he told it in secret, and Bernard told the townsmen what he
wanted them to do, and told all the knights that he found within the
town. Then he came before the king and spoke of this and that.
Each had his own thoughts but hid them from the other.
    The news went crowding through the town that the king held
Richard and was hiding him away. Bretons and Normans were all

Chevalier et borgeois, vilain et païsant.
A lor armes corurent, sis pristrent maintenant,
Qui hache, qui guisarme, qui espee tranchant:
Armes neuves et viés veïssiez traire avant:
Ce que lor vint as mains, ne vont mie querant.
Looïs et les suens vont souvent menaçant;
Tel noise a par ces rues n'oïssiez Dieu tonant.
Es vous vile estormie, hautement vont criant:
Se li rois ne lor rent vistement tost l'enfant,
Jamais ne traïra ne seigneur ne serjant.

Grant noise font borgeois et autres gens menues;
Nes les legieres femmes, les vieilles, les chenues,
O bastons, o tinels, o barres, o maçues
Toutes eschevelees vont cerchant par les rues,
Droit vers l'ostel le roi sont toutes acorues;
De menacier le roi ne se font mie mues,
Moult demandent où est; s'els en fussent creües,
Les maisons où il ert fussent tost abatues.
Ja estoient as portes des maisons avenues;

distressed to hear it, knights and burgesses, serfs and peasants. They
ran to their arms and took them up at once, one an axe, another a
halberd, another a keen sword; new arms and old arms you could
have seen brought out, whatever came to their hands, they lost no
time in searching. They pour out threats against Louis and his sup-
porters; there is such a noise in the streets you could not have heard
God thundering. See! the whole town is in a tumult. They go
shouting aloud that if the king does not give the boy back to them
at once he will never live to betray lord or serving-man again.

The burgesses and the common people make a great commotion,
even the harlots and old women with white hair, bearing sticks and
clubs and bars and bludgeons, with streaming hair go crowding
through the streets, and all making straight for the king's lodgings.
[The women] threaten the king in no uncertain voice, they keep
asking where he is; and if it had depended on them, the houses
where he was lodged would soon have been torn down. They had
already come to the doors of the houses, and without asking leave

Sans congié demander ens fussent embatues,
Quant cil qui dedans erent les ont aperceües;
Les portes ont barrees et par dedans tenues.

Li rois oï la noise qui ert en la cité.
Les serjanz apela si lor a demandé:
«Qu'a li peuple qui crie? Qui l'a si esfreé?
A il feu ou meslee? A il homme affolé?»
Si distrent cil qui sorent: «Tout ont autre pensé:
S'il vous poent ateindre, ja vous avront tué.»
«Pourquoi? dist Looïs, sont il donc forsené?»
«Ja tenez en prison Richart, nostre avoé.»
«Jel tenoie, dist il, par bone lealté,
Pour courtoisie aprendre le tenoie en chierté.»
«Par mon chief, distrent cil, ne vous en savons gré.»

«Bernart, dist Looïs, n'estuet avoir paour.»
«Oïl, ce dist Bernart, j'en sui en grant freour
Que il ne vous ocient ou facent deshonour.
Là fors a maint borgeois et maint bon vavasour,
S'il commencent meslee, ja verrez grant dolour;
S'il damage vous font, ja nel plaindront le jour.

were on the point of rushing in, when those who were inside saw them coming, barred the doors, and held them from within.

The king heard the noise that there was in the city; he called his servants and asked them: 'What is the matter with the people who are shouting? What has alarmed them so? Is there a fire or a riot? Has someone gone mad?' And those who knew told him: 'They have something very different in mind: if they can get at you they will soon have you killed.' 'Why?' said Louis, 'are they out of their senses?' 'You are keeping prisoner our sworn lord Richard.' 'I was keeping him,' said he, 'in all good faith; in order to teach him courtesy and out of affection I was keeping him.' 'By my head,' they replied, 'we do not thank you for it.'

'Bernard,' said the king, 'there is no need to be afraid.' 'Yes, there is,' said Bernard, 'I am in great fear lest they should kill you or do you dishonour. Out there is many a burgess and many a good vavasour; if they start a fight you will soon see serious trouble.

Se vous voulez garir, rendez tost lor seignour.»
«Jel tenoie, dist il, pour bien et pour honour.»
«Par foi, ce dist Bernart, ne semble mie amour;
Trop le tenez destroit quant des hier n'ot loissour.»

Li rois de France vit que Richart estut rendre.
Ne l'ose retenir, se la mort n'en volt prendre.
Moult par est entrepris qu'il ne s'ose defendre.
Richart lor a rendu, puis lor a fait entendre
Qu'il l'avoit tant tenu pour courtoisie apprendre
Et nourrir en sa court, tant com le veïst tendre.
«Chier li voulez, font il, la nourriture vendre;
S'uns autres l'eüst fait, moult feïst à reprendre.» ...

Today, they will not care what harm they do to you. For your
safety's sake, give them back their lord at once.' 'I was holding
him,' said he, 'for his own good and honour.' 'On my faith,' said
Bernard, 'it does not look like kindness: you keep him too close,
when he has not been at liberty since yesterday.'

The king of France saw that he would have to give Richard up;
he dared not keep him and risk being killed. He was furious that he
dared not defend himself. He gave Richard back to them, and then
told them that he had kept him so long with the intention of teach-
ing him courtesy and educating him in his own court, while he saw
that he was young. 'Dearly,' said they, 'you would charge him for
his keep. If anyone else had done it, he would have been much to
blame.' ...

BENOÎT DE SAINTE-MAURE

Le Roman de Troie
[Medea and Jason]

... La pucelle respont a tant:
«Or sai, fait el, vostre talant.
Ce remaindra jusqu'enevois
Que se sera couchiés li rois.
En ma chambre vendrez touz sous:
Ja compagnon n'avrez o vous.
La me ferez tel seürance
Que vers vous n'aie plus doutance;
Puis vous dirai comfaitement
Pourrez les bués et le serpent
Veintre et donter et justisier:
Ja puis n'avrez d'eus encombrier.»
«Dame, fait il, ainsi l'otroi,
Mais envoiez, s'ous plaist, pour moi;
Car ne savroie où je alasse,
Ne à quel heure je levasse.»
Dist la pucelle: «C'ert bien fait.»
Congié a pris, puis si s'en vait;

The Romance of Troy

At that, the maiden replies. 'Now,' she says, 'I know what you wish. This must wait until later when the king has gone to bed. You must come to my room alone, you must have no companion with you. There you will make me such vows that I shall have no doubt of your good faith, then I shall tell you how you can conquer and tame and overcome the oxen and the serpent: you will never more have any trouble with them.'

'Lady,' he said, 'I grant it so. But send for me, if you please, for I shall not know where to go, nor at what time I should rise.' Said the maiden: 'That will be well done.' She took her leave and went away.

38

Arriere en ses chambres s'en entre.
Moult li tressaut li cuers el ventre;
Esprise l'a forment Amours.
Moult li ennuie que li jours
Ne s'en vait à greignour esploit;
Moult se merveille que ce doit.
Tant a le soleil esgardé
Que elle le vit esconsé.
Moult li tarja puis l'anuitier,
Que son plait li fait pourloignier;
Et quant le jour en vit allé,
N'ot elle pas tout achevé:
Soventes fois a esgardee
La lune s'elle estoit levee.
Crient que sempres s'en aut la nuit:
Ne li tourne mie à deduit
Ce que par la salle veillierent
Et ce que pas ne se couchierent.
Son vueil fussent tuit endormi:
Moult par en a son cuer marri.
As uis des chambres vait oïr
S'encor parolent de dormir;
Iluec escoute, iluec estait.
N'en ot tenir conte ne plait.

She goes back into her apartments; her heart is beating wildly in her breast; love has set her all on fire. She is quite distracted that the day does not pass more quickly, and wonders much why this should be. She watched the sun so long that at last she saw it set, and then the darkness seemed to tarry and still delay her business. And when she saw daylight had gone, she still had not achieved her end. Often she looked to see if the moon had risen. She is afraid that the night will be over too soon. It does not please her at all that in the hall people are still awake and not going to bed; she longs for them all to be asleep and her heart is tormented. She goes to listen at the doors of her chambers, to see if they are talking of going to sleep yet. There she listens, there she stands; she hears no word or

«Ïço, fait elle, que sera?
Ceste gent quant se couchera?
Ont il juré qu'il veilleront
Et que mais ne se coucheront?
Qui vit mais gent qui tant veillast
Que de veillier ne se lassast?
Mauvaise gent, folle prouvee,
Ja est la mie nuit passee;
Moult a mais peu deci qu'au jour.
Certes moult a en moi folour:
De quoi me sui je entremise?
Mieuz en devroie estre reprise
Que cil qui est trovés emblant.
Fol corage et mauvais semblant
Pourroit on or trouver en moi,
Que ci m'estois ne sai pour quoi.
Estuet me il estre en esfroi
Que volentiers ne veigne à moi
Jason, quel heure qu'i envoi?
O il, moult volentiers, ce croi.
Que fais je ci, ne qui atent?
Tant en ai fait qu'or m'en repent.»
De l'uis se part en itel guise.
Vint à son lit, si s'est assise;

mention of such a thing. 'What will this come to?' she says, 'when will these people go to bed? Have they sworn to stay up all night and never go to sleep? Whoever saw people stay awake so long and never get tired? Wretched people! Idiots! Already it is after midnight, there is very little time from now to daybreak.

'Indeed, I am behaving very foolishly. What have I undertaken? I am more deserving of reproof than a thief caught red-handed. How foolish and ill-conducted people would think me now, standing here I know not why. Need I be afraid that Jason will not willingly come to me at any time that I send for him? He will, most gladly, I think. What am I doing here and what am I waiting for? I have gone so far that now I regret it.' She goes away from the door in this frame of mind, she comes to her bed and sits down, but

Mais je cuit bien certainement
Qu'el n'i serra pas longuement.
Relieve s'en, n'i peut plus estre,
S'alla ouvrir une fenestre.
Vit la lune, que ert levee,
Lores li est s'ire doublee:
«Dès or, fait elle, est il ennuiz:
Passee est ja la mie nuiz.»
Clot la fenestre, arriere torne;
Iriee est moult, pensive et morne.
En mi la chambre s'arresta
Tout en estant, si escouta:
La noise oï auques baissiee,
Car ja departoit la maisniee.
A l'uis s'en va pensive et pale,
Si esgarda par mi la sale.
As chamberlens vit les liz faire:
Lores li est bien à viaire
Que jusqu'à peu se coucheront
Et que gaires plus n'i serront.
Par la chambre va sus et jus,
Et souvent regarde au pertus,
Tant que trestuit furent couchié.
Bien a veü et agaitié
Le lit où Jason se coucha.

I am sure that she will not sit there long. She gets up, she can sit no longer, and goes to open a window. She sees the moon, which has risen, and then her anxiety is doubled. 'Now,' she says, 'this is maddening, it is already past midnight.' She shuts the window and turns away; she is full of misgivings, anxious and troubled. She stopped in the middle of the room and stood and listened; she heard the noise somewhat abated, for the people of the household were separating. Thoughtful and pale, she went to the door; she sees the chamberlains making the beds. Then it seems to her that people will soon go to bed and will not sit up much longer. She paces up and down the room, and often looks through the opening until they are all in bed; she saw and noted well the bed where Jason lay. She

Une soue maistre apela:
Tout son conseil li a gehi,
Car el se fioit moult en li.
«Droit à cel lit, fait elle, iras
Tout souavet, le petit pas;
Celui qu'i gist m'ameine o toi;
De noise te garde et d'esfroi.» ...

[Briseida's Monologue]

... QUANT Diomedès fu navrés
Et la fille Calcas le sot,
Conforta s'en tant com plus pot;
Mais n'en pot pas son cuer couvrir
Que plor et lermes et souspir
N'issent de li à nesun fuer.
Semblant fait bien que de son cuer
L'aime sor toute rien vivant:
N'en avoit onc fait grant semblant,
Jusqu'a cel jor, de lui amer,
Mais lores ne s'en pot celer;
Moult a grant duel et grant pesance.
Ne laisse pas pour reparlance
Qu'el nel voie dedans sa tente;

called one of her women to her, and told her all her mind, for she trusted her completely. 'Straight to that bed,' she said, 'you must go, quietly and softly. The one who lies there bring back with you: be careful not to make any noise or disturbance.'

... WHEN Diomedes was wounded and Calchas' daughter heard of it, she comforted herself as best she could; however, she could by no means so hide her feelings but that sobs and tears and sighs would out. It was clearly to be seen that she loved him above every living thing; up to that time, she had never shown much sign of loving him, but now she could not hide it; great were her grief and sorrow. She does not hesitate, for fear of slander, to go and see him

Dès or est toute en lui s'entente,
Dès or l'aime, dès or le tient,
Mais de lui perdre moult se crient.
Moult fu perilleuse la plaie;
Li oz des Greus moult s'en esmaie,
Et ele en plore o ses deus ieuz.
Ne remaint pour Calcas le vieuz,
Ne pour chasti ne pour manace,
Ne pour devié que il l'en face,
Que ne l'aille sovent veoir.
Dès or peut on apercevoir
Que vers lui a tout atorné
S'amour, son cuer et son pensé.
Si set el bien certainement
Qu'el se mesfait trop laidement.
A grant tort et à grant boisdie
S'est si de Troïlus partie,
Mesfait a moult, ce li est vis,
Et trop a vers celui mespris
Qui tant est beaus, riches et prouz
Et qui as armes les vaint touz.

in his tent; henceforth her mind is wholly set on him, henceforth she loves him, henceforth she clings to him; but she is very much afraid of losing him, for his wound is very dangerous; the Grecian army is in great dismay about it, and it brings tears to her two eyes. She will not desist because of old Calchas – neither for his admonishments nor for his threats, nor however much he forbids her to do so – from going often to see Diomedes. From now on it can clearly be seen that she has quite turned to him her love, her heart, and all her thoughts. And yet she knows very well how badly she is behaving. It is a great wrong and great treachery to have abandoned Troilus so; she has done very ill, it seems to her, and treated him very badly who is so handsome, noble, and full of valour, and who outshines them all in arms.

A soi meïsmes pense et dit:
«De moi n'ert ja fait bon escrit
Ne chantee bonne chançon.
Tel aventure ne tel don
Ne vousisse ja jour avoir.
Mauvais sen oi et fol, espoir,
Quant je trichai à mon ami
Qui onc vers moi nel deservi.
Ne l'ai pas fait si com je dui:
Mes cuers deüst bien estre en lui
Si atachiés et si fermés
Qu'autre n'en fust ja escoutés;
Fausse fui, et legiere et fole
Là où j'en entendi parole.
Qui loiaument se veut garder
N'en doit ja parole escouter:
Par parole sont engeignié
Li sage et li plus veziié.
Dès or avront pro que retraire
De moi cil qui ne m'aiment gaire;
Lor paroles de moi tendront
Les dames qui à Troie sont.
Honte i ai fait as damoiseles
Trop lait, et as riches puceles;

She thinks to herself and says: 'Of me nothing good will ever be written, and no good song be sung. Such a trick of fortune, such a gift of fate I never would have wished myself. It was wickedness in me – madness, perhaps – to be false to my lover who never deserved to be treated so; I have not behaved as I ought to have done: my heart should have been so fixed and so bound up in him that it would never listen to another. Faithless I was, wanton and foolish when I listened to another's words. She who would keep herself in loyal faith must never hear such words, for by words are deceived the wisest and the most cunning. Henceforth they will have plenty to say about me, those who do not like me. The ladies in Troy will be talking about me; I have brought great shame upon the maidens

44

Ma tricherie et mes mesfais
Lor sera mais tous jours retrais.
Peser m'en doit, et si fait el.
Trop est mes cuers muable et fel,
Qu'ami avoie le meillour
Cui mais pucele doint s'amour;
Ceus qu'il amast deüsse amer
Et ceus haïr et eschiver
Qui pourchaçassent son damage.
Ici pert il com je sui sage,
Quant à celui qu'il plus haoit,
Contre raison et contre droit,
Ai ma fine amor otroiee;
Trop en serai mais desproisiee.
Et que me vaut, se m'en repent?
En ço n'a mais recovrement.
Serai donc à cestui loiaus
Qui moult est prous et bons vassaus.
Je ne puis mais là revertir,
Ne de cestui moi resortir;
Trop ai ja en lui mon cuer mis,
Por c'en ai fait ce que j'en fis.
Et n'eüst pas ainsi esté,
Se fusse encore en la cité:

and the noble girls there; my treachery and my misdeeds will be a reproach to them for evermore. It should be a grief to me, and indeed it is. My heart is very wicked and fickle; for I had the best lover to whom a maiden ever gave her love. I should have loved those he loved and hated and avoided all who sought to do him evil. Here can be seen the measure of my worth, when on the man he hated most I have bestowed my love, against all reason and all right. But what good is it to repent of it? There is no going back now. So I will be true to this one, who is a noble and a valiant knight. I can no longer turn back, nor withdraw myself from him: I am already too much in love with him, that is why I have behaved as I have done. None of this would have happened if I had still been in the city: the thought would never have come into my

Ja jor mes cuers ne se pensast
Qu'il tressaillist ne qu'il changeast.
Mais ci estoie sans conseil
Et sans ami et sans feeil;
Si m'ot mestier tel atendance
Que m'ostast d'ire et de pesance.
Trop peüsse ore consirer
Et plaindre et moi desconforter
Et endurer jusqu'à la mort:
N'eüsse ja de là confort.
Morte fusse, pieça, ce croi,
Se n'eüsse merci de moi.
Sans ce que je ai fait folor,
Des jeus partis ai le meillor:
Tel ore avrai joie et leece
Que mes cuers fust en grant tristece;
Tels en porra en mal parler
Que me venist tart conforter.
Ne doit on mie por la gent
Estre en dolor et en torment.
Se touz li mondes est haitiés
Et mes cuers soit triste et iriés,
Iço ne m'est nule gaaigne;

heart of faltering or changing. But I was here without advice, without a friend or anyone to trust in, and in great need of such a consolation to save me sorrow and sad thoughts. Very sad indeed they might have been, and bitterly I might be complaining and lamenting now, and suffering until my death, but I should never have had any comfort from there. I should have died long since, I think, if I had not had pity on myself. Leaving aside the folly of my conduct, I have chosen the best way out of my dilemma. I shall have joy and gladness when my heart would have been in great sorrow; many a one perhaps will blame me for it who would not have hastened to my help. One is not bound to suffer grief and torment for the sake of other people's opinion. If everyone else is well pleased but my own heart is sad and sorrowful, that is no gain for me; but all the

Mais moult me deut li cuers et saigne
De ce que je sui en error;
Car nule rien qui a amor
Là où ses cuers soit point tiranz,
Troubles, doutos ne repentanz,
Ne peut estre ses jeus verais.
Sovent m'apai, sovent m'irais;
Sovent m'est bel et bien le vueil;
Sovent resont ploros mi ueil:
Ainsi est or, je n'en sai plus.
Dieus donge bien à Troïlus!
Quant nel puis avoir, ne il moi,
A cestui me doing et otroi.
Moult voudroie avoir cel talent
Que n'eüsse remembrement
Des euvres faites d'en arriere;
Ce me fait mal à grant maniere.
Ma conscience me reprent,
Qui à mon cuer fait grant torment.
Mais or m'estuet à ce torner
Tout mon corage et mon penser,
Veuille ou ne veuille, dès or mais,
Comfaitement Diomedès
Soit d'amor à moi atendanz,

same, my heart bleeds and grieves because I have done wrong. For no one who is in love, if his heart is divided, disturbed, uncertain, or troubled by remorse, can give free play to his affections. Often I feel at peace, but often full of care; often my love seems right and I accept it wholeheartedly, but then again my eyes are wet with tears; so it is now, I cannot help it. God send good fortune to Troilus, since I cannot have him nor he me, to the other I give and bind myself. How gladly would I have a mind that could banish all memory of things done in the past. This causes me great suffering; my conscience reproaches me and brings suffering to my heart. But now I must concentrate all my heart and all my thought, whatever I may wish, on making Diomedes confident of my love, so that he

Si qu'il en soit liez et joianz,
Et je de lui, puis qu'ainsi est.
Or truis mon cuer hardi et prest
De faire ce que lui plaira;
Ja plus orgueil n'i trovera.
Par parole l'ai tant mené
Qu'or li ferai sa volenté
Et son plaisir et son voloir.
Dieus m'en doint joie et bien avoir.» ...

CHRÉTIEN DE TROYES

Le Conte du Graal (*Le Roman de Perceval*)

... CE fu au tens qu'arbre foillissent,
Que glai et bois et pré verdissent,
Et cil oisel en lor latin
Chantent doucement au matin
Et toute rien de joie aflamme,
Que li fils à la veve femme
De la gaste forest soutaine
Se leva; et ne li fu paine

may be happy and glad because of me, and I because of him, as things have come about. Now I feel my heart bold and ready to do what will please him; no longer will he find any resistance in it. So far I have put him off with words, now I shall do all his will and his pleasure and desire. God grant that I may have joy and good from him.' ...

The Story of the Grail (*The Romance of Perceval*)

... IT was in the season when trees break into leaf, when iris plants and woods and meadows become green, when the birds in their own language sing sweetly in the morning, when everything is aflame with joy, that the son of the widow of the wild and lonely forest arose; it was no trouble to him to saddle his horse and take

Que il sa sele ne meïst
Sor son chaceor, et preïst
Trois javelos; et tout ainsi
Fors du manoir sa mere issi.
Il pensa que veoir iroit
Herceors que sa mere avoit,
Qui ses avaines li herçoient;
Bués douze et sis herces avoient.
Ainsi en la forest s'en entre,
Et maintenant li cuers du ventre
Pour le dous tens li resjoï,
Et pour le chant que il oï
Des oiseaus qui joie faisoient;
Toutes ces choses li plaisoient.
Pour la douçor du tens serain,
Osta au chaceor le frain,
Si le laissa aler paissant
Par l'herbe fresche verdoiant.

    Et cil qui bien lancier savoit
Des javelos que il avoit,
Aloit environ lui lançant,
Une heure arriere, l'autre avant,
Une heure bas et autre haut,
Tant qu'il oï parmi le gaut
Venir cinc chevaliers armés,

three darts; and thus he went out from his mother's dwelling. He thought he would go and see his mother's labourers, who were harrowing his oats; they had twelve oxen and six harrows. And so he went out into the forest; and immediately his heart was glad within him for the lovely weather and the song he heard from the rejoicing birds; all these things pleased him. The weather was so soft and mild that he took off the horse's bridle and let it loose to graze on the fresh green grass.

And he, who was skilled at throwing with the darts that he had, went along hurling them now here, now there, now high, now low, until he heard coming through the wood five armed knights, equipped with all their arms; and the arms of the approaching

De toutes armes adoubés.
Et moult grant noise demenoient
Les armes de ceus qui venoient,
Que souvent hurtelent as armes
Li raim des chaisnes et des charmes.
Les lances as escus hurtoient
Et tout li hauberc fresteloient;
Sonent li fust, sone li fers
Et des escus et des haubers.
Li vallés ot et ne voit pas
Ceus qui vers lui vienent le pas;
Moult se merveille et dist: «Par m'ame,
Voir se dist ma mere, ma dame,
Qui me dist que diable sont
Les plus laides choses du mont;
Et si dist por moi enseignier
Que pour eus se doit on seignier,
Mais cest ensaing desdaignerai,
Que ja voir ne m'en seignerai,
Ainz ferrai si tout le plus fort
D'un des javelos que je port
Que ja n'aprochera vers moi
Nuls des autres, si com je croi.»

knights made a very great noise, for often the branches of the oaks
and the hornbeams clashed against their armour, and the lances
struck against the shields, and all the hauberks jingled; both wood
and iron resounded, from the shields and from the hauberks. The
boy heard, but could not see, the men coming towards him at a
walking pace. He marvelled greatly and said, 'On my soul, she told
me the truth, my mother, my lady, when she said that devils are the
most hideous things in the world. And she said too, to instruct me,
that we should cross ourselves on meeting them. But I will scorn
this counsel, for indeed I will not cross myself, but will strike the
very strongest of them with one of the darts that I am carrying so
hard that none of the others will come near me, as I think.' So said

Ainsi à soi meïsmes dist
Li vallés, ainz qu'il les veïst;
Et quant il les vit en apert,
Que du bois furent descovert,
Et vit les haubers fremians
Et les helmes clers et luisans,
Et vit le blanc et le vermeil
Reluire contre le soleil,
Et l'or et l'azur et l'argent,
Si li fu moult bel et moult gent,
Et dist «Ha! sire Dieus, merci!
Ce sont angle que je voi ci.
Et voir or ai je moult pechié,
Or ai je moult mal esploitié,
Qui dis que c'estoient diable.
Ne me dist pas ma mere fable,
Qui me dist que li angle estoient
Les plus beles choses qui soient,
Fors Dieus qui est plus beaus que tuit.
Ci voi je Damedieu, ce cuit,
Car un si bel en i esgart
Que li autre, se Dieus me gart,
N'ont mie de beauté la disme.

the boy to himself before he saw them. And when he saw them clearly as they came out of the trees, and saw the glittering hauberks, and the bright shining helmets, and saw the white and the scarlet flashing in the sun, and the gold and the blue and the silver, it seemed to him most beautiful and noble, and he said, 'Ah Lord God, mercy! these are angels that I see here, and truly now have I sinned greatly; I did very wrong just now, when I said that they were devils. My mother was not deceiving me when she said that angels were the most beautiful things in existence except God, who is more beautiful than all. And here I see the Lord God, I think, for one so handsome I see among them that the others (so help me God!) have not a tenth of his beauty. My mother herself told me

Ce me dist ma mere meïsme
Qu'on doit Dieu sor tous aorer
Et supplier et honorer;
Et je aorerai cestui
Et tous les angles après lui.»
Maintenant vers terre se lance
Et dist trestoute sa creance
Et oroisons que il savoit,
Que sa mere apris li avoit.
Et li maistres des chevaliers
Le voit, et dist «Estez arriers!
A terre est de paor cheüs
Uns vallés qui nous a veüs.
Se nous alions tuit ensemble
Vers lui, il avroit, ce me semble,
Si grant paor que il morroit,
Ne respondre ne me porroit
A rien que je li demandasse.»
Cil s'arestent et il s'en passe
Vers le vallet grant aleüre,
Si le salue et asseüre
Et dist «Vallet, n'aiez paor.»
— «Non ai je, par le Salveor,

that we must worship God above all others, and pray to him and honour him, and I shall worship this being and all the angels after him.' Straightway he threw himself on the ground and said all his creed and the prayers that he knew, that his mother had taught him. And the leader of the knights saw him and said, 'Stay behind! A boy who has seen us has fallen to the ground in fear; if we all went towards him together, I think he would be so terrified that he would die and would not be able to reply to anything I asked him.' They stopped, and he went on quickly towards the boy and greeted and reassured him, and said, 'Do not be afraid, boy.' 'I am not afraid,' said the boy, 'by the Saviour in whom I believe. Are you not

Fait li vallés, en qui je croi.
N'estes vous Dieus?» – «Naie, par foi.»
«Qui estes donc?» – «Chevaliers sui.»
– «Ainc mais chevalier ne conui,
Fait li vallés, ne nul n'en vi
N'onques mais parler n'en oï,
Mais vous estes plus beaus que Dieus.
Car fuisse je or autretieus,
Aussi luisanz et aussi fais.»
Maintenant pres de lui s'est trais,
Et li chevaliers li demande:
«Veïs tu hui par ceste lande
Cinc chevaliers et trois puceles?»
Li vallés à autres nouveles
Enquerre et demander entent;
A sa lance sa main li tent,
Sel prent et dist «Beaus sire chiers,
Vous qui avez nom chevaliers,
Que est or ce que vous tenez?»
– «Or sui je moult bien assenez,
Fait li chevaliers, ce m'est vis.
Je cuidoie, beaus dous amis,
Nouveles aprendre de toi,
Et tu les veus oïr de moi;
Sel te dirai: ce est ma lance.»

God?' 'Not I, by my faith.' 'Who are you, then?' 'I am a knight. 'I never knew a knight before,' said the boy, 'nor saw one, or ever before heard tell of one. But you are more beautiful than God. How I wish I were such another, just as shining and just like you.' At this he drew near to him and the knight asked him, 'Have you seen today on this moor five knights and three maidens?' The boy was intent on asking and inquiring about other matters; he stretched out his hand to the lance, grasped it, and said, 'Fair dear lord, you who are called "knight", now what is this that you are holding?' 'Now I am being very well directed,' said the knight, 'it seems to me. I thought, fair sweet friend, to learn news from you, and you want to hear news from me. And I will tell you: that is my lance.' 'Do

— «Dites vous, fait il, qu'on la lance
Si com je fais mes javelos?»
— «Naie, vallet, tu es tous sos!
Ainz en fiert on tout demanois.»
— «Donc vaut mieus li uns de ces trois
Javelos que vous veez ci;
Que quanques je vueil en oci,
Oiseaus et bestes au besoing,
Et si les oci de si loing
Come on porroit d'un bojon traire.»
— «Vallet, de ce n'ai je que faire,
Mais des chevaliers me respont.
Di moi se tu sez où il sont,
Et les puceles veïs tu?»
Li vallés au pié de l'escu
Le prent et dist tout en apert
«Ce que est et de quoi vous sert?»
— «Vallet, fait il, ce est abés:
En autre nouvele me mes
Que je ne te quier ne demant.
Je cuidoie, se Dieus m'avant,
Que tu nouveles me deïsses
Ainz que de moi les apreïsses,
Et tu veus que je tes apreigne.

you mean,' said he, 'that you throw it as I do my darts?' 'No, boy.
How foolish you are! On the contrary, you strike with it directly.'
'Then one of these three darts you see here is more use, for I kill
whatever I want with it, birds and beasts according to my need;
and I kill from as far away as you can shoot an arrow.' 'Boy, that
does not concern me. But give me an answer about the knights.
Tell me if you know where they are, and if you saw the maidens.'
The boy seized him by the bottom of his shield and said boldly,
'What is this, and what is it for?' 'Boy,' he said, 'this is a trick;
you are changing the subject from what I ask and seek of you. I
thought, so God amend me, that you would give news to me rather
than learn news from me, and you want me to tell them to you. I

Je te dirai, coment qu'il preigne,
Car à toi volentiers m'acort:
Escu a nom ce que je port.»
– «Escu a nom?» – «Voire, fait cil,
Ne le doi mie tenir vil,
Car il m'est tant de bone foi
Que se nuls lance ou trait à moi,
Encontre tous les coups se met.
C'est li services qu'il me fet.»
    Atant cil qui furent arriere
S'en vindrent toute la charriere
Vers leur seigneur plus que le pas,
Si li dient isnellepas:
«Sire, que vous dist cist Galois?»
– «Il ne set pas toutes les lois,
Fait li sire, se Dieus m'ament,
Qu'a rien nule que li demant
Ne me respont il ainc à droit,
Ainz demande de quanqu'il voit
Coment a nom et qu'on en fait,»
– «Sire, sachiez tout entresait
Que Galois sont tout par nature
Plus fol que bestes en pasture;
Cist est aussi come une beste.

will tell you, come what may, for I have taken a liking to you: what I am carrying is called a shield.' 'It is called a shield?' 'Yes, indeed,' he replied, 'I must by no means scorn it, for it is so faithful to me that if anyone attacks me with lance or arrow it intercepts every blow. That is the service that it does me.' At this point, those that were behind came briskly up along the track towards their lord, and said to him without delay, 'Sire, what is this Welsh boy saying to you?' 'He is not quite right in his mind,' said the leader, 'so God amend me, for to nothing I ask him will he give a straight answer, but asks about everything he sees, what it is called and what it is used for.' 'Sire, you may know for certain that Welshmen are all by nature more stupid than the cattle in the fields. This boy

Fols est qui dalez lui s'areste,
S'à la muse ne veut muser
Et le tens en folie user.»
— «Ne sai, fait il, mais se Dieu voie,
Ainz que soie mis à la voie,
Quanqu'il voudra tout li dirai;
Ja autrement n'en partirai.»
Lors li demande de rechief:
«Vallet, fait il, ne te soit grief,
Mais des cinc chevaliers me di
Et des puceles autresi
S'hui les encontras ne veïs.»
Et li vallés le tenoit pris
Par le hauberc, et si le tire.
«Or me dites, fait il, beaus sire,
Que c'est que vous avez vestu?»
— «Vallet, fait il, donc nel sez tu?»
— «Je non.» — «Vallet, c'est mes haubers,
S'est aussi pesans come fers,
Qu'il est de fer, ce vois tu bien.»
— «De ce, fait il, ne sai je rien,
Mais moult est beaus, se Dieus me saut.
Qu'en faites vous, et que vous vaut?»

is just like a beast. It is useless to stay with him, unless we want to play the fool and waste our time on nonsense.' 'I don't know about that,' said he, 'but, as I hope to see God, before I set off again I will tell him everything he wants to know. Otherwise I will not leave him.' Then he asked him again, 'Boy,' he said, 'I do not want to bother you, but tell me about the five knights and also about the maidens, if you met them or saw them today.' And the boy was holding him by the hauberk, and pulled at it. 'Now tell me,' said he, 'fair sir, what is this thing that you are wearing?' 'Boy,' said he, 'do you not know then?' 'Not I.' 'Boy, it is my hauberk, and it is as heavy as iron, for it is made of iron, as you see.' 'I don't know anything about that,' he said, 'but it is very beautiful, so God save me. What do you do with it, and what use is it to you?'

— «Vallet, c'est à dire legier.
Se voloies à moi lancier
Javelot ou saiete traire,
Ne me porroies nul mal faire.»
— «Dans chevaliers, de tels haubers
Gart Dieus les biches et les cers,
Que nule ocirre n'en porroie
Ne jamais après ne courroie.»
Et li chevaliers li redit:
«Vallet, se Damedieus t'aït,
Se tu me sez dire nouveles
Des chevaliers et des puceles?»
Et cil qui petit fu senés
Li dist: «Fustes vous ainsi nés?»
— «Naie, vallet, ce ne peut estre
Qu'ainsi peüst ja nuls hom nestre.»
— «Qui vous atorna donc ainsi?»
— «Vallet, je te dirai bien qui.»
— «Dites le donc.» — «Moult volentiers:
N'a pas encor cinc ans entiers
Que tout cest harnois me dona
Li rois Artus qui m'adouba.
Mais or me redi que devindrent
Li chevalier qui par ci vindrent,

'Boy, that is easy to say. If you wanted to throw a dart or shoot an arrow at me, you could not do me any harm.' 'Sir knight, may God keep hinds and stags from such hauberks, for I should never be able to kill any of them and I should no longer hunt them.' And the knight said to him once more, 'Boy, so may God help you, can you tell me news of the knights and the maidens?' And he, who had but little sense, said, 'Were you born like this?' 'No, boy, that could not be, for no man can be born like this.' 'Who equipped you then like this?' 'Boy, I will tell you who.' 'Tell it then.' 'Willingly. It is not yet five whole years since all this harness was given to me by King Arthur, who dubbed me knight. But now you tell me: what has become of the knights who passed this way, those who

Qui les trois puceles conduient.
Vont il le pas, ou il s'en fuient?»
Et cil dist: «Sire, or esgardez
Le plus haut bois que vous veez,
Qui cele montaigne avironne.
Là sont li destroit de Valbone.»
— «Et que de ce, fait il, beaus frere?»
— «Là sont li herceor ma mere,
Qui ses terres sement et erent,
Et se ces gens i trespasserent,
S'il les virent, sel vous diront.»
Et cil dient qu'il i iront
Avec lui, se il les i maine,
Jusqu'à ceus qui hercent l'avaine.

    Li vallés prent son chaceor
Et va là où li herceor
Herçoient les terres arees
Où les avaines sont semees.
Et quant il virent lor seignor,
Si tremblerent tout de paor.
Et savez pour quoi il le firent?
Pour les chevaliers que il virent,
Qui avec lui armé venoient,

were leading the three maidens? Are they going slowly or are they in flight?' And he said, 'Sire, now look at the highest wood that you see surrounding that hill. That is the Pass of Valbone.' 'And what of that,' said he, 'fair brother?' 'There are my mother's harrowers, who sow and plough her land; and if those people passed that way and they saw them, they will tell you.' And the knights said that they would go there with him if he would take them as far as the men who were harrowing the oats.

The boy took his horse, and went to where the harrowers were harrowing the ploughed land where the oats were sown, and when they saw their lord they all trembled with fear. And do you know why they did so? Because of the knights that they saw coming with him in armour. For they knew well that if they had told him their

Que bien savent, s'il li avoient
Lor afaire dit et lor estre,
Que il voudroit chevaliers estre;
Et sa mere en istroit du sen,
Car destorner l'en cuidoit l'en
Que ja chevalier ne veïst
Ne lor afaire n'apreïst. ...

BEROUL

Le Roman de Tristran

... Tristrans s'appuie sor son arc;
Souvent regrete le roi Marc,
Son oncle, cui a fait tel tort,
Sa femme mise à tel descort.
Tristran au soir se dementoit;
Oiez d'Iseut com li estoit:
Souvent disoit: «Lasse, dolente,
Pour quoi eüstes vous jovente?
En bois estes comme autre serve,
Petit trouvez qui ci vous serve.
Je sui reïne, mais le nom
En ai perdu par ma poison
Que nous beümes en la mer.

business and their way of life he would want to be a knight, and
this would drive his mother out of her mind, for they had hoped to
prevent him from ever seeing a knight or finding out anything
about them. ...

The Romance of Tristram

... Tristram leans on his bow; repeatedly he grieves for King
Mark, his uncle, whom he has so wronged, and his wife, whom he
has so estranged from him. Tristram lamented that evening; listen
how it was with Iseult. Often she cried: 'Alas, poor wretch, what
have you done with your youth? You are in the woods like any
peasant woman, and little can you find to do you service here. I am
a queen, but the name of queen I have lost through my potion that

Ce fist Brengain, qu'i dut garder.
Lasse! si male garde en fist!
El n'en pot mais, car trop mesprist.
Les damoiseles des honors,
Les filles as frans vavasors,
Deüsse ensemble o moi tenir
En mes chambres, pour moi servir,
Et les deüsse marier
Et as seignors pour bien donner.
Ami Tristran, en grant error
Nous mist qui le boivre d'amor
Nous aporta ensemble à boivre;
Mieus ne nous pot il pas deçoivre.»
Tristran li dist: «Reïne gente,
En mal usons nostre jovente.
Bele amie, se je peüsse,
Par conseil que je en eüsse,
Faire au roi Marc acordement,
Qu'il pardonnast son mautalent
Et qu'il preïst nostre escondit,
Qu'onques nul jour, n'en fait n'en dit,
N'oi à vous point de druerie
Qui li tornast à vilenie,
N'a chevalier en son roiaume,
Ne de Lidan tresqu'en Dureaume,

we drank on the sea. This Brengain did, for she was in charge of it; alas! how ill she guarded it! She could not help it, for she made a great mistake. Maidens of noble houses and daughters of free vavassours I should have with me in my own rooms to serve me, and I should arrange marriages for them and honourably bestow them on their lords. Tristram, my love, she who brought us the love potion to drink together led us into great sin; she could not have deceived us more grievously.' Tristram said to her: 'Noble queen, how ill we wear out our youth. My sweet love, if I could, by any plan that I could make, come to an agreement with King Mark that he should forgo his wrath and accept our assurance that never at any time, by word or deed, have I loved you in a way to bring dishonour on him, there is no knight in his realm, not from Lidan to

S'il vouloit dire que amour
Eüsse o vous pour deshonour,
Ne m'en trouvast en champ, armé.
Et s'il avoit en volenté,
Quant vous avriez desresnie,
Qu'il me soufrist de sa mesnie,
Jel serviroie à grant honour,
Comme mon oncle et mon seignour;
N'avroit soudoier en sa terre
Qui mieus le servist de sa guerre.
Et s'il estoit à son plaisir
Vous à prendre et moi de guerpir,
Qu'il n'eüst soin de mon servise,
Je m'en iroie au roi de Frise,
Ou m'en passeroie en Bretagne,
O Governal, sans plus compagne.» ...

«Reïne franche, où que je soie,
Vostre tous jours me clameroie.
Ne volsisse la departie,
S'estre peüst la compagnie,
Ne fust, bele, la grant soufraite
Que vous soufrez et avez faite
Tous dis, pour moi, par desertine.

Durham, who, if he should say that I had loved you dishonourably, would not find me armed in the field. And if it were the king's will, when you had cleared your name, to accept me into his household, I would serve him with great honour, as my uncle and my lord; he would have no warrior in his land who would serve him better. And if it were his pleasure to take you and to be rid of me, and he had no wish for my service, I should go to the king of Frisia, or cross to Brittany with Governal and no other company.' ...

'Noble queen, wherever I may be, I shall always call myself yours. I should not wish to part from you if we could stay together, if it were not, fair love, for the great ills you suffer, and have always suffered for me in the wilderness. For me you lose the name of

Pour moi perdez nom de reïne;
Estre peüsses à honour
En tes chambres, o ton seignour,
Ne fust, dame, li vins herbés
Qui à la mer nous fu donnés.
Iseut, franche, gente façon,
Conseille moi que nous feron.»

«Sire, Jesu soit graciés
Quant deguerpir voulez pechiés!
Amis, membre vous de l'ermite
Ogrin, qui de la loi escrite
Nous preëcha et tant nous dist,
Quant tornastes à son abit,
Qui est el chief de cel boschage.
Beaus amis douz, se ja corage
Vous ert venus de repentir,
Or ne peüst mieus avenir;
Sire, courons à lui ariere.
De ce sui toute fianciere:
Conseil nous donroit honorable
Par quoi à joie pardurable
Pourrons encore bien venir.» ...

queen. You could be held in honour, in your own halls, with your lord, were it not, lady, for the herb-charmed wine which was given to us on the sea. Iseult, noble and beautiful lady, advise me what we should do.'

'My lord, Jesu be thanked that you wish to cast off your sin. My friend, remember Ogrin, the hermit who preached to us of the law of the scriptures and talked to us for so long when you went to his cell, which is at the end of this wood. Fair sweet love, if now it were in your heart to repent, nothing better could happen; my lord, let us hasten back to him. Of this I am sure, he will give us honourable counsel, through which we may well come to eternal joy.' ...

MARIE DE FRANCE

Le Lai de Chevrefeuil

ASSEZ me plaist et bien le veuil
Du lai qu'on nomme Chevrefeuil
Que la verité vous en cont,
Et pour quoi il fu fait et dont.
Plusours le m'ont conté et dit
Et je l'ai trouvé en escrit
De Tristran et de la reïne,
De leur amour qui tant fu fine,
Dont il eurent mainte dolour,
Puis en moururent en un jour.

Li reis Mark esteit coroucié,
Vers Tristran son neveu irié;
De sa terre le congëa
Pour la reïne qu'il ama.
En sa contree en est alés;
En Suhtwales, où il fu nés,
Un an demoura tout entier,
Ne pot ariere repairier;

The Lay of the Honeysuckle

I AM very glad and willing to tell you the true story of the lay called 'Honeysuckle', and why it was made and how it arose. Many people have told and recited it to me, and I have seen it written down about Tristram and the Queen and their love which was so true, for which they suffered many a sorrow, and for which in the end both died on the same day.

King Mark was full of wrath and angry with Tristram his nephew; he drove him from his country because of the Queen, whom he loved. Tristram went away to his own country in South Wales, where he was born. He stayed there a whole year, he was not able to return; but afterwards he put himself in peril of death

63

Mais puis se mist en abandon
De mort et de destruction.
Ne vous esmerveilliez neant:
Car qui aime moult lealment,
Moult est dolenz et trespensés,
Quant il nen a ses volentés.
Tristran est dolent et pensis:
Pour ço se met de son païs.
En Cornewaille va tout dreit,
Là où la reïne maneit.
En la forest tout seul se mist,
Ne vouleit pas qu'on le veïst;
En la vespree s'en eisseit,
Quant tens de herberger esteit.
O païsans, o povre gent
Preneit la nuit herbergement.
Les noveles lor enquereit
Du rei com il se conteneit.
Ce li dient qu'il ont oï
Que li baron erent bani,
A Tintagel doivent venir,
Li rois i veut sa cort tenir,
A pentecoste i seront tuit;
Moult i avra joie et deduit,
Et la reïne i sera.

and destruction. Do not be amazed at that, for whoever loves truly is in great grief, and heavy-hearted, when he cannot have what he desires. Tristram was sad and downcast, therefore he left his own land and went straight to Cornwall, where the Queen was living. He hid himself all alone in the forest, he did not want anyone to see him; he came out only at nightfall, when it was time to seek lodging; with peasants and with poor people he sought shelter at night. He asked them for news of what the King was doing. They told him that they had heard that the barons had been summoned. They were to come to Tintagel; there the King wished to hold his court. At Whitsuntide they would all be there, and there was to be great joy and celebration, and the Queen was to be there.

Tristran l'oï, moult se haita:
Ele ne pourra mie aler
Qu'il ne la voie trespasser.
Le jour que li rois fu meüs,
Et Tristran est al bois venus
Sur le chemin que il saveit
Que la route passer deveit;
Une codre trencha par mi,
Toute carree la fendi.
Quant il a paré le baston,
De son coutel escrit son nom.
Se la reïne s'aparceit,
Qui moult grant gardë en preneit
(Autre fois li fu avenu
Que si l'aveit aparceü)
De son ami bien conoistra
Le baston quant el le verra.
Ce fu la somme de l'escrit
Qu'il li aveit mandé et dit:
Que longes ot ilec esté
Et atendu et sojorné
Pour espier et pour savoir
Comment il la peüst veoir,
Car ne pot nient vivre sans li;

Tristram heard it, and was very glad. She would hardly be able to go there without his seeing her pass by. The day the King set out, Tristram came to the wood on the road where he knew the company must pass. He cut off a hazel branch and squared it off completely. When he had prepared the stick, he wrote his name upon it with his knife. If the Queen saw it, and she would be looking carefully for it (at other times it had happened that she had become aware of his presence in this way) she would easily recognize the stick left by her lover when she saw it. This was the matter of the letter which he had sent and told her that he had been a long time waiting and lingering there to spy out and discover some way of seeing her, for he simply could not live without her. They two

D'eus deus fu il tout autresi
Comme du chevrefeuil esteit
Qui à la codre se preneit:
Quant il s'i est laciés et pris
Et tout entour le fust s'est mis,
Ensemble peuvent bien durer;
Mais qui puis les veut desevrer,
La codre meurt hastivement
Et li chevrefeuil ensement.
«Bele amie, si est de nous:
Ne vous sans moi, ne moi sans vous.»

La reïne va chevauchant;
Ele esgarda tout un pendant,
Le baston vit, bien l'aparçut,
Toutes les letres i conut.
Les chevaliers qui la menoient,
Qui ensemblë o li erroient,
Commanda tous à arrester:
Descendre veut et reposer.
Cil ont fait son commandement.
Ele s'en va loin de sa gent;
Sa meschine apela à soi,
Brengain, qui fu de bonne foi.

were like the honeysuckle and the hazel which it clings to, when it is all enlaced and caught up in it, and wreathed around the wood; together they can long endure, but if anyone should try to separate them, the hazel dies at once and the honeysuckle too. 'My sweet love, so it is with us: you cannot live without me, nor I without you.'

The Queen came riding along; she looked along a slope, she caught sight of the stick, she saw it clearly, she made out all the letters. She told all the knights who were conducting her and riding along with her to stop: she wished to dismount and rest. They did as she told them. She went away from her people; she called to her side her maid Brengain, who was trustworthy, she went a little way

Du chemin un peu s'esloigna;
Dedans le bois celui trouva
Qui plus l'amoit que rien vivant.
Entre eus meinent joie moult grant.
A li parla tout à leisir,
Et ele li dit son plaisir;
Puis li mostre confaitement
Del roi avra acordement,
Et que moult li aveit pesé
De ce qu'il l'ot si congeé;
Par encusement l'aveit fait.
Atant s'en part, son ami lait;
Mais quant ce vint au desevrer,
Donc comencerent à plorer.
Tristran à Wales s'en rala,
Tant que ses oncles le manda.

Pour la joie qu'il ot eüe
De s'amie qu'il ot veüe
Et pour ce qu'il aveit escrit,
Si com la reïne l'ot dit,
Pour les paroles remembrer,
Tristran, qui bien saveit harper,

from the path. In the wood she found him who loved her above all
living things. Great was their joy to be together. He talked to her
at his leisure, and she to him as much as she wished, and then she
told him how he could come to an agreement with the king, and
how much it had grieved her that the king had banished him in that
way – he had done it because of an accusation. Then she went away
and left her lover, but when it came to parting, then they began to
weep. Tristram went back to Wales until his uncle sent for him.

Because of the joy it had given him to see his love, and because of
what he had written, just as the Queen had directed him so as to
keep his words in memory, Tristram, who was a skilled harpist,

En aveit fait un nouvel lai;
Assez brefment le nommerai:
«Gotelef» l'apelent en engleis,
«Chevrefeuil» le noment Franceis.
Dit vous en ai la verité
Del lai que j'ai ici conté.

from LA FOLIE TRISTRAN

... TRISTRAN, quant ot Iseut nommer,
Du cuer comence à souspirer;
Pourpense soi d'une voidie
Com il pourra veoir s'amie.

Bien set qu'il n'i pourra parler
Pour nul engin qu'il peut trover.
Prouesse ne lui peut valoir,
Sens, ne cointise, ne savoir;
Car Mark li rois, ce set il bien,

made a new lay about it all. I will soon tell you its name: 'Goatleaf'
they call it in English, and 'Chevrefeuil' in French. Now I have
explained to you the origin of the lay I have just told you.

from TRISTRAM'S MADNESS

... WHEN Tristram hears them speak of Iseult, he begins to sigh
from his heart; he tries to think of some device by which he will be
able to see his love.

Well he knows that he will not be allowed to speak to her by any
means; neither bravery nor wisdom will avail him, neither skill nor
knowledge; for King Mark, as he is well aware, hates him above

Le haoit sur trestoute rien,
Et s'il vif prendre le pooit,
Il set bien que il l'ociroit.
Donc se pourpense de s'amie
Et dit: «Cui en chaut s'il m'ocie?
Bien doi mourir pour soue amour.
Las! Ja me muir je chascun jour.
Iseut, pour vous tant par me deuil,
Iseut, pour vous bien mourir veuil.
Iseut, se ci me saviez,
Ne sai s'à moi parleriez.
Pour vostre amour sui afolés,
Ci sui venu et nel savez.
Ne sai comment parler o vous,
Pour ce sui je tant angoissous.
Or veuil esprouver autre rien,
Savoir se ja me vendroit bien:
Feindre moi fol, faire folie
Donc n'est ce sens et grant voidie?» ...

everything, and if he could take him alive he knows very well that he would kill him. Then he thinks of his love and says: 'What does it matter if he kills me? I ought to be willing to die for her. Alas! I die for her every day; Iseult, I long for you so much, Iseult, for you I will gladly die. Iseult, if you knew I was here, I do not know whether you would speak to me. I am driven mad for love of you; I have come here and you do not know it. I do not know how I can speak with you, and that is why I feel such anguish. Now I will try something else to see if it will succeed. I will pretend to be mad: to play the fool, is that not wisdom and great subtlety?' ...

Li fols entre ens par le guichet;
Contre lui courent li valet.
Il l'escrient com on fait lou:
«Veez le fol! hou! hou! hou! hou!»
Li vallet et li escuier
De bois le cueillent arocher.
Par la cort le vont convoiant
Li fol valet quil vont sivant.
Il leur trestourne moult souvent,
Estre qu'il i jacte à talent:
Se nuls l'asaut devers le destre,
Il tourne et fiert devers senestre.
Vers l'uis de la sale aprocha,
Le pel el col dedans entra.
Senes s'en aperçut li rois,
Là où il sist al maistre dois.
Il dit: «Or voi un bon sergeant:
Faites le moi venir avant.»
Plusors saillent, contre lui vont,
En sa guise salué l'ont,
Puis si amenerent le fol
Devant le roi, le pel el col.

The madman goes in at the gate; the boys run to meet him and shout at him as people do at a wolf: 'Look at the madman! Hou! hou! hou! hou!' The boys and squires start throwing pieces of wood at him; they go with him and follow him through the court-yard. He often rounds on them, but he has his own special way of laying about him: if one of them attacks him on the right, he turns and strikes out to the left. He went up to the door of the hall; with his stake on his shoulder he went in. At once the king saw him from where he sat at the high table. He said: 'I see a good fellow there; make him come up here in front of me.' Several jumped up and went to meet him; they greeted him in his own fashion, then they brought the fool before the king, his stake still on his shoulder.

Markes dit: «Bien vegnez, amis!
Dont estes vous? Qu'avez ci quis?»
Li fols respont: «Bien vous dirai
Dont sui et que je ci quis ai:
Ma mere fu une baleine,
En mer hanta come sereine,
Mais je ne sai où je nasqui.
Moult sai je bien qui me nourri.
Une grant tigre m'alaita
En une roche où me trouva.
El me trouva sur un perron,
Cuida que fusse son faon,
Si me nourri de sa mamele.
Mais une seur ai je moult bele,
Cele vous dorrai, se voulez,
Pour Iseut que vous tant amez.»
Li rois s'en rit et puis respont:
«Que dit la merveille du mond?»
— «Roi, je vous dorrai ma seror
Pour Iseut que aim par amor.
Faisons bargaine, faisons change:
Bon est à essaier estrange.

Mark said: 'Welcome, friend! Where are you from and what do you seek here?' The fool replies: 'Indeed, I will tell you where I come from and what I came to seek. My mother was a whale; she lived in the sea like a mermaid, but I do not know where I was born; I know very well who brought me up: a huge tigress suckled me on a rock where she found me. She found me on a great stone, thought I was her cub, and fed me from her udder. But I have a sister who is very beautiful; I will give her to you, if you wish, in exchange for Iseult whom you love so much.'

The king laughed, and then replied: 'What says the Wonder of the World?' 'King, I will give you my sister for Iseult, whom I love. Let's make a bargain, let's exchange them; it is a good thing

D'Iseut estes tout ennuiés:
A une autre vous acointez!
Baillez m'Iseut, je la prendrai;
Reis, par amour vous servirai.»

Li rois l'entent et si s'en rit,
Et dit au fol: «Si Dieu t'aït,
Se je te doinse la reïne
Avoir, et mette en ta saisine,
Or me di que tu en feroies,
Ou en quel part tu la menroies.»
— «Rois, fait li fols, là sus en l'air
Ai une sale où je repair.
De verre est faite, bele et grant;
Li soleil va parmi raiant,
En air est et par nues pent,
Ne berce ne crolle pour vent.
Delès la salle a une chambre
Faite de cristal et de lambre.
Li soleil, quant par main levra,
Leans moult grant clarté rendra.» …

to try a foreign woman. You are quite tired of Iseult, you ought to take another woman. Give Iseult to me, I will take her. King, I will do this for you for love.'

The king hears him and laughs at him. He says to the fool: 'So may God help you, if I gave you the queen in your possession and put her in your hands, now tell me what you would do with her, and where you would take her?' 'King,' said the fool, 'up there in the sky I have a hall where I dwell; it is all made of glass, both fair and wide; the sunshine comes pouring through it. It is in the air, and hanging from the clouds; it will not rock nor stir in any wind. Beside the hall there is a chamber made of crystal and precious panelling. The sun rising in the morning will fill it with great brightness.' …

THOMAS

Le Roman de Tristran

... LA nef desirent à la rive;
Encore ne la virent pas.
Tristrans en est dolenz et las,
Souvent se plaint, souvent sospire
Pour Iseut que il tant desire;
Plore des ieus, son cors deteurt,
A poi que du desir ne meurt.
En cele angoisse, en cel ennui
Vient sa femme Iseut devant lui.
Pourpensee de grant engin,
Dit: «Amis, or vient Kaherdin.
Sa nef ai veüe en la mer,
A grant peine l'ai veu sigler;
Nequedent je l'ai si veüe
Que pour la soe l'ai conue.
Dieus doint que tel novele aport
Dont vous au cuer aiez confort.»

Tristrans tresaut de la novele,
Dit à Iseut: «Amie bele,

The Romance of Tristram

... ON shore they are longing for the ship to come; as yet they
have not seen it. Tristram is full of grief and weariness; often he
moans, often he sighs for Iseult, whom he so longs to see. His tears
fall down, he tosses about, he almost dies from his longing. In this
anguish, in this trouble, his wife Iseult comes before him; her mind
full of great treachery, she says: 'My love, now Kaherdin is coming: I have seen his ship on the sea; I could only just see it, but still
I saw it well enough to know that it was his. God grant it brings us
some news that will give comfort to your heart.'
Tristram starts up at this; he says to Iseult: 'Fair love, are you

Savez pour voir que c'est sa nef?
Or me dites quel est le tref.»
Ce dit Iseut: «Jel sai pour voir.
Sachez que le sigle est tout noir.
Trait l'ont amont et levé haut
Pour ice que li venz lor faut.»
Donc a Tristrans si grant dolour
Onques n'ot ne n'avra maour,
Et torne soi vers la paroi;
Donc dit: «Dieus saut Iseut et moi!
Quant à moi ne voulez venir,
Pour vostre amour m'estuet mourir.
Je ne puis plus tenir ma vie;
Pour vous muer, Iseut, bele amie.
N'avez pitié de ma langour,
Mais de ma mort avrez dolour.
Ce m'est, amie, grant confort
Que pitié avrez de ma mort.»
«Amie Iseut» trois fois a dit,
A la quarte rent l'espirit.

Idonc plorent par la maison
Li chevalier, li compaignon.
Li criz est haut, la plainte grant.

sure that it is his ship? Tell me, what kind of sail has it?' Iseult
says: 'I am sure of it, and I can tell you that the sail is all black;
they have hoisted it and raised it high because they have not wind
enough.' Then Tristram feels so sharp a pang as he had never felt
before, nor ever will again, and he turns his face to the wall and
says: 'God help Iseult and me! Since you will not come to me, I
must die for your love. I can cling to life no longer. I am dying for
you, Iseult, my fair love; you will not take pity on my suffering,
but my death will be a grief to you. My love, it is a great consolation to me that you will mourn my death.' 'Iseult, my love,' he says
three times, and at the fourth gives up his spirit.

Then the knights his companions weep throughout the house;
the cry is loud, the lamentation great. Knights and servants leap

Saillent chevalier et sergent
Et portent le cors de son lit,
Puis le couchent sur un samit,
Couvrent le d'un paile roié.

Li venz est en la mer levé
Et fiert soi en milieu du tref;
A terre fait venir la nef.
Iseut est de la nef issue,
Ot les grans plaintes en la rue,
Les seins as mostiers, as chapeles;
Demande as homes quels noveles,
Pourquoi il font tel soneïs,
Et de quoi soit li ploreïs.
Uns anciens donques li dit:
«Bele dame, si Dieu m'aït,
Nous avons issi grant dolour
Que onques genz n'orent maour.
Tristran li prouz, li francs, est mort.
A tous ceus du regne ert confort.
Larges estoit as bosognous
Et grant aïe as dolorous.

forward to carry the body from his bed and lay it down on a samite
cloth and cover it with one of striped silk.

The wind has risen over the sea and hurled itself upon the midst
of the sail, and it brings the ship to shore. Iseult has come out of
the ship, she hears the great lamentations in the street and the bells
in churches and chapels, and she asks the people what the news is
for which they make such ringing and what the cause of the
lamentations. An old man then says to her: 'Fair lady, as God may
help me, we have such a sorrow that no people ever had a greater.
Tristram the brave, the good, is dead. He was the comfort of all in
the kingdom. Generous he was to the needy, and full of help to those

D'une plaie qu'en son cors ut
En son lit orendroit morut.
Onques si grant chaitiveson
N'avint à ceste region.»

Tres que Iseut la novele ot,
De dolour ne peut soner mot.
De sa mort est si adolee
La rue va desafublee
Devant les autres el palais.
Breton ne virent onques mais
Femme de la soe beauté:
Merveillent soi par la cité
Dont ele vient, qui ele soit.
Iseut va là où le cors voit,
Si se tourne vers orient,
Pour lui prie pitousement:
«Amis Tristran, quant mort vous voi,
Par raison vivre puis ne doi.
Mort estes pour la moie amour,
Et je muer, amis, de tendrour,
Quant je à tens ne poi venir
Pour vous et vostre mal garir.
Amis, amis, pour vostre mort

in trouble. He died just now in his bed from a wound he had in his body. Never so great a calamity befell this country.'

When Iseult hears the news, she cannot speak a word for sorrow. She is so grief-stricken at his death that she goes without a cloak along the street to the palace before the others. The Bretons had never before seen a woman of her beauty; throughout the city they are wondering whence she comes and who she may be. Iseult goes to the place where she sees the body, and she turns towards the East and prays for him tenderly. 'Tristram, my love, when I see you dead, it is not reasonable that I should live any longer. You have died for my love and I am dying for sorrow that I could not come in time to cure you and heal your sickness. My love! my love!

N'avrai jamais de rien confort,
Joie, ne hait, ne nul deduit.
Icil orages soit destruit
Qui tant me fist, amis, en mer,
Que n'i poi venir, demourer!
Se je i fusse à tens venue,
Vie vous eüsse rendue,
Et parlé doucement à vous
De l'amour qui fu entre nous;
Plainte eüsse nostre aventure,
Nostre joie, nostre envoisure,
Et la peine et la grant dolour
Qui a esté en nostre amour,
Et eüsse ice recordé
Et vous baisié et acolé.
Se je n'ai peü vous garir,
Qu'ensemble puissons donc mourir.
Quant je à tens venir n'i poi
Et je l'aventure ne soi,
Et venue sui à la mort,
De meisme boivre avrai confort.
Pour moi avez perdu la vie,
Et je frai com veraie amie:
Pour vous veuil mourir ensement.»

because of your death nothing can ever give me consolation nor joy nor gladness nor any pleasure. A curse upon the storm that kept me so long on the sea that I could not come. If I had been in time, I would have brought you back to life and talked softly with you of the love that was between us. I should have spoken tenderly of all that has come to us, our joy and our delight, and all the sorrow and the great grief that there has been in our love. I should have recalled all this and kissed you and embraced you. Since I have not been able to heal you, let us then die both together; since I could not get here in time and did not know that this was happening, and have come at your death, I too will drink from the same cup. You have lost your life for me, and I shall do as a true lover should: I too shall die for you.' She embraces him and lies down beside

Embrace le et si s'estent,
Baise li la bouche et la face
Et moult estroit à li l'embrace,
Cors à cors, bouche à bouche estent,
Son espirit à itant rent,
Et meurt dejoste lui ainsi
Pour la dolour de son ami.
Tristrans morut pour son desir,
Iseut, qu'à tens n'i pot venir.
Tristrans morut pour soe amour
Et la bele Iseut pour tendrour. ...

HÉLINAND

Les Vers de la Mort

... MORT, Mort, qui ja ne seras lasse
De muer haute chose en basse,
Trop volentiers fesisse aprendre
Ambesdeus les rois, se j'osasse,
Com tu trais raseor de chasse
Por rere ceus qui ont que prendre.
Mort qui les montés fais descendre
Et qui des cors as rois fais cendre,

him, kisses his mouth and his face and draws him very closely to
her, body to body, mouth to mouth. Then she gives up her spirit,
and so dies beside him, for grief for her lover. Tristram died of his
longing, Iseult because she could not come in time; Tristram died
for love of her, and the fair Iseult for sorrow. ...

Lines on Death

DEATH, Death, you who tirelessly cast down the highest to the
depths, very gladly would I make known to the kings of France
and England, if I dared, how you draw out your razor from its
sheath to shave those who have good things to lose. Death, you
who bring the exalted low, and turn the bodies of kings to ashes,

Tu as tramail et roiz et nasse
Pour devant le haut homme tendre
Qui por sa poesté estendre
Son ombre tressaut et trespasse.

Mort, tu abaz à un seul tour
Aussi le roi dedans sa tour
Com le povre dedans son toit:
Tu erres adès sanz sejour
Pour chascun semondre à son jour
De paier Dieu trestout son droit.
Mort, tu tiens tant l'ame en destroit
Qu'ele ait paié quanqu'ele doit,
Sanz nul restor et sanz retour.
Pour c'est fous qui sor s'ame acroit,
Qu'ele n'a gage qu'ele ploit,
Puis qu'ele vient nue à l'estour. ...

Mort, qui est à veüe escrite
En la vieille face despite,
Se repont bien es jovenceaus;
Et plus entour ceus se delite
Qui par fierté li dient: «Fui te!»

you have your nets and toils and snares to set in the path of the
great man while he, in order to extend his power, is striving to
overleap his own shadow.

Death, you strike down, at one same time, both the king in his
tower and the poor man beneath his thatch. You go ceaselessly from
place to place to summon every man, as his day falls due, to pay his
debt in full to God. Death, you hold the soul in your grip till it has
paid all that it owes without return or restitution. Therefore he is a
fool who seeks credit for his soul, for it has never a pledge to give,
but must come all naked to the test. ...

Death, which is written for all to see on the pitiable visage of the
old, hides well behind the face of youth, and takes his pleasure
above all among those who proudly cry to him 'Be off', these

— C'est en ces cointes damoiseaus
Qui vont as chiens et as oiseaus,
Et font homage as bons morseaus,
Qui plus ardent que leschefrite:
A ceus jue Mort de couteaus,
Et leur afuble tels manteaus
Qu'en plein miedi leur anuite.

Mort, où tuit sommes en atente
Que tu nous somoignes ta rente,
Bien nous as fort loié le point:
Tu prenz celui en sa jovente,
A vint et huit anz, ou à trente,
Qui cuide estre en son meilleur point.
Com plus s'acesme et plus se joint,
Tost l'as de ton aguillon point
Qui plus entosche que tarente.
Por c'est droit que chascuns ressoint,
Car cui deliz du siecle voint
Mout part de lui s'ame dolente. ...

Que vaut quanque li siecles fait?
Mort en une heure tout desfait,
Qui ne jue pas à refaire.

dainty lordlings, hunting with dogs and with hawks, devoted to
the pleasures of the table, and hot as dripping spitting from the
roast – at these Death throws his daggers for his sport, and wraps
around them such a cloak as turns their bright midday to night.

Oh! Death, from whom we all await a summons to pay our dues
to you, well and strongly you have tied our hands! You take that
man in his youth, at twenty-eight or thirty years, who thinks himself in his prime. Just when he most bedizens and bedecks himself,
you have pricked him with your sting, more poisonous than the
tarantula. Therefore it is right that every man beware; for if a man
is conquered by the delights of this world, in great sorrow shall his
soul depart from him. ...

What good is all that this world can create? Death in an hour
can destroy it all, and building up again is not his game. What is

Que vaut quanqu'avarice atrait?
Mort en une heure tout fortrait,
Qui nul jeu ne pert par mestraire.
Mort fait les plus emparlés taire,
Les enrisés plorer et braire;
Mort fait tous jours de bel tens lait;
Mort fait valoir et sac et haire
Autant com porpre et robe vaire;
Mort contre tous desrainne à plait.

Que vaut beauté, que vaut richece,
Que vaut honeur? que vaut hautece,
Puis que Mort tout à sa devise
Fait sor nous pluie et secherece,
Puis qu'ele a tout en sa destrece,
Quanqu'on despise et quanqu'on prise?
Qui paor de mort a jus mise,
C'est cil cui la Mort plus atise
Et vers qui ele ançois s'adrece.
Cors bien norri, char bien alise
Fait de vers et de feu chemise:
Qui plus s'aaise plus se blece. . . .

the good of all that avarice heaps up? Death in an hour can snatch
it back, Death who never loses the game by making a false move.
Death silences the readiest of speech, and makes the quick to
laughter weep and wail. Death every day turns fair weather to foul;
Death makes sackcloth and a hairshirt the equals of purple and fur-
lined robes; Death has the law on every man.

   What use is beauty? What use is riches? What use is honour?
What use is nobility? Since Death at his own sweet will can call
down rain or drought upon us, since everything is in his sway, all
that we despise and all that we value. He who has suppressed the
fear of death is the very one who most excites Death's notice, and
to whom Death turns first of all. The well-fed body and the delicate flesh, for them he makes a shirt of worms and of fire: he who
most seeks his ease most harms himself. ...

Mort est la roiz qui tout atrape,
Mort est la main qui tout agrape;
Tout li remaint quanqu'ele aert.
Mort fait à toz d'isembrun chape
Et de la pure terre nape,
Mort à tous oniement sert,
Mort tous secrez met en apert,
Mort fait franc homme de cuivert,
Mort acuivertist roi et pape,
Mort rent chascun ce qu'il desert,
Mort rent au povre ce qu'il pert,
Mort tolt au riche quanqu'il hape.

Mort fait à chascun sa droiture,
Mort fait à tous droite mesure,
Mort poise tout à juste pois,
Mort venge chascun de s'injure,
Mort met orgueil à porreture,
Mort fait faillir la guerre as rois,
Mort fait garder decrez et lois,
Mort fait laissier usure et crois,
Mort fait de soëf vie dure,
Mort as porees et as pois
Donne saveur de bon craspois
Es cloistres où l'on crient luxure. ...

Death is the all-capturing snare, Death is the all-grasping hand;
whatever he touches is his. Death makes for all men a cloak of
russet brown and a covering of simple earth. Death serves all men
alike, Death reveals all secrets, Death makes a freeman of the serf,
Death makes slaves of king and Pope. Death gives everyone his
deserts; Death gives the poor man back his losses, and robs the rich
of all that he has snatched.

Death gives every man his rights, Death gives fair measure to
all, Death weighs everything by true weight, Death avenges every
insult, Death turns pride to rottenness, Death puts an end to the
wars of kings, Death makes men observe decrees and laws and
relinquish usury and profit, Death turns an easy life into a hard
one, Death gives to the monastic peas and soup the savour of
finest whalemeat in the cloisters where luxury is shunned. ...

ANONYMOUS CHANSONS DE TOILE

QUANT vient en mai, que l'on dit as lons jors,
Que Franc de France repairent de roi cort,
Raynauz repaire devant el premier front,
Si s'en passa lez le mès Erembor,
Ainz n'en deigna le chief drecier amont.
        E! Raynauz amis!

Bele Erembor, à la fenestre, au jor,
Sor ses genouz tient paile de color;
Voit Frans de France qui repairent de cort
Et voit Raynaut devant el premier front;
En haut parole, si a dit sa raison.
        E! Raynauz amis!

«Amis Reynauz, j'ai ja veü cel jor,
Se passissez selon mon pere tor,
Dolenz fussiez se ne parlasse à vos.»
– «Jal mesfeïstes, fille d'empereor:
Autrui amastes, si obliastes nos.»
        E! Raynauz amis!

WHEN the time is come in May, which we call the month of long days, that the Franks of France come back from the king's Court, Raynaud rides back first, in the forefront, and he has passed by the house of Erembor, but never deigned to lift up his head. Ah! Raynaud, my love!

Fair Erembor at the window, in the sunlight, holds on her knees her bright silk embroidery; she sees the Franks of France coming back from the Court, and sees Raynaud first in the forefront, and speaks aloud and says her say. Ah! Raynaud, my love!

'Raynaud, my love, I have seen that day when if you had passed before my father's tower you would have been grieved if I had not spoken to you.' 'You have done wrong, daughter of the emperor, you have loved another and forgotten me.' Ah! Raynaud, my love!

«Sire Raynauz, je m'en escondirai:
A cent puceles sor sainz vos jurerai,
A trente dames que avec moi menrai,
Qu'onques nul home fors vostre cors n'amai.
Prenez l'emende et je vos baiserai.»
      E! Raynauz amis!

Li cuens Raynauz en monta le degré.
Gros par espaules, greles par le baudré,
Blont ot le poil, menu recercelé,
En nule terre n'ot si beau bacheler.
Voit l'Erembor, si comence à plorer.
      E! Raynauz amis!

Li cuens Raynauz est montés en la tor,
Si s'est asis en un lit point à flors.
Dejoste lui se siet bele Erembors,
Lors recommencent lor premieres amors.
      E! Raynauz amis!

'Sir Raynaud, I will prove my innocence: with a hundred maidens I will swear on the saints, with thirty ladies that I shall bring with me, that never a man but you have I loved. Accept this proof, and I will kiss you.' Ah! Raynaud, my love!

Count Raynaud has come up the steps – broad in the shoulders, slim in the waist – his hair was fair and tightly curling. In no land was there so handsome a youth. Erembor sees him and begins to weep. Ah! Raynaud, my love!

Count Raynaud has come up into the tower and has sat down on a flower-embroidered couch. At his side sits fair Erembor. Then their first love begins again. Ah! Raynaud, my love!

ORIOLANT en haut solier
Sospirant prist à lermoier
Et regrete son dru Helier.
«Amis, trop vous font esloignier
De moi felon et losengier.»
Dieus! tant par vient sa joie lente
A celui cui ele atalente!

«Amis, beaus douz amis Helier,
Quant me membre de l'embracier,
De l'acoler et du baisier,
Du douz parlement sans noisier,
Comment me puis vivre laissier?»
Dieus! tant par vient sa joie lente
A celui cui ele atalente!

«Amis, je vous fis esloignier
De moi plus que li losengier.
Quant je onques vous fis dangier,
De m'amour vous fis estrangier.
Or en reçoi si dur loier!»
Dieus! tant par vient sa joie lente
A celui cui ele atalente!

ORIOLANT in her high bower sighing starts to weep, and laments her lover Helier: 'My love, too far from me they have kept you, the cruel slanderers.' God! with how slow a step comes joy to one who longs for it!

'My love, my fair sweet love Helier, when I remember being in your arms, our embraces and our kissing, and our sweet speech without discord, how can I let myself go on living?' God! with how slow a step comes joy to one who longs for it!

'My love, I drove you away from me, more than the slanderers did. It was my own refusal that made you cease to love me. Now I am paying dearly for it.' God! with how slow a step comes joy to one who longs for it!

«Amis, la nuit en mon couchier
En dormant vous cuit embracier,
Et quant j'i fail au resveillier,
Nule riens ne m'i puet aidier.
Lors me reprent au souhaidier.»
Dieus! tant par vient sa joie lente
A celui cui ele atalente!

«Amis, or vueil à Dieu proier,
S'il me doit jamais conseillier,
Que je vous voie sans targier.
Mais à ce vient plus d'encombrier
Dont on a plus grant desirier.»
Dieus! tant par vient sa joie lente
A celui cui ele atalente!

Que que la bele fait ses criz,
Heliers est de court departiz;
Vient chevauchant par un larriz,
Si a les douz plainz entr'oïz.
Durement s'en est resjoïz.
Dieus! tant par vient sa joie lente
A celui cui ele atalente!

'My love, in my bed at night, when I am asleep, I think I have
you in my arms, and when I waking lose you, nothing can help me.
Then I fall once more to longing.' God! with how slow a step
comes joy to one who longs for it!

'My love, now I will pray to God, if ever he will help me, that
I may see you without delay, but the greatest obstacles are always
in the way of what we most desire.' God! with how slow a step
comes joy to one who longs for it!

While the fair lady makes her complaint, Helier has left the
Court; he comes riding over the fell, and has half heard her gentle
lament, and greatly rejoices at it. God! with how slow a step comes
joy to one who longs for it!

La bele sosleva son vis,
Voit que c'est Heliers ses amis.
Baisier et acoler l'a pris,
Si l'a entre ses beaus braz mis.
Assez i ot joué et ris.
Dieus! tant par vient sa joie lente
A celui cui ele atalente!

Oriolant li dist: «Amis,
Malgré losengeors chaitis,
Estes vos or de moi saisiz.
Or parleront à leur devis,
Et nos ferons tout nos plaisirs.»
Dieus! tant par vient sa joie lente
A celui cui ele atalente!

Ne sai que plus vous en devis;
Ensi aviegne à touz amis.
Et je, qui ceste chançon fis,
Sur la rive de mer pensis,
Commant à Dieu bele Aelis.
Dieus! tant par vient sa joie lente
A celui cui ele atalente!

The fair lady lifts her head and sees that it is her lover Helier; she has fallen to kissing and embracing him, and has taken him in her lovely arms, and long they play and laugh together. God! with how slow a step comes joy to one who longs for it!

Oriolant says to him: 'My love, in spite of the wretched slanderers, see, I am now your own. Now let them talk as they like, we will have all our delight.' God! with how slow a step comes joy to one who longs for it!

I know not what to tell you more; may it be thus with all lovers. And I who made this song, on the sea shore, heavy with thought, commend to God the lovely Aelis. God! with how slow a step comes joy to one who longs for it!

ANONYMOUS AUBES

Entre moi et mon ami,
En un bois qu'est lès Betune,
Alames jouant mardi,
Toute la nuit à la lune,
   Tant qu'il ajourna
Et que l'aloue chanta
Qui dit: «Amis, alons ent.»
Et il respont doucement:
    «Il n'est mie jours,
   Saverouse au cors gent;
    Si m'aït amours,
   L'alouette nous ment.»

Adonc se trait près de mi,
Et je ne fui pas enfrune;
Bien trois fois me baisa il,
Ainsi fis je lui plus d'une,
   Qu'ainz ne m'enoia.
Adonc vousissions nous là
Que celle nuit durast cent,
Mais que plus n'alast disant:
    «Il n'est mie jours,
   Saverouse au cors gent;
    Si m'aït amours,
   L'alouette nous ment.»

My love and I, in a wood beside Béthune, went playing on Tuesday, all night, by the moon, until day broke and the lark sang, saying, 'Beloved, let us go.' And my love answered softly: 'It is not day, my sweet, my beautiful; so may Love help me, the lark is lying to us.'

Then he drew closer to me, and I was not unwilling; a good three times he kissed me, and I him more than once, for that was no sorrow to me. Then we could have wished that that night would last a hundred nights, and that he would never again say: 'It is not day, my sweet, my beautiful; so may Love help me, the lark is lying to us.'

QUANT voi l'aube du jour venir,
Nulle rien ne doi tant haïr;
Qu'elle fait de moi departir
Mon ami que j'aim par amour.
Or ne hé rien tant com le jour,
Ami, qui me depart de vous.

Je ne vous puis de jour veoir,
Car trop redout l'apercevoir,
Et si vous di trestout pour voir
Qu'en agait sont li envious.
Or ne hé rien tant com le jour,
Ami, qui me depart de vous.

Quant je me gis dedans mon lit
Et je regarde encoste mi,
Je n'y truis point de mon ami,
Si m'en plaing à fins amorous:
Or ne hé rien tant com le jour,
Ami, qui me depart de vous.

Beaus dous amis, vous en irez:
A Dieu soit vo corps commandés.
Pour Dieu vous pri, ne m'oubliez:

WHEN I see the dawn of day appearing, that is the thing I hate above all, for it separates me from my lover, whom I dearly love. There is nothing I hate so much as the daylight, which parts me from you, my love.

I cannot see you in the daytime, for I am too much afraid that our love will be discovered; and I tell you most truly that envious people are on the watch. There is nothing I hate so much as the daylight, which parts me from you, my love.

When I lie in my bed and look beside me and do not find my lover there, then I make my lament to all true lovers: there is nothing I hate so much as the daylight, which parts me from you, my love.

My fair sweet love, you must go, may God watch over you. In God's name I beg of you, do not forget me, for I love you above all

Je n'aim nulle rien tant com vous.
Or ne hé rien tant com le jour,
Ami, qui me depart de vous.

Or pri à tous les vrais amans
Ceste chançon voisent chantant
Ens en despit des mesdisans
Et des mauvais maris jalous:
«Or ne hé rien tant com le jour,
Amis, qui me depart de vous.»

GACE BRULÉ

Chanson d'Amour

Li consirrers de mon païs
Si longuement me trait à mort,
Qu'en estranges terres languis,
Las, sans deduit et sans confort,
Et si dout moult mes enemis
Qui de moi mesdient à tort,
Mais tant sent mon cuer vrai et fort
Que, se Dieu plaist, ne m'en ert pis.

else. There is nothing I hate so much as the daylight, which parts
me from you, my love.

Now I beg of all true lovers that they will go singing this song,
in despite of all the gossips, and the cruel, jealous husbands: 'There
is nothing I hate so much as the daylight, which parts me from you,
my love.'

Love Song

So long an absence from my own country is bringing my life to an
end, for I languish in foreign lands, weary, without delight or consolation. And I greatly dread my enemies who wrongly slander me,
but I feel my heart so strong and true, that, please God, no harm
will come to me from their slanders.

Ma douce dame, ne creez
Touz ceus qui de moi mesdiront.
Quant vous veoir ne me poez
De vos beaus yeuz qui souspris m'ont,
De vostre franc cuer me veez.
Mais ne sai s'il vous en semont,
Car tant ne dout rien en cest mont
Com ce que vous ne m'oubliez.

Par cuer legier de femme avient
Que li amant doutent souvent,
Mais ma loiauté me soustient,
Donc fusse je mors autrement!
Et sachiez de fine amour vient
Qu'il se doutent si durement,
Car nuls n'aime seürement,
Et fausse est amours qui ne crient.

Mes cuers m'a gari et destruit,
Mais de ce va bien qu'à li pens,
Et ce que je perdre la cuit
Me fait doubler mes pensemens.

My sweet lady, do not believe all those who speak ill of me.
When you cannot see me with those lovely eyes that took me captive, you can see me with your true heart. But I do not know
whether your heart urges you to do so, for I dread nothing in this
world so much as that you should forget me.

The fickleness of women's hearts often makes lovers afraid, but
my own loyalty keeps me from despairing; but for that I should
have died. And you must know that it is true love that makes
lovers go in such grievous fear, for no true lover is confident, and
false is the love that does not fear.

My heart first comforts me, then casts me down; but it is good
that it makes me think of her; and the dread of losing her makes
me dwell doubly on my thoughts. Thus comfort comes and then

Ainsi me vient soulaz et fuit,
Et nepourquant, selon mon sens,
Penser à ma dame tous tens
Tieng je, ce sachiez, à deduit.

Chançon, à ma dame t'envoi
Ançois que nuls en ait chanté,
Et si li dites de par moi
(Gardez que ne li soit celé):
«Se trecherie n'a en foi
Et trahison en loiauté,
Donc avrai bien ce qu'avoir doi,
Car de loial cuer ai amé.»

Chanson d' Amour

DE bonne amour et de loial amie
Me vient souvent pitié et remembrance,
Si que jamais à nul jour de ma vie
N'oublierai son vis ne sa semblance;
Pouroec, s'Amours ne s'en veut plus soufrir
Qu'ele de tous ne face à son plaisir
Et de toutes, mais ne peut avenir
Que de la moie aie bone esperance.

withdraws again, and yet, in my opinion, thinking of my lady is always a delight for me, as you must know.

My song, I send you to my lady before anyone has sung a word of you; and tell her from me (take care it is not hidden from her): 'Unless there is treachery in Faith and treason in Loyalty, then I must win what I deserve, for I have loved with a loyal heart.'

Love Song

I AM often haunted by the sad longing for true love and a faithful lover, for never any day of my life shall I forget her face and her form. Therefore, unless Love will henceforth refrain from making his sport of all men and all women, never can it come to pass that I may have good hope of my true love.

Coment pourroie avoir bonne esperance
A bonne amour ne à loial amie,
Ne à vairs yeuz, n'à la douce semblance
Que ne verrai jamais jour de ma vie?
Amer m'estuet, ne m'en puis plus soufrir,
Celi cui ja ne venra à plaisir;
Et si ne sai comment puist avenir
Qu'aie de li ne secours ne aïe.

Coment avrai ne secours ne aïe
Vers fine amour, là où nuls n'a puissance?
Amer me fait ce qui ne m'aime mie,
Dont ja n'avrai fors ennui et pesance;
Ne ne li os mon corage gehir
Celi qui tant m'a fait de maus sentir,
Que de tel mort sui jugiés à morir
Dont ja ne quier veoir ma delivrance.

Je ne vois pas querant tel delivrance
Par quoi amour soit de moi departie;
Ne ja nul jour n'en quier avoir puissance,
Ainz amerai ce qui ne m'aime mie,
N'il n'est pas droit que li doie gehir
Pour nul destroit que me face sentir;

How can I ever have good hope of true love and a faithful lover, or of her bright eyes or of her sweet form that I shall never see again in all my life? I cannot refrain, but I must love her who will never be pleased to accept my love. And I do not know how it can come to pass that I should have from her either succour or help.

How can I have succour or help in face of Love, against whom no man has power? Love makes me love one who does not love me; therefore I shall have nothing but sorrow and sadness; and I dare not confess my feeling to her who makes me suffer so many ills, for I am condemned to die a death from which I do not seek deliverance.

I am not seeking such a deliverance as would release me from my love, and never do I wish to have the power to free myself, but I will still love her who does not love me. It is not right that I should

N'avrai confort, n'i voi que du mourir,
Puis que je sai que ne m'ameroit mie.

Ne m'ameroit? Ice ne sai je mie;
Que fins amis doit par bone atendance
Et par soffrir conquerre haute amie.
Mais je n'i puis avoir nulle fiance,
Que cele est tel pour qui plaing et sopir
Que ma dolor ne daigneroit oïr;
Si me vaut mieuz garder mon bon taisir
Que dire rien qui li tort à grevance.

Ne vous doit pas trop torner à grevance
Se je vous aim, dame, plus que ma vie,
Car c'est la rien où j'ai greignor fiance
Quant par moi seul vos os nommer amie,
Et pour ce fais maint dolorous sopir
Que ne vous puis ne veoir ne oïr;
Et quant vous voi, n'i a que du taisir,
Que si sui pris que ne sai que je die.

confess my love to her, whatever anguish she may make me suffer.
I shall have no consolation; I can see nothing but death, since I
know that she would never love me.

   Never love me? This I do not know. For a true lover ought by
long patience and by suffering to win a noble lady. But I cannot put
my trust in this, for she for whom I weep and sigh would not deign
to listen to my sorrow; and I had better keep a wise silence rather
than say a thing which might offend her.

   Lady, it should not offend you if I love you better than my life,
for it is the one comfort I rely upon to dare, when speaking to myself alone, to call you my love, and I heave many a grievous sigh
because I cannot see you nor hear you. And when I do see you,
silence is best for me, for I am so overcome that I do not know what
I am saying.

Mais biaus confors ne m'en pourra garir;
De vous amer ne me pourrai partir
N'à vous parler, ne ne m'en puis taisir
Que mon maltrait en chantant ne vous die.

Par Dieu, Huet, ne m'en puis plus soffrir,
Qu'en Bertree est et ma mors et ma vie.

LE CHÂTELAIN DE COUCY

Chanson d'Amour

La douce voiz du rossignol sauvage,
Qu'oi nuit et jour cointoier et tentir,
Me radoucist mon cuer et rassouage:
Lors ai talent que chant pour esbaudir.
Bien doi chanter, puis qu'il vient à plaisir
Celi cui j'ai de cuer fait lige homage;
Si doi avoir grant joie en mon corage
S'ele me veut à son oés retenir.

Onques vers li n'oi faus cuer ne volage,
Si m'en devroit pour ço mieus avenir;

Sweet consolation will never come to heal me; I shall never be
able to cease to love you, nor to keep silent, for I cannot help telling
you my grief in my song.

Oh God! Huet, I cannot be silent any longer, for in Bertree lies
both my death and my life.

Love Song

The sweet voice of the woodland nightingale that I hear night and
day trilling and calling softens and soothes my heart, and then I
have a mind to sing for joy. Well should I sing, since it is her
pleasure to whom I have done homage with my heart, and my soul
should be filled with joy if she is willing to accept me into her
service.

I never had a false or fickle thought towards her – and this should

Ainz l'aim et serf et aour par usage,
Si ne li os mon penser descovrir,
Car sa beauté me fait si esbahir
Que je ne sai devant li nul langage,
Ne regarder n'os son simple visage,
Tant en redout mes yeus à repartir.

Tant ai vers li ferm assis mon corage
Qu'ailleurs ne pens, et Dieus m'en laist joïr;
Qu'onques Tristans, cil qui but le bevrage,
Si coraument n'ama sans repentir;
Car j'i met tout, cuer et cors et desir,
Sens et savoir, ne sai se faz folage;
Encor me dout qu'en trestout mon eage
Ne puisse assez li et s'amour servir.

Je ne di pas que je face folage,
Nis se por li me devoie mourir;
Qu'el mont ne truis si belle ne si sage,
Ne nule rien n'est tant à mon plaisir.
Moult aim mes yeus qui m'i firent choisir;
Lués que la vi, li laissai en ostage

make my case more hopeful – but I love and serve and adore her
with constancy; and yet I dare not disclose my thoughts to her, for
her beauty so dazzles me that I can find no words in her presence.
And I dare not even look at her sweet face, so much I dread to take
my eyes away.

I have so firmly set my heart on her that I can think of no one
else, and God grant that I may win her; for never Tristram, he who
drank the potion, loved so deeply or with such constancy; for I
give up all to loving, heart and body and every wish, all sense, all
reason; I do not know whether I am behaving like a madman – and
even so I fear that in all my life I shall not be able to serve her and
her love enough.

I do not say I am behaving like a fool, even if I were to die for
her, for in all the world I cannot find another so beautiful or so wise,
nor anyone to cause me such delight. I love my eyes for having
made me see her. As soon as I saw her, I left my heart a hostage in

Mon cuer, qui puis i a fait lonc estage,
Ne jamais jour ne l'en quier departir.

Chançon, va t'en pour faire mon message
Là où je n'os trestorner ne guenchir;
Que tant redout la male gent ombrage
Qui devinent, ainz que puist avenir,
Les biens d'amour. Dieus les puist maleïr,
Qu'à maint amant ont fait ire et outrage,
Mais de ç'ai je touz jours mal avantage,
Qu'il les m'estuet sor mon gré obeïr.

Chanson d'Amour

COMMENCEMENT de douce saison bele
Que je voi revenir,
Remembrance d'amours qui me rapele,
Dont ja ne quier partir,
Et la mauvis qui comence à tentir,
Et li dous sons du ruissel sor gravele
Que je voi reclarcir,
Me fait resouvenir
De là où tuit mi bon desir
Sont et seront jusqu'au finir.

her keeping, and there it has already made a long stay, and I never wish to remove it from her.

Go, Song, and bear my message to that place where I myself dare neither go nor turn my steps, for I so greatly fear the wicked jealous people who guess the sweets of love before they can be savoured; God's curse upon such people: they have brought sorrow and injury to many a lover, but I am always unfortunate in this, that I have to obey them against my will.

Love Song

WHEN I see spring's first lovely days come round again, and feel myself called back by memory of that love I never will abandon, and hear the thrush's song ring out anew, and the sweet noise of water on the gravel where I watch the shining stream, then my thoughts return where all my heart's desires are now and will ever be till my life's end.

Touz tens m'est plus s'amour fresche et novele
      Quant recort à loisir
Ses yeus, son vis qui de joie sautele,
      Son aler, son venir,
Son bel parler et son gent contenir,
Son dous regart, qui vient d'une estencelle
      Mon cuer el cors ferir,
      Sans crieme de perir;
      Et quant je plus plaing et souspir,
      Plus sui joianz quant plus m'aïr.

Loial amour et fine et droituriere
      M'a si en son vouloir,
Que ne m'en puis partir ne traire arriere,
      Ne je n'en ai pooir.
N'est pas amour dont on se peut movoir,
Ne cil amis qui en nule maniere
      La bee à decevoir;
      Or sai je bien de voir
      Qu'ensemble covient remanoir
      Moi et amour par estovoir.

My love for her springs always fresh and new when memory dwells upon her eyes, her face alight with happiness, her going and her coming, her fair speech and her noble manner, and her sweet look which sends a burning spark to strike the heart within me, but never puts my life in peril; and when I most complain and sigh, then the more I suffer, the greater is my joy.

True, loyal love, love duly merited, has so enslaved my will that I cannot tear myself away or draw back: it is beyond my strength. Love is not love that can be shaken off at will, nor is that man a lover who has any thought of cheating love. Now well I know in truth that love and I must dwell together out of sheer necessity.

Se li envis de la gent malparliere
Ne me feïst doloir,
J'eüsse bien joie fine et entiere,
D'esgarder, de veoir;
Mais ce que n'os por eus ramentevoir,
Conoissiez, belle, au vis et à la chiere;
Que je n'os mon vouloir
Dire pour parcevoir,
Mais bonne dame doit savoir,
Conoissance et merci avoir.

Chanson d' Amour

Bien cuidai vivre sans amour
Dès ore en pais tout mon aé,
Mais retrait m'a en la folour
Mes cuers, dont l'avoie eschapé.
Empris ai greignor folie
Que li fols enfes qui crie
Pour la bele estoile avoir
Qu'il voit haut et cler seoir.

If the envy of the slanderers did not work my woe, how full and how complete would be my joy in watching you, in seeing you; but what because of them I dare not mention, you know, sweet lady, by my face and by my looks – for I dare not tell my longing lest others should discover it, but wisdom, perception, and mercy must be the attributes of a lover's lady.

Love Song

I thought to live without love henceforth in peace for all my life, but my heart has dragged me back into the madness from which I had rescued it. I have undertaken a greater folly than the foolish child who cries for the beautiful star he sees shining above him.

Coment que je me desespoir,
Bien m'a amour guerredonné
Ce que je l'ai, à mon pooir,
Servie sans desloiauté,
  Qui roi m'a fait de folie.
  Si se gart bien qui s'i fie;
  Que si haut don set merir
  Ceus qui servent sans trahir.

Nen est merveilles se m'aïr
Vers amour qui tant m'a grevé.
Dieus! car la peüsse tenir
Un seul jour à ma volenté:
  El comperroit sa folie,
  Si me face Dieu aïe!
A mourir li convenroit,
  Se ma dame ne vaincoit.

Aï! frans cuers qui tant connoit,
Ne beez à ma foleté.
Bien sai qu'en vous amer n'ai droit,
S'amour ne mi eüst doné;
  Mais esforcier fait folie,
  Si com fait nef que vens guie,
  Qui va là où vens l'empaint,
  Si que toute esmie et fraint.

However little hope I have, Love has rewarded me well for having served him to the best of my power and without treachery, by
making me the King of Folly! Let everyone beware of putting trust
in him, who can give such a fine gift to those that loyally serve him!

And it is not surprising that I should be angry with Love, who
has served me so ill. God! if I could have him in my power for a
single day, he would pay for his folly, as God may be my help. He
would have to die unless he could conquer my lady.

Oh! noble heart, you who are so wise, do not look too severely
on my madness! I know full well that I have no right to love you,
except such right as Love has given me; for folly leads to wildness,
as a ship is swept before the wind and goes where the wind drives
it until it is all wrecked and broken up.

Ma dame où nuls biens ne soffraint,
Merci, par franchise et par gré:
Puis qu'en vous sont tuit mal estaint,
Et tuit bien à droit alumé,
      Connoissiez dont la folie
      Me vient qui me tolt la vie.
      Où en doi faire clamour,
      S'à vous non, de ma dolour?

      Chançon, ma bele folie
      Me salue, et si li prie
      Que pour Dieu et pour s'honour
      N'ait ja l'us de traïtour.

Chanson de Croisade

A vous, amans, plus qu'à nule autre gent
Est bien raison que ma dolor complaigne,
Quant il m'estuet partir outreement
Et desevrer de ma loial compaigne;
Et quant li pert, n'est rien qui me remaigne.
Et sachiez bien, Amour, seürement
S'ainc nuls morut por avoir cuer dolent,
Jamais par moi n'ert meüs vers ne lais.

My lady in whom no good quality is lacking, I beg for mercy by
your generosity and by your kindness. Since in you all evil is extin-
guished and all good shines forth, you know whence this folly
comes which is taking my life: to whom can I call for help if not to
you in my grief?

Song, salute my lovely folly, and beg her for God's sake, and
her honour's, never to prove a traitor to me.

Song of the Crusade

To you, oh! lovers, more than to any others, it is very fitting that
I should lament my sorrow, since I am forced to part from my true
love and leave her altogether; and if she is lost to me, nothing remains. Oh! Love, you may be sure that if ever a man died from a
grieving heart, verses and lays will never more be made by me.

Beaus sire Dieus, qu'ert il donc et coment?
Convenra il qu'en la fin congié praigne?
Oïl, par Dieu, ne peut estre autrement,
Sans li m'estuet aler en terre estraigne.
Or ne cuit mais que grans mals me sofraigne,
Quant de li n'ai confort n'alegement,
Ne de nule autre amor joie n'atent,
Fors que de li; ne sai se c'ert jamais.

Beaus sire Dieus, qu'ert il du consirrer
Du grant solas et de la compaignie
Et des deduis que me soloit mostrer
Cele qui m'ert dame, compagne, amie?
Et quant recort sa simple cortoisie,
Et les dous mos que seut à moi parler,
Coment me peut li cuers el cors durer?
Quant ne s'en part, certes, moult est mauvais.

Ne me veut pas Dieus por noient doner
Tous les deduis qu'ai eüs en ma vie,
Ainz les me fait chierement comparer,
S'ai grant paor cist loiers ne m'ocie.

Dear Lord God, what will come of it and how can it be? Shall I
in the end have to take leave of her? Yes, by God, it cannot be
otherwise. Without her I must go to a foreign land. Henceforth, I
think, I cannot escape great sorrows, when I have neither comfort
nor solace from her; and I cannot hope for joy from any other love
except from hers, and I do not know if that will ever come to me
again.

Dear Lord God, how shall I do without the great comfort and
the companionship and the delight that she used to give me, she
who was my lady, my comrade, and my love? When I recall her
simple courtesy and the sweet words she used to speak to me, how
can my heart endure within my body? It is indeed a coward not to
leave me.

God does not wish to give me for nothing all the pleasures that
I have had in my life, but makes me pay dearly for them; and I

Merci, Amour! S'ainc Dieus fist vilenie,
Que vilains fait bone amour desevrer;
Ne je ne puis l'amor de moi oster,
Et si m'estuet que je ma dame lais.

Or seront lié li faus losengeor
Cui tant pesoit des biens qu'avoir soloie;
Mais ja de ce n'ere pelerins jor
Que ja vers eus bone volenté aie:
Por tant porrai perdre tote ma voie;
Que tant m'ont fait de mal li traïtor
Se Dieus voloit qu'il eüssent m'amor
Ne me porroit chargier plus pesant fais.

Je m'en vois, dame; à Dieu le creator
Comant vo cors, en quel lieu que je soie;
Ne sai se ja verrai mais mon retor:
Aventure est que jamais vous revoie.
Par Dieu vos pri, quel part que li cors traie,
Que vos covens tenez, vegne ou demor;
Et je pri Dieu qu'ainsi me doinst honor
Com je vos ai esté amis verais.

greatly fear that this payment will kill me. Have pity, Love; if ever God did wrong, He does so now in parting our true love. I cannot put this love away from me, and yet I must leave my lady.

Now those false tale-bearers can rejoice, who were so envious of the joys I used to have; but I shall never be so much a pilgrim as to have any good will towards them. Indeed, through them my journey may well be wasted; for the traitors have done me so much harm that if God willed that they should have my love, He could not lay on me a harder task.

Lady, I go; to God the Creator I commend you, wherever I may be. I do not know whether I shall ever see the day of my return: perhaps I shall never see you again. In God's name I beg you, wherever I may go, that you will keep your promise, whether I come back or whether I stay; and I pray to God so to give me honour as I have been a true lover to you.

CONON DE BÉTHUNE

Chanson d' Amour

Sɪ voirement com cele dont je chant
Vaut mieuz que toutes les bonnes qui sont,
Et je l'aim plus que rien qui soit el mont,
Si me doint Dieus s'amour sans decevoir;
Que tel desir en ai et tel vouloir,
Ou tant ou plus, Dieus en set la verté,
Si com malades desirre santé,
Desir je li et s'amour à avoir.

Or sai je bien que rien ne peut valoir
Tant com celi de qui j'ai tant chanté,
Qu'or ai veü et li et sa beauté,
Et si sai bien que tant a de valor
Que je doi faire et outrage et folor
D'amer plus haut que ne m'avroit mestier;
Et, nonporquant, maint povre chevalier
Fait riches cuers venir à haute honor.

Ainz que fusse sospris de ceste amor,
Savoie je autre gent conseillier,

Love Song

As truly as she of whom I sing surpasses all other women in goodness, and as I love her more than anything in the world, so may
God grant me her love without fail; for I desire and wish for it so
much that I long to have her and her love as much – or more – God
knows the truth of it, as a sick man longs for health.

Now I know well that none can be the equal of her whose praises
I have sung so long, for now I have seen her and her beauty, and I
know too that she is of such worth that I must be guilty of presumption and folly in loving higher than I ought to do. And nevertheless a noble heart brings many a lowly knight to high honour.

Before this love had taken possession of me, I could give counsel

104

Et or sai bien d'altrui jeu enseignier
Et si ne sai mie le mien juër;
Si sui com cil qui as eschés voit cler
Et qui tres bien ensengne as autres gens,
Et, quant il jue, si pert si son sens
Qu'il ne se set escore de mater.

Hé! las, dolanz, je ne sai tant chanter
Que ma dame parçoive mes tormenz,
N'encor n'est pas si granz mes hardemenz
Que je li os dire les maus que trai,
Ne devant li n'en os parler ne sai;
Et quant je sui aillors devant autrui,
Lors i parol, mais si peu m'i dedui
Qu'un anui vaut li deduiz que j'en ai.

Encor devis comment je li dirai
La grant dolor que j'en trais senz anui;
Que tant l'ador et desir quant j'i sui,
Que ne li os descouvrir ma raison;

to other people, and now I can teach another his game but cannot play my own, and I am like a man who sees clearly at chess and teaches others very well, but when he plays, then he so loses his head that he cannot escape being checkmated.

Alas, poor wretch, I know not how to sing so that my lady shall perceive my torments, nor yet is my boldness so great that I dare tell her of the sufferings I endure, and in her presence I dare not and cannot speak of them. And when I am elsewhere before another, then I can speak, but it gives me so little pleasure that any joy I find there is no better than sorrow.

And still I plan how I shall tell her, without giving her offence, of the great pain I suffer for her; for I adore her and long for her so when I am with her, that I dare not tell her what is in my mind, and

Si va de moi com fait du champion
Qui de lonc tens aprent à escremir,
Et quant il vient ou champ as cous ferir,
Si ne set rien d'escu ne de baston.

Chanson

L'AUTRIER avint en cel autre païs
Qu'uns chevaliers eut une dame amee.
Tant com la dame fu en son bon pris,
Li a s'amor escondite et veee.
Puis fu un jor qu'ele li dist: «Amis,
Mené vous ai par parole mains dis;
Or est l'amor coneüe et prouvee.
Desormais sui tout à vostre devis.»

Li chevaliers la regarda el vis,
Si la vit moult pale et descoulouree.
«Dame, fait il, certes mal sui baillis
Que n'eüstes pieça ceste pensee.

it is with me as it is with the champion who has long studied sword-play, but when he comes into the field and to the striking of blows, then he knows not a thing of either shield or weapon.

Song

THE other day it came about in a certain country that a knight had loved a lady. As long as the lady was at her best, she refused her love and denied it to him, until one day she said to him: 'My friend, for many a day I have put you off with words; now your love is known and tested, henceforth I hold myself entirely yours.'

The knight looked her full in the face and saw that she was very pale and faded. 'Lady,' he said, 'I am really out of luck that you did not have this idea some years ago. Your lovely face that was like

Vostre cler vis, qui sembloit flors de lis,
Est si alés, dame, de mal en pis
Qu'il m'est avis que me soïez emblee.
A tart avez, dame, cest conseil pris.»

Quant la dame s'oï si ramprosner,
Grant honte en eut, si dist par sa folie:
«Par Dieu, vassal, jel dis pour vous gaber.
Quidiez vous donc qu'à certes le vous die?
Onques nul jor ne me vint en penser.
Savriez vous donc dame de pris amer?
Nenil, par Dieu! ainz vous prendroit envie
D'un bel vallet baisier et acoler.»

«Dame, fait il, j'ai bien oï parler
De vostre pris, mais ce n'est ore mie;
Et de Troie rai je oï conter
Qu'ele fu ja de moult grant seignorie;
Or n'i peut on fors les places trover.
Et si vous lo ainsi à escuser
Que cil soient reté de l'iresie
Qui desormais ne vous voudront amer.»

the lily has so far gone, lady, from bad to worse that it seems to me that you have been stolen from me. Too late, lady, you have come to this decision.'

When the lady heard herself so taunted, she was overcome with shame, and said in her rage: 'By God, sir knight, I said it to mock you. Did you really think I meant it seriously? Such a thing never entered my head. Would you be capable of loving a lady of rank? No, by God! You would be much more likely to want to kiss and embrace some handsome youth.'

'Lady,' said he, 'I have certainly heard you highly praised, but that was not recently. Of Troy too I have heard it said that it was once a mighty city; now only its site can be found. And so I advise you to refrain from making accusations of immorality against all those who henceforth do not wish to love you.'

«Par Dieu, vassal, moult avez fol pensé,
Quant vous m'avez reprové mon eage.
Se j'avoie tout mon jovent usé,
Si sui je riche et de si haut parage
Qu'on m'ameroit à petit de beauté.
Encor n'a pas un mois entir passé
Que li Marchis m'envoia son message
Et li Barrois a pour m'amour josté.»

«Par Dieu, dame, ce vous a moult grevé
Que vous fiez tous jours en signorage;
Mais tel cent ont ja pour vous souspiré,
Se vous estiez fille au Roi de Cartage,
Qui ja mais jour n'en avront volenté.
On n'aime pas dame pour parenté,
Mais quant ele est belle et cortoise et sage.
Vous en savrez par tens la verité.»

Chanson de Croisade

AHI! Amors, com dure departie
Me convenra faire de la meillor
Qui onques fust amee ne servie!

'By God, sir knight, you are a fool to reproach me for my age. Even if I had quite worn out my youth, still I am rich and of such high birth that I could be loved with very little beauty. Within this last month, the Marquis has sent his messenger to me and the Barrois has jousted for my love.'

'By God, my lady, it has gone much against you that you have always put your trust in rank; but a hundred have sighed for you in the past who, if you were the daughter of the king of Carthage, would now no longer desire you. A lady is not loved for her lineage, but when she is beautiful and courteous and wise. You will soon learn the truth of this.'

Song of the Crusade

ALAS! oh Love, how hard it will be for me to part from the best lady who was ever loved or served. God in his goodness bring me

Dieus me ramaint à li par sa douçor,
Si voirement com j'en part à dolor!
Las! qu'ai je dit? Ja ne m'en part je mie.
Se li cors va servir Nostre Seignor,
Mes cuers remaint del tout en sa baillie.

Pour li m'en vois sospirant en Surie,
Car je ne doi faillir mon Creator.
Qui li faura à cest besoing d'aïe,
Sachiez que il li faura à greignor;
Et sachent bien li grant et li menor
Que là doit on faire chevalerie
Où on conquiert Paradis et honor
Et pris et los et l'amor de s'amie.

Dieus est assis en son saint hiretage;
Or i parra com cil le secourront
Cui il jeta de la prison ombrage,
Quant il fu mis en la crois que Turc ont.
Honi soient tout cil qui remandront,
S'il n'ont poverte ou vieillece ou malage!
Et cil qui sain et jeune et riche sont
Ne peuvent pas demorer sans hontage.

back to her as surely as I grieve to leave her. Alas! what have I said?
I do not leave her: for though my body goes to serve our Lord, my
heart remains entirely in her keeping.

Sighing for her I leave for Syria, for I must not fail my Creator.
If a man fails Him in this hour of need, be sure that God will fail
him in a greater. And let both great and small know well that the
place for knightly deeds is where a man can win Paradise and honour
and glory and praise and the love of his lady.

God is besieged in His holy heritage. Now we shall see how He
will be succoured by those He rescued from the gloomy prison when
He was put on the cross the Turks now hold. Be sure that those
who do not go will be dishonoured, unless they have the excuse of
poverty or age or sickness; those who are healthy and young and
rich cannot stay behind without shame.

Tout li clergié et li home d'eage
Qui en ausmogne et en bienfais manront
Partiront tout à cest pelerinage,
Et les dames qui chastement vivront
Et loiauté feront ceus qui iront;
Et s'eles font par mal conseil folage,
A lasches gens mauvaises le feront,
Car tout li bon iront en cest voiage.

Qui ci ne veut avoir vie ennuieuse
Si voist pour Dieu morir liés et joieus,
Car cele mort est douce et savereuse
Dont on conquiert le regne presieus,
Ne ja de mort n'en i mourra uns seus,
Ainz naistront tout en vie glorieuse;
Et sachiez bien, qui ne fust amoreus,
Moult fust la voie et bone et deliteuse.

Dieus! tant avons esté preus par huiseuse,
Or i parra qui à certes ert preus;
S'irons vengier la honte doloreuse
Dont chascuns doit estre iriés et honteus;

All the clergy and the old men who continue here in charity and
good works will have their share in this crusade, and all the ladies
who live chastely and keep faith with those who go. And if by evil
counsel they fall into sin, they will do so with cowards and worthless men, for all the brave will have gone on this journey.

Let him who does not wish to lead a life without renown go and
die for God in joy and happiness; for sweet and pleasant is that
death by which the heavenly kingdom is won. And not a single one
of them will die in death, but they will all be born again to glorious
life. And be assured that if a man was not in love, this would be an
enterprise of great delight and joy.

God! for so long our prowess has been unproved; now it will be
seen who is really worthy, and we shall go and avenge the grievous
reproach which should make each of us angry and ashamed, for it

Car à no tans est perdus li sains lieus
Où Dieus soffri pour nous mort angoisseuse.
S'or i laissons nos enemis morteus,
A tous jours mais ert no vie honteuse.

GUIOT DE DIJON

Chanson de Croisade

CHANTERAI por mon corage
Que je vueil reconforter,
Car avec mon grant damage
Ne quier mourir n'afoler,
Quant de la terre sauvage
Ne voi nului retorner
Où cil est qui m'assoage
Le cuer, quant j'en oi parler.
Dieus, quant crieront «Outree»,
Sire, aidiez au pelerin
Pour qui sui espoentee,
Car felon sont Sarrazin.

Soufrerai en tel estage
Tant quel voie rapasser.

is in our day that the holy places have been lost where God for our
sake suffered a cruel death. If we now let our mortal enemies stay
there, our life will be disgraceful for ever more.

Song of the Crusade

FOR my heart's consolation I will sing, since I do not want to die
or go out of my mind in my great suffering: for I see none returning from that wild country where he is who soothes my heart when
I hear him spoken of. God, when they cry 'Outree', help, oh Lord,
that crusader for whose sake I go in fear, for cruel are the Saracens.
I will patiently keep my present state until I see him come back.

Il est en pelerinage,
Dont Dieus le lait retorner.
Et maugré tout mon lignage
Ne quier ochoison trouver
D'autre face mariage;
Fols est qui j'en oi parler.
Dieus, quant crieront «Outree»,
Sire, aidiez au pelerin
Pour qui sui espoentee,
Car felon sont Sarrazin.

De ce sui au cuer dolente
Que cil n'est en Beauvoisis
Qui si souvent me tormente:
Or n'en ai ne jeu ne ris.
S'il est beaus, et je sui gente.
Sire Dieus, pour quel feïs?
Quant l'uns à l'autre atalente,
Pour quoi nous as departis?
Dieus, quant crieront «Outree»,
Sire, aidiez au pelerin
Pour qui sui espoentee,
Car felon sont Sarrazin.

He is on pilgrimage: God grant he may return. And in spite of all
my kindred I do not wish to seek occasion to marry any other; he
is a fool whom I hear speaking of it. God, when they cry 'Outree',
help, oh Lord, that crusader for whose sake I go in fear, for cruel
are the Saracens.

What grieves my heart is that he is not here in Beauvaisis, he
for whom I long so often. Now I have neither joy nor laughter. If
he is handsome, I too am comely. Lord God, why did you do it?
When one desires the other, why have you parted us? God, when
they cry 'Outree', help, oh Lord, that crusader for whose sake I go
in fear, for cruel are the Saracens.

De ce sui en bone atente
Que je son homage pris,
Et quant la douce ore vente
Qui vient de cel dous païs
Où cil est qui m'atalente,
Volentiers i tor mon vis;
Adonc, m'est vis que jel sente
Par desous mon mantel gris.
Dieus, quant crieront «Outree»,
Sire, aidiez au pelerin
Pour qui sui espoentee,
Car felon sont Sarrazin.

De ce sui moult deceue
Que ne fui au convoier.
Sa chemise qu'ot vestue
M'envoia pour embracier;
La nuit, quant s'amor m'argue,
La met deles moi couchier
Moult estroit à ma char nue
Pour mes maus assoagier.
Dieus, quant crieront «Outree»,
Sire, aidiez au pelerin
Pour qui sui espoentee,
Car felon sont Sarrazin.

What gives me hope is that I have received his homage; and
when the gentle breeze blows from that sweet country where my
love is, I gladly turn my face towards it; and then, it seems to me,
I feel his touch beneath my grey mantle. God, when they cry
'*Outree*', help, oh Lord, that crusader for whose sake I go in fear,
for cruel are the Saracens.

What I regret is that I was not there to escort him at his starting
out. The pilgrim's gown he wore, he sent for me to hold in my
arms. At night, when love of him assails me, I put it beside me in
my bed, close to my naked flesh, to allay my grief. God, when they
cry '*Outree*', help, oh Lord, that crusader for whose sake I go in
fear, for cruel are the Saracens.

ANONYMOUS CHANSONS DE CROISADE

Por joie avoir perfite en paradis
M'estuet laissier le païs que j'aim tant
Où celle maint cui je merci touz dis,
A gent cors gai, à vis fres et plaisant;
Et mes fins cuers du tout à li s'otroie,
Mais il covient que li cors s'en retraie:
Je m'en irai là où Deus mort sofri
Por nos raembre à jor du vendredi.

Douce amie, j'ai à cuer grant dolour
Quant me covient enfin de vos partir
Où j'ai trové tant bien, tante douçour,
Joie et soulaz, du tout à mon plaisir;
Mais Fortune m'a fait par sa puissance
Changier ma joie à duel et à pesance
Qu'avrai por vos mainte nuit et maint jour:
Ensi irai servir mon creatour.

Ne plus qu'enfes ne puet la faim sofrir,
Ne l'on nel peut chastoier d'en plourer,

To gain perfect joy in Heaven, I am forced to leave the land I love so much, where she lives to whom I give thanks each day, that gay and noble lady with fresh and charming face; my true heart gives itself entirely to her, but my body must tear itself away: I am going to the place where God suffered death on Good Friday to redeem us.

Sweet love, I have great grief in my heart, now that I must at last leave you, in whom I have found so much goodness, so much gentleness, joy, and solace, entirely as I wished it. But Fortune by her power has made me change my joy for grief and sorrow that I shall suffer for you many a night and many a day. It is thus that I shall go to serve my Creator.

No more than a child can suffer hunger and be restrained from

Ne croi je pas que me puisse tenir
De vous, que suel baisier et acoller,
Ne je n'ai pas en moi tant d'astenance;
Cent fois la nuit remir vostre semblance;
Tant me plaisoit vostre cors à tenir
Quant ne l'avrai, si morrai de desir.

Biaus sire Deus, ainsi com je por vous
Lais le païs où celle est cui j'aim si,
Vous nous doigniez en ciel joie à tous jours,
M'amie et moi par la vostre merci,
Et li doigniez de moi amer poissance,
Que ne m'oublit por longue demourance;
Que je l'aim plus que rien qui soit el mont,
S'en ai pitié tel que li cuers m'en font.

Belle Isabel, à cors Deu vos comant.
Je ne puis plus avec vos demorer:
En paenime, à la gent mescreant
M'estuet ainsi por l'amour Dieu aler.
Por sauver m'ame i vois en bone entente;

*

weeping when he is hungry, no more, I think, can I deprive myself
of you and your accustomed kisses and embraces; there is not so
much abstinence in me. A hundred times a night I call up your
image; to hold you in my arms was such delight that without it I
shall die of longing.

Fair Lord God, as for Thy sake I leave the country where she
is whom I love so much, so I beseech Thee, in Thy mercy, grant
eternal joy in Heaven to my love and me; grant her power to love
me, so that long absence may not make her forget me, for I love
her more than anything in the world, and my grief is so great that
it melts my heart.

Fair Isabel, I commend you to God Himself; I can stay with
you no longer: for the love of God, I must go to pagan lands,
among the miscreant people. I go most willingly, for my soul's

Mais bien sachiez, amie belle et gente,
Se nuls morut por lealment amer,
Ne cuit vivre jusqu'à havre de mer.

Car autresi com la flors naist de l'ente,
Naist li grans duez de vous qui me tormente;
Mais, s'en revien, sour sainz le puis jurer,
Que c'ert por vous servir et honorer.

Je chant d'amors leaus où j'ai m'entente,
Ne je ne quier que mes cuers s'en repente;
Mais mon seignor de Gisour vueil mander
Que c'est honours de lealment amer.

JERUSALEM, grant damage me fais,
Qui m'as tolu ce que je plus amoie;
Sachiez de voir ne vous amerai mais,
Car c'est la rien dont j'ai plus male joie,
Et bien souvent en sospir et pantais,
Si qu'a bien peu que vers Dieu ne m'irais
Qui m'a osté de grant joie où j'estoie.

salvation, but know well, fair and noble lady, that if ever a man
died for true love I do not think to live till we reach the seaport.

For just as the flower springs from the shoot, so springs the
great longing for you which tortures me. But if I come back, I can
swear on the saints that it will be to love and honour you.

I sing of true love where my heart is fixed, nor do I wish it ever
to repent; rather I would send this message to my lord of Gisour:
honour demands that a man should love truly.

JERUSALEM, you do me a great wrong, you who have taken from
me what I loved the best; know in truth that I shall never love you,
for this it is that robs me of my joy, and often makes me sigh and
gasp, until I almost quarrel with my God, who has snatched me
from the great joy I was in.

Beaus dous amis, com pourrez endurer
La grant peine pour moi en mer salee,
Quant rien qui soit ne pourroit deviser
La grant douleur qui m'est el cuer entree?
Quant me remembre du douz viaire cler
Que je souloie baisier et acoler,
Grant merveille est que je ne sui dervee.

Si m'aït Dieux, ne puis pas eschaper:
Mourir m'estuet, tel est ma destinee;
Si sai de voir que qui meurt pour amer
Jusques à Dieu n'a pas qu'une journee.
Lasse, mieux vueil en tel journee entrer
Que je puisse mon douz ami trouver,
Que je ne vueil ci remaindre esgaree.

ANONYMOUS REVERDIES

En avril au tens pascour,
Que sur l'herbe naist la flour,
L'aloete au point du jour
Chante par moult grant baudour,
Pour la douçor du tems nouvel,
Si me levai par un matin,

My fair sweet love, how will you ever bear your great longing
for me on the salt sea, since nothing in the world could tell how
great a grief has entered into my heart? When I recall the dear
bright face I used to kiss and caress it is a wonder I do not go mad.

As God may help me, I cannot escape, but I must die, such is my
destiny; and yet I truly know that one who dies for love flies up to
God in but a single day. Alas! I would rather venture on that day
so that I may find my sweet love again, than linger here forlorn.

In April, in the Easter season, when flowers are budding in the
grass, the lark at daybreak sings with hearty joy, for the sweetness

S'oï chanter sur l'arbrissel
Un oiselet en son latin.
     Un petit me soulevai
     Pour esgarder sa faiture;
     N'en soi mot, que des oiseaux
     Vi venir à desmesure.
        Je vis l'oriou,
        Et le rossignou,
        Si vi le pinçon
        Et l'esmerillon,
Dieu, et tant des autres oiseaux,
De quoi je ne sai pas les noms,
     Qui sur cel arbre s'assistrent
     Et commencent leur chançon.
     Je m'en alai sous la flour
     Pour oïr joie d'amour.
Tout belement par un prael
Li dieus d'Amours vis chevauchier.
Je m'en alai à son appel,
De moi a fait son escuier.
     Ses chevaus fu de depors,
     Sa selle de ses dangiers,

of spring. I rose early one morning, and on the little tree I heard a small bird singing its own song.

I raised my head a little to see what sort of bird it was, and the next moment I saw birds coming in hundreds. I saw the oriole and the nightingale, the chaffinch and the merlin, and God knows how many other birds, whose names I do not know, who sat on that tree and began their song.

I went beneath the flowery branches to hear [them sing] of the joy of love, and there I saw the god of Love come riding slowly across a meadow. I went to join him at his call, and he made me his

Ses escus fut de quartiers
De baisier et de sourire.
    Ses haubers estoit
    D'acoler estroit,
    Ses heaumes de flours
    De pluseurs colours.
Dieu, sa lance est de cortoisie,
    Espee de flour de glai,
    Ses chauces de mignotie,
    Esperons de bec de jai.
    Tuit chanterent à un son,
Onc n'i ot autre jongleör.

VOULEZ vous que je vous chant
Un son d'amours avenant?
    Vilain nel fist mie,
Ainz le fist un chevalier
Sous l'ombre d'un olivier
    Entre les bras s'amie.

squire. His horse was made of love's delight, his saddle of love's delays; his shield was quartered with kisses and sighs, his hauberk was made of close embracing, his helmet of flowers of many colours. God! his lance was of courtesy, an iris flower for his sword, his hose of caresses and jay's beaks for his spurs. All the birds sang to a single tune, with never another musician.

SHALL I sing you a sweet song of love? Not made by some uncourtly boor, but by a knight, under the shade of an olive tree, in the arms of his love.

Chemisete avoit de lin
Et blanc peliçon hermin
   Et bliaut de soie;
Chauces ot de jaglolai
Et solers de flours de mai,
   Estroitement chauçade.

Ceinturete avoit de feuille
Qui verdist quant li tens meuille,
   D'or est boutonade.
L'aumosniere estoit d'amour,
Li pendant furent de flour:
   Par amours fu donade.

Et chevauchoit une mule;
D'argent ert la ferreüre,
   La sele ert dorade;
Sus la croupe par derriers
Avoit planté trois rosiers
   Pour faire li ombrage.

She had a linen kirtle, and a white ermine tunic, and a gown of silk. She had stockings of iris and shoes of mayflower, close fitting to her feet.

She had a leafy girdle that freshened after rain and was buttoned with gold. Her purse was of love, with flowery pendants; she had it for a love-token.

She was mounted on a mule, with silver shoes and golden saddle. Behind her on the crupper she had three rose-trees planted to give her shade.

Si s'en va aval la pree.
Chevaliers l'ont encontree,
    Beau l'ont saluade:
«Belle, dont estes vous nee?»
«De France sui la loee,
    Du plus haut parage.

«Li rossignol est mon pere,
Qui chante sor la ramee
    El plus haut boscage.
La seraine elle est ma mere,
Qui chante en la mer salee,
    El plus haut rivage.»

«Belle, bon fussiez vous nee!
Bien estes emparentee
    Et de haut parage.
Pleüst à Dieu nostre pere
Que vous me fussiez donee
    A femme esposade.»

As thus she goes along the meadow, she has met some knights, and fairly they have greeted her: 'Sweet Lady, where were you born?' 'I come from France, that noble land, and am of highest lineage.

'My father is the nightingale, who sings in the branches of the highest wood; my mother is the mermaid, who sings in the salt sea on the steepest shore.'

'Fortune attend you, fair one! You come from a good family and a noble lineage. I would to God our Father that you could be given to me as my wedded bride.'

PASTOURELLE

[attributed to Hue de Saint-Quentin, and to
Jean de Braine]

Par desous l'ombre d'un bois
Trovai pastoure à mon chois;
Contre hiver ert bien garnie
La tousete o les crins blois.
Quant la vi sanz compaignie,
Mon chemin lais, vers li vois.
　　Aé!

La touse n'ot compaignon,
Fors son chien et son baston;
Pour le froit en sa chapete
Se tapist lès un buisson;
En sa flahute regrete
Garinet et Robeçon.
　　Aé!

Quant la vi, soudainement
Vers li tour, et si descent,
Si li dis: «Pastoure amie,
De bon cuer à vos me rent;
Faisons de feuille courtine,
S'amerons mignotement.»
　　Aé!

Beneath the shade of a wood, I found a shepherdess to my liking.
She was well protected against the winter, this girl with the golden
hair. When I saw her all alone, I left my path and went towards her.
　　The girl had no companion except her dog and her staff; because of the cold, she sat wrapped in her cloak, close beside a bush;
on her flute she played a plaintive tune of Garinet and Robin.
　　When I saw her, straight away I made towards her and dis-
mounted, and said to her, 'Sweet shepherdess, heartily I give myself to you; let us build a bower of leaves and tenderly make love.'

«Sire, traiez vous en là,
Car tel plait oï je ja.
Ne sui pas abandonee
A chascun qui dist «Vien ça!»
Ja pour vo sele doree
Garinel rien n'i perdra.»
          Aé!

«Pastourele, si t'est bel,
Damę seras d'un chastel.
Desfuble chape grisete,
S'afuble cest vair mantel;
Si sembleras la rosete
Qui s'espanist de novel.»
          Aé!

«Sire, ci a grant covent,
Mais molt est fole qui prent
D'homme estrange en tel maniere
Mantel vair ne garniment,
Se ne li fait sa proiere
Et ses bons ne li consent.»
          Aé!

'Sir, go your way, for I have heard that tale before; I do not give myself to everyone who says, "Come hither," and I will never be false to Garinet for the sake of your gilded saddle.'

'Shepherdess, if it seems good to you, you shall be lady of a castle. Take off your cape of grey and wrap yourself in this mantle of miniver, and you will look like the rose-bud newly blooming.'

'Sir, here is a fine promise! But foolish indeed is she who would take from a stranger in this way a mantle of miniver or any other garment, unless she does as he wishes and lets him have his way.'

«Pastorele, en moie foi,
Pour ce que bele te voi,
Cointe dame noble et fiere,
Se tu veus, ferai de toi.
Laisse l'amour garçoniere,
Si te tien du tout à moi.»
        Aé!

«Sire, or pais, je vous en pri,
N'ai pas le cuer si failli,
Que j'aim mieus povre deserte
Sous la feuille o mon ami
Que dame en chambre coverte,
Si n'ait on cure de mi!»
        Aé!

JEAN RENART

L'Escoufle

... Que qu'il en vont parlant, tout droit
Vers la cité, grant aleüre,
Il a oï par aventure
Lès le chemin, en un jonchois,
Un ruisselet qui n'ert pas cois,
Ainz murmure sor la gravele.

'Shepherdess, on my faith, because you look so lovely to me, if
you wish, I will make of you a fine lady, noble and proud. Give up
your shepherd lad and be mine only.'

'Peace now, sir, I beg of you. I have not so treacherous a heart
but that I had rather have my poor living beneath the trees with my
true love, than be a lady in a well-roofed hall, where no one cares
anything for me.'

The Kite

... As they rode on talking, straight towards the city, at a good
speed, he heard by chance, beside the way, in a bed of rushes, a little
stream that was not silent but murmured over the gravel. He heard

124

Il a oï la fontenele
Dont l'eaue est plus clere qu'argens.
Fait il: «Or est ce li plus gens
Lieus d'eaue douce et de flors;
Ainc mais ne vi de tans colors
En si peu de terre autretant.»
Il esgardent tout en estant
Le lieu delitable en esté.
La rosee ot si grans esté
Qu'encore en sont tout plein li oeil
Des flors, et li rais del soleil
Feroit si en chascune flor
Que l'eaue en reçoit la color
De chascune tel comme el l'a.
«Beaus dous amis, fait ele, là
Vueil je descendre pour mangier.»
De tant la veut cil losengier
Qu'il li otroie volentiers.
Atant uns mout soutius sentiers
Ambedeus les conduit et maine
Du chemin jusqu'à la fontaine.

Il saut jus, si l'a descendue;
La pucele s'est estendue
As flouretes et au deduit.

the spring with water brighter than silver. Said he: 'This is the
loveliest place of sweet water and flowers. Never before have I
seen such a quantity of flowers of so many different colours in such
a small space.' They stopped and looked at this place, so delightful
in the summer weather. The dew had been so heavy that the eyes
of the flowers were still full of it, and the sunlight shone into every
flower so that the water took on the colour of each one. 'Fair sweet
friend,' said she, 'this is where I should like to dismount to eat.'
He wished to please her so much that he willingly agreed. Then a
very winding path took them both from the road to the spring.
    He leaped down and helped her to dismount. The girl gladly

Pour le chaut qui li grieve et nuit
Tolt sa chape et sa jupe fors:
Ele remest en pur le cors,
Tout desliee et desceinte.
Sa cote li fait grant aceinte
Tout entour li, sor l'erbe drue.
(Moult est garis qui a tel drue;
Ne doit avoir nule destrece!)
Pour ce que sa bende destrece,
Li cort kavelet et li blont
Par moult grant maistrie li vont
Par devant le tour des oreilles
Desci jusqu'as faces vermeilles;
Sor son blanc col en rot floceaux. ...

Guillaume de Dole

... QUE qu'il sont amdui acosté
As fenestres, vers un vergier
Où il oient, après mangier,
Des oisillons les chans divers,
L'emperere en fist luès ces vers:

stretched herself out among the flowers. Because of the oppressive heat that was troubling her, she took off her cloak and her riding-skirt and sat in indoor clothes, her robe loosened and ungirt, her gown making a great circle round her on the thick grass. (He is a fortunate man who has such a lover; he should never have any sorrows!) As she had unbraided her hair, the short, fair tresses fell charmingly round her ears and on to her rosy cheeks; and some curled on her white neck. ...

Guillaume de Dole

.. WHILE they were both leaning out of the window, looking to-wards an orchard and listening, after their meal, to the varied songs of the birds, the Emperor forthwith composed these verses:

Quant de la feuille espoissent li vergier,
Que l'erbe est vert et la rose espanie,
Et au matin oi le chant commencier
Du rossignol qui par le bois s'escrie,
Lors ne me sai vers Amours conseillier,
Car onques n'oi d'autre richece envie,
       Fors que d'amours,
Ne rien fors li ne m'en peut faire aïe.

Ja fine amours ne sera sans torment,
Que losengier en ont corrouz et ire.
Et se je puis servir à son talent,
Qu'ele me veuille à son servise eslire,
Je soufferai les faus diz de la gent
Qui n'ont pooir, sanz plus, fors de mesdire
       De bone amour,
Ne rien fors li ne me peut geter d'ire.

When orchards thicken with leaf, and grass is green, and the rose full-blown, and early in the morning I hear the nightingale begin his song and shout it through the wood, then for me there is no escape from love, for I never desired any other riches, and none but love can come to my help.

True love can never be without its storms, for it fills envious tale-bearers with spite and anger, and, if I can do love's will so well that he will choose me for his service, I will endure the false reports of those who have no power to use love except as a target for slander; for none but love can soothe my troubled heart.

JEAN RENART

Galeran de Bretagne

... T<small>OUT</small> sagement et deduisant
Entre Galeran en la ville
Où il ot de destriers dix mille
Parmi ces rues cler hennir,
Chevaliers aller et venir
Sur chevaux reposés et fres.
Cil autre y jouent aux eschés,
Et cil aux tables se deportent;
Cil varlet ces presens y portent
Par les hostels à ces pucelles
Et aux dames vaillans et belles.
Plenté y a de damoiseaux
Qui font gorges à leurs oiseaux.
Si sont fichees ces banieres
Et cil escu teint de manieres
Sus fenestres de tours perrines;
De covertoirs vairs et d'ermines,
Et d'autres chiers draps trais de malles
Ont pourtendues ces grans salles;
Autres ront mise leur entente
De jonchier ces rues de mente

Galeran of Brittany

... I<small>N</small> good array and full of high spirits, Galeran enters the town,
where he can hear the whinnying of ten thousand steeds ring out
along the streets, as knights ride up and down on fresh well-rested
horses. Others can be seen playing chess and still others back-
gammon; servants are going from house to house carrying presents
to maidens and to noble lovely ladies. There are young noblemen
in plenty feeding their hawks. Banners with shields painted to
match them are fixed outside the windows of stone turrets. Great
halls have been draped with miniver and ermine rugs, and other
precious hangings brought out of chests. Other people have made
it their business to strew the streets with mint, and green rushes,

Et de vers joncs et de jagleux.
Ci sont à vendre cist chevreux
Et cerfs et autres venoisons,
Et de là est la grant foisons
D'oues, de jantes et de grues,
Qu'on va portant parmi ces rues,
Et d'autres volailles assez;
Trop repourroie estre lassez
De nommer et de mettre en nombre
Les poissons que l'on vent en l'ombre;
Si pouez veoir el chemin
Plenté de poivre et de coumin,
D'autres espices et de cire.
Ci sont les changeürs en tire
Qui devant eux ont leur monnoie:
Cil change, cil conte, cil noie,
Cil dit «C'est voir,» cil «C'est mençonge.»
Onques ivres, tant fust en songe,
Ne vit en dormant la merveille
Que cil peut ci veoir qui veille.
Cil n'i resert mie d'oiseuses
Qui y vent pierres precieuses,
Et images d'argent et d'or.

and wild iris. Here roebucks are for sale, and stags and other venison, and over there great stocks of geese, wild geese, and cranes are
being hawked through the streets, and other fowl in plenty. It
would be too wearisome a task to name and detail all the kinds of
fish that are being sold in the shade; and you can see on your way
plenty of pepper, and cummin and other spices, and beeswax. Here
there are rows of money-changers, each with his coins before him:
this one is changing money, this one is counting up, the next dis-
putes the sum: one cries, 'It's true,' another, 'It's a lie.' Never a
man in drunken dream saw half the wonders in his sleep that you
could see here while still wide awake. And the merchant is not
wasting his time who deals in precious stones, and gold and silver

Autre ont devant eux grant tresor
De leur riche vesselement.
Là en a vint, là en a cent
Qui braire font lions et ours;
En mi la ville, es quarrefours,
Viele cil, et cist y chante,
Cil y tumbe, cist y enchante.
Ci orrïez cors et buisines,
Et les couteaux par ces cuisines
Dont cil queu les viandes coupent
(Qui des meilleurs morseaux s'en coupent.)
Ci a grant noise de mortiers,
Et des cloches de ces moustiers
Qu'on sonne par la ville ensemble.
Telle feste court, ce me semble,
Mais or est morte en nostre eage:
Pas ne regnent li seigneurage. ...

images. Still others have before them a wealth of costly vessels.
Here twenty people, there a hundred in a crowd set bears and lions
roaring. In the middle of the town, at the cross-roads, one man is
playing on the viol, another singing; here is an acrobat and there
a conjurer; the noise of horns and trumpets mingles with that of
sharpening knives in kitchens where cooks are carving up the joints
(and cutting for themselves bits from the choicest parts). And there
is a great noise of gongs and the church bells which are all being
rung at once throughout the town. Such festival is being kept, it
seems to me, as is no longer known in our times, for lordly living
is a thing of the past. ...

THIBAUT D'AMIENS

Prière

J'AI un cuer trop lait
Qui souvent mesfait
Et peu s'en esmaie,
Et li tens s'en vait
Et je n'ai rien fait
Où grant fiance aie.
Assez ai musé
Et mon tens usé,
Dont j'atent grief paie,
Se par sa bonté
La flor de purté
Son fil ne m'apaie.

Mes cuers est trop vains
Et vils et vilains
Et gais et volages.
Il n'est mie sains,
Ains est faus et fains,
Pleins de grans outrages.

Prayer

I HAVE a very wicked heart, prone to do wrong and slow to repent, and time is slipping by, and I have achieved nothing in which I can put my trust. I have played the fool and wasted my life, for which I fear a heavy retribution, unless, of her goodness, the flower of purity makes my peace with her Son.

My heart is very empty, vile and coarse, and careless and incon-stant: not a heart in good health, but false and cowardly and full of

Il est fors du sens,
De povre porpens,
De mauvais usages, –
Uns chaitis dolans,
Pereceus et lens,
Oscurs et ombrages.

Cil est fous à droit
Qui assez acroit
Et petit veut rendre.
Souvent se deçoit:
Tel present reçoit
Qui le fait mesprendre.
Bien set en joer,
En rire, en moquer
Sa cure despendre,
Mais en bien plorer
Ne en bien orer
Ne set il entendre.

Il veut peu veillier
Et peu traveillier
Et doute poverte.
Il veut peu proier
Et veut grant loier
Avoir sans deserte.

pride. It is crazy and thoughtless and full of bad habits: a miserable
wretch, idle and slow, gloomy and sombre.

He is a fool indeed who accepts much on credit and expects to
repay with little. Often he deludes himself, he gets such a gift as
sets him astray. Well he knows how to waste his living in play and
laughter and mockery. But on repenting well and praying well he
cannot set his mind.

He wants to watch but little, and work but little; and he is afraid
of poverty. He wants to pray but little, and have a great income
without earning it. He wants, without sowing seed, to gather in

Il veut sans semer
Assez moissoner;
C'est folie aperte:
Nuls ne peut trouver
Grant fruit sans ouvrer
En terre deserte.

Hé! Dieus, que ferai?
Comment finerai
Au jour de juïse?
Comment conterai
Au juge verai,
Au roi de justise?
Nul conseil n'i voi
Se ne m'en porvoi
Devant cele assise:
Adonc prit pour moi
La mere le roi
Par sa grant franchise.

Hé! las, je comment,
Par quel hardement,
Requerrai s'aïe,
Quant à escïent
Et hardïement
L'ai tant messervie?

good harvest: it is the plainest madness; no one can get much fruit
from neglected land, unless he tills it.

Ah! God, what shall I do? How shall I pay my debts at the Day
of Judgement? How shall I give account to the righteous Judge, to
the King of Justice? I see no other course but to make provision
against those Assizes; therefore may the mother of the King pray
for me of her great goodness.

Alas! how shall I, by what great presumption, ask for her help,
when knowingly and boldly I have served her so ill? I will gather

Je m'enhardirai
Et si li dirai:
«Tres douce Marie,
Je m'amenderai
Et vous servirai
Trestoute ma vie.

«Ma joie, m'amours,
Ma vie, m'honours,
Ma pais, ma lumiere,
Qui de grant secours
Faire as pecheours
Estes coustumiere, –
Mon cuer mehaignié
Met à vostre pié,
Noble tresoriere:
Faites le haitié,
Vous qui de pitié
Estes boutilliere.

«Pucele roiaus,
Reïne loiaus,
Mere debonaire,
Precieus vaissiaus,
Esmerez cristaus
Pleins de saintuaire,

up my courage, and I will say to her, 'Sweetest Mary, I will amend my ways, and I will serve you all my life.

'My joy, my love, my life, my honour, my peace, and my light, you who are accustomed to give great help to sinners, I lay my wounded heart at your feet, oh! noble Keeper of the Treasure; make it whole again, oh! you who are the dispenser of pity.

'Royal maiden, loyal queen, noble mother, precious vessel, shining crystal full of holiness, temple richly adorned, tabernacle

Temples aornez,
Tres enluminez
De grant luminaire,
M'ame confortez,
Douce qui portez
Le dous laituaire.

«Cele de piment
Qui fait doucement
Le cuer sobre vivre,
Clef de l'oignement
Qui la morte gent
Peut faire revivre,
Grant est vostre odor
Et vostre douçor:
Nus ne peut descrivre
Comme vostre amor
Humble pecheor
Volentiers delivre.

«Tres nobles paumiers,
Tres dous oliviers
Pleins de medecine,
Tres gentis rosiers,
Souëf aiglentiers
Qui n'a nule espine,

illuminated by the great Light, comfort my soul, gentle lady, you who bear the sweet electuary.

'Storehouse of spiced wine to sweeten the life of the sober heart, key to the balm which can bring back the dead to life, great is your savour and your sweetness; none can tell the way in which your love delights to save the humble sinner.

'Noblest of palm trees, sweetest of olives, full of healing, loveliest rose tree, gentle eglantine without a single thorn, delectable

Deliteus cyprès,
Qui loin giete et près
Odor si tres fine,
Purgiez m'ame adès
Et la tenez pres
En vostre doctrine.

«Arbre de haut fruit
Qui à nostre nuit
Aportastes joie,
Mout a de deduit
Et seür conduit
Qui à vous s'apoie.
Tres sainte clartez
Qui les esgarez
Ramenez à voie,
Ne me trespassez:
Voir, j'avroie assez
Se je vous avoie.

«Estoile de mer,
A mon cuer amer
Ne soiez amere.
Daigniez l'entamer
A vous bien amer,
Bele douce mere.

cypress casting far and near your most delicate scent, purge my soul now and guard it safely in your keeping.

'Tree of noble fruit, who to our night brought joy, happy is the man and safe his steps who leans upon you. Holiest light, you who bring back the lost ones to the way, do not pass me by. In truth, I should have all I need, if I had you.

'Star of the Sea, to my hard heart do not be hard; deign to open it up, so that it may love you well, oh! fair Sweet Mother. Now hear

Pour Dieu, car m'oiez,
Et si ne soiez
Vers ce povre avere:
Clarté m'envoiez
Si me ravoiez,
Tres sage et tres clere.

«Saphirs esprovez,
Jaspes alosez,
Esmeraude pure,
Rubiz alumez,
Diamanz amez
De noble nature,
Chasteaus de refui,
A vous m'en afui
Comme à tour seüre;
Dame, à vous m'apui,
Du tout à vous sui,
Or en prenez cure.

«Donez moi du pain
Qui fait le cuer plein
De leesce pleine,
Du pain sans levain
Qui les filz Evain
Jeta hors de paine.

me in the name of God and do not withhold your wealth from this poor man. Shed your light on me and put me back in the right way, oh! wisest and brightest.

'Sapphire of proven worth, renowned jasper, pure emerald, glowing ruby, beloved diamond of noble nature, oh! castle of refuge, I fly to you as to a sure tower. Lady, on you I lean, and wholly yours I am, now take me in your care.

'Give me of the Bread that fills the heart with fullness of joy, that unleavened Bread that redeemed the sons of Eve. I beseech you

Je cri à vostre huis
Si comme je puis:
Besoins m'i amaine.
Grans ert mes ennuis
Se pitié ne truis
A si grant fontaine.

«Rendez moi l'amour
De mon bon seignour
Avant que je muire:
Que il toute errour
Par sa grant douçour
Veuille en moi destruire.
Gardez m'à la mort
De l'ennemi fort
Qu'il ne me puist nuire,
Mais à seür port,
O joie, o confort,
Me daigniez conduire.»

Tybaut congié prent;
La mort le sorprent
Qui le contralie;
Chetif et dolent
Se claime souvent,
A Dieu merci crie.

at your door, as best I can, brought there by my need. Deep will be
my grief if I do not find pity at so great a fountain.

'Bring back to me the love of my good Lord before I die. May
He of His great sweetness, destroy all sin in me. Keep me at my
death from the strong Enemy, that he may not hurt me, but to the
safe harbour, with joy and with comfort, vouchsafe to guide me.'

Tybaut takes his leave, for death is besetting and tormenting
him; often he laments in his misery and cries to God for mercy. Ah!

Hé! Tybaut d'Amiens,
Mout as eü biens
Les jours de ta vie.
Or n'en portes riens
Qu'un fessel de fiens:
C'est ta char pourrie.

GUILLAUME LE VINIER

Chanson à la Vierge

GLORIEUSE Vierge pucele,
Qui Dieu fustes mere et ancele
Et encore vous est pere et fieus,
Qui vous sert de cuer sans favele
Amender en doit sa querele.
Secourez moi, dame gentieus!
Priez vo fil, beaus dous cuer pieus,
Qui rien que veuilliez ne rapele,
Qu'en la sainte clarté des cieus
Soit fais et devisés mes lieus
Et chascun qui de cuer l'apele.

Tybaut of Amiens, much wealth you have had in the days of your life. Now you take nothing with you but a little bundle of filth which is your corrupted flesh.

Song to the Virgin

GLORIOUS Virgin Maid, you who were both God's mother and His handmaiden, and He is both your Father and your Son, the man who serves you with a guileless heart must thereby mend his case. Succour me, oh! gentle Lady. Pray to your Son, sweet gentle pious heart! for He refuses nothing that you ask, that in the holy brightness of the Heavens a place may be made and planned for me, and for everyone who calls upon Him from his heart.

Precieuse dame tres bele,
Talent ai que vos biens espele
Selon ce que pourrai au mieus.
Vo douceur est la fontenele
Qui sourt sous la plaisant gravele,
Qui rent talent as maladieus.
Les mors cuers pereceus et vieus
Esprendez d'ardant estincele
D'estre en l'amour Dieu talentieus.
Vo douceur dont tant croit li rieus
Le monde arose et renovele.

De tout est dame et damoisele
Cele dont issi la flourcele
Et la source des fontenieus
Dont li cours n'estanche n'engele;
Terre gaste arose, et praiele;
La où court est tempres avrieus;
Les durs cuers negligens targieus
Font et molie et esquartele
Com fait contre soleil gresieus;
Repentance, rosee et mieus,
L'amour Dieu i ferme et seële.

Precious and most beautiful Lady, it is my wish to set out all
your virtues as best I am able to do. Your sweetness is the spring
that rises in delightful sands and gives back to the sick the desire to
live. Hearts dead in indolence and vileness you light up with a burning spark so that they long for the love of God. Your sweetness,
with its swelling stream, waters and refreshes the world.

She is the sovereign lady of all, she from whom arose the very
flower and the source of the springs whose course never dries up
and never freezes. It waters both the waste land and the meadow:
wherever it flows, April is quickly come; it melts and softens and
breaks down the hard, neglectful, over-tardy hearts, as hail melts
in the sun. The dew and honey of repentance fastens and seals in
them the love of God.

De dous trenchant est l'alemele
Qui le cuer desous la mamele
Fent sans angoisse et sans perieus;
Si souef le roisne et quarele
Que sons de harpe ne viele
N'est plus dous ne plus melodieus;
Clarté remet en orbes yeus
Et parole en langue muele;
Les mors membres fait poestieus
Et fers et sentables quant Dieus
Les surrexist de grace isnele.

Bien peut mestraire la merele
Cil qui si sa char n'afincele
Et estraint qu'il ne soit decieus.
Sire en qui tous biens amoncele,
Gardez mon cors qu'il ne chancele.
Trop est cist siecles malaisieus,
Tant i a article doutieus
Dont la char soronde et revele.
Se vo secours ne m'est hastieus,
Tost puis estre atains et consieus
Au tournoi sans frein et sans sele.

A gentle sharpness has that knife which opens up the heart within the breast without anguish and without danger; it probes and pierces so softly that the sound of harp and viol is not sweeter or more melodious; it puts back light into blind eyes and the word into the mute tongue and makes dead limbs strong and firm and sentient when God reanimates them with His swift grace.

A man may play his game very badly if he does not master and control the flesh so that he is not led astray. Ah! Lord in whom all virtue is amassed, keep my body from stumbling. This world is very wicked; it holds so many dreadful things to lead the flesh into excesses and rebellion. If your help does nòt come speedily I may soon find myself attacked and caught up in the tournament without bridle or saddle.

Seigneur, la gaitans mors soutieus
Tient la queue de la paiele.
Ainsi à s'eslite et son kieus
Aussi tost prent jeunes et vieus.
Pour ce a bien fait la martele.

Chantez, arcangles sains Mikieus,
Devant Dieu ma chançon nouvele
Tant qu'il vous commant que recieus
Soit de vous mes espris doutieus
Quant mors li toudra sa cotele.

ANONYMOUS

Chanson pieuse

Li soleus qui en moi luist est mes deduis,
　　Et Dieus est mes conduis.

Et que me demandez vous, amis mignos?
Car à vous ai tout donné et cuer et cors.
Et que voulez vous de moi? Voulez ma mort,
　　Savoureus Jesu Crist?
Li soleus qui en moi luist est mes deduis,
　　Et Dieus est mes conduis.

My Lords, Death, cunning and ever watchful, is master of us all[?]. He chooses at his own good pleasure the young as readily as the old, and for this purpose his club[?] is well prepared.

Sing! Archangel, Holy Michael, sing before God my new song, so that he may order you to receive my fearful spirit when Death has snatched away its mortal clothing.

Religious Song

The sun that shines within me is my joy, and God is my guide.

What do you ask of me, my darling love? For I have given you my heart and my body. What do you want of me? Do you require my death, sweet Jesus Christ? The sun that shines within me is my joy, and God is my guide.

Je li ferai une tour en mon cuerçon,
Ce sera el plus beau lieu de ma maison;
Il n'en istra ja nul jour, mon ami dous,
      Ainz sera en deduit.
Li soleus qui en moi luist est mes deduis,
      Et Dieus est mes conduis.

Dieus! or ardent cil buisson par paradis;
Amours les font jubiler et tressaillir.
Fins amans ont tout le temps en Jesu Crist,
      Car c'est tout leur desir.
Li soleus qui en moi luist est mes deduis,
      Et Dieus est mes conduis.

Hé! mi, lasse, que ferai? N'i puis aler.
Esperance et fine amour, car m'i portez,
Qu'après ceste mortel vie i puisse aler:
      Ce est tous mes deduis.
Li soleus qui en moi luist est mes deduis,
      Et Dieus est mes conduis.

I will build him a tower in my heart, it shall be in the finest place in my house; he shall never depart from it, my sweet love, but live there in delight. The sun that shines within me is my joy, and God is my guide.

God! how the bushes are burning in Paradise! Love makes them sparkle with jubilation. And their true love is ever Jesus Christ, for He is all they long for. The sun that shines within me is my joy, and God is my guide.

Alas for me! what shall I do? I cannot go there. Hope and true love, I will ask you to carry me there, that after this mortal life I may go there: that is all my delight. The sun that shines within me is my joy, and God is my guide.

Dame Marie, priez à vostre fil
Que tant com vivrons en cest mortel essil
Sa grace nous doint, par quoi soions si fil,
   Et en son livre escrit.
Li soleus qui en moi luist est mes deduis,
   Et Dieus est mes conduis.

GUILLAUME DE LORRIS

Le Roman de la Rose (First Part)

... JOLIS, gais et pleins de leece,
Vers une riviere m'adrece
Que j'oï pres d'ilueques bruire;
Car ne me soi aller deduire
Plus bel que sus celle riviere.
D'un tertre qui pres d'iluec iere
Descendoit l'eaue grant et roide.
Clere estoit l'eaue et aussi froide
Comme puiz ou comme fontaine;
Si estoit peu mendre de Seine,
Mais qu'elle estoit plus espandue.
Onques mais n'avoie veüe
Cele eaue qui si bien seoit;

Lady Mary, pray to your Son that as long as our mortal exile lasts, He may grant us grace to be His children, and that our names may be written in His book. The sun that shines within me is my joy, and God is my guide.

The Romance of the Rose (First Part)

... BLITHE and gay and full of gladness, I made my way towards a river that I heard flowing near by, for I could not have a better place to take my pleasure than by that river. From a hillock close at hand, the water flowed down wide and swift. The river was clear, and as cold as if it came from a well or a spring, and it was a little smaller than the Seine, although it was wider spread. Never before had I seen this river in its lovely setting, and it rejoiced and glad-

Si m'abelissoit et seoit
A regarder le lieu plaisant.
De l'eaue clere et reluisant
Mon vis rafreschi et lavai;
Si vi tout covert et pavé
Le fonz de l'eaue de gravele.
La praerie grant et bele
Tres au pié de l'eaue batoit.
Clere et serie et bele estoit
La matinee, et atempree;
Lors m'en alai par mi la pree,
Contreval l'eaue esbanoiant,
Tout le rivage costoiant.

Quant j'oi un peu avant alé,
Si vi un vergier grant et lé,
Tout clos de haut mur bataillié,
Portrait dehors et entaillié
A maintes riches escritures.
Les images et les peintures
Du mur volentiers remirai,
Si vous conterai et dirai
De ces images la semblance,
Si com moi vient en remembrance. ...

dened me to gaze at this beautiful place. With the clear and shining
water I refreshed and washed my face, and I saw the bottom of the
river all covered and paved with gravel. A beautiful wide meadow
came right to the water's edge. Clear and calm and lovely was the
morning, and temperate. Then I went on through the meadow,
happily wandering downstream, all along the river bank.

When I had gone a little way, I saw an orchard great and wide,
all enclosed with a high battlemented wall, painted and carved on
its outer side with many richly adorned inscriptions. I looked with
great pleasure at the images and paintings on the wall, and I will
describe to you the appearance of these pictures as I remember
them. ...

Après fu Vieillece portraite,
Qui estoit bien un pié retraite
De tel comme ele soloit estre;
A peine qu'el se pooit paistre,
Tant estoit vieille et redotee.
Mout estoit sa beauté gastee,
Mout estoit laide devenue.
Toute sa teste estoit chenue
Et blanche com s'el fust florie.
Ce ne fust mie grant morie
S'ele morist, ne granz pechiés,
Car touz ses cors estoit sechiés
De vieillece, et aneientiz.
Mout estoit ja ses vis flestiz,
Qui fu jadis soués et plains;
Or estoit tous de fronces pleins.
Les oreilles avoit moussues,
Et toutes les denz si perdues
Qu'ele n'en avoit mais nesune.
Tant par estoit de grant vieillune
Qu'el n'alast mie la montance
De quatre toises sanz potence.
Li Tens qui s'en va nuit et jour
Sanz repos prendre et sanz sejour,

Next, Old Age was portrayed, shrunk a full foot from what she used to be; hardly could she feed herself, she was so old and doddering. Her beauty was all wasted away, and very ugly had she become. Her head was all hoary and white, as if it was in blossom. It would not be much of a death if she died, nor much of a pity, for all her body was dried up with age and shrunk to nothing. Her face was now all withered, which once was soft and smooth, but now was full of wrinkles. Her ears were hairy, and she had lost all her teeth until she had not a single one left. She was so far gone in age that she could not walk the length of four ells without a stick. Time, who speeds on both night and day, never resting, never staying,

Et qui de nous se part et emble
Si celeement qu'il nous semble
Qu'il s'arrest adès en un point,
Et il ne s'i arreste point,
Ainz ne fine de trespasser,
Que l'on ne puet neïs penser
Quels tens ce est qui est presenz,
Sel demandez as clers lisanz,
Car ainz que l'on l'eüst pensé
Seroient ja troi tens passé;
Li Tens qui ne peut sejourner,
Ainz va tousjours sans retourner,
Com l'eaue qui s'avale toute,
N'il n'en retourne arriere goute;
Li Tens vers qui neienz ne dure,
Ne fer ne chose tant soit dure,
Car Tens gaste tout et manjue;
Li Tens qui toute chose mue,
Qui tout fait croistre et tout norrist
Et qui tout use et tout porrist;
Li Tens qui envieilli nos peres,
Qui vieillist rois et empereres
Et qui tous nous envieillira,
Ou Mort nous desavancira;

and flees from us, and steals away so secretly that it seems to us
that he is always standing still, and yet he never stops but endlessly
flies past, so that you cannot even seize the thought of present time
if you inquire of learned men, for before you have thought it three
separate presents will have passed away; Time, who cannot stay,
but travels ever onwards without returning, as water flows for ever
down and never a drop turns back; Time, against whom nothing
endures, not iron or anything however hard, for Time spoils all,
eats everything away; Time, who changes all things, makes all
things grow, nourishes all, then wears all out and turns all to decay;
Time, who has aged our fathers, who ages kings and emperors, and
who will age us all, unless death halts us first; Time, who is all-

Li Tens, qui tout a en baillie
Des genz vieillir, l'avoit vieillie
Si durement qu'au mien cuidier
El ne se pouoit mais aidier,
Ainz retournoit ja en enfance;
Car certes el n'avoit puissance,
Ce cuit je, ne force ne sen,
Ne plus que uns enfes d'un an.
Neporquant, au mien escientre,
Ele avoit esté sage et entre,
Quant ele ert en son droit eage;
Mais je cuit qu'el n'ere mais sage,
Ainz estoit toute rassotee. ...

... Des roses i ot grant monceaus,
Aussi beles n'avoit sous ceaus;
S'i ot boutons petis et clos,
Et tels qui sont un peu plus gros;
Si en i a d'autre moison,
Qui se traient à lor saison
Et s'aprestent d'espaneïr:
Icil ne font pas à haïr;
Les roses ouvertes et lees
Sont en un jour toutes alees,

powerful to make all men old, had made her so very old that it
seemed to me she could no longer help herself, but was already
turning back to childhood. For certainly she had not power, I
think, nor strength nor sense, more than a year-old child. None the
less, she surely had been wise and judicious when she was in her
prime, but I think she was no longer in her right mind, but was
quite in her dotage. ...

... There were great masses of those roses, more beautiful than
any under Heaven: small tight buds and others just a little bigger,
and some of yet another size, just coming to their season and almost
ready to bloom; these last are not to be despised. The wide-open
roses are all gone in a day, but the buds stay quite fresh at least for

Mais li bouton durent tuit frois
A tout le moins deus jours ou trois.
Icil bouton moult m'abelurent:
Onques si bel nul lieu ne crurent;
Qui en pourroit un acrochier,
Il le devroit avoir moult chier;
Se chapel en peüsse avoir,
Je n'amasse tant nul avoir.

Entre ces boutons en eslui
Un si tres bel qu'envers celui
Nul des autres rien ne prisai,
Puis que je l'oi bien avisé,
Car une color l'enlumine
Qui est si vermeille et si fine
Com Nature la pot plus faire.
De feuilles i ot quatre paire,
Que Nature par grant maistire
I ot assises tire à tire;
La queue est droite come jons,
Et par dessus siet li boutons
Si qu'il ne cline ne ne pent.
L'odor de lui entor s'espant:
La suatume qui en ist
Toute la place replenist.
Et quant jel senti si flairier,

two days or three. These buds seemed most beautiful to me; never such lovely ones grew anywhere. If a man could get hold of one of them, he ought to treasure it most dearly; if I could have a garland of them, no wealth on earth would give me such delight.

Among these buds one I espied so beautiful that, matched with it, all the others seemed to me worthless, when once I had looked well on it; for through it shone the colour of the very purest red that Nature could fashion. It had four pairs of leaves, placed with Nature's consummate art one following another; its stalk was straight as a reed, and the bud installed above it without the slightest droop or bending. Its scent spread all about it: the fragrance from

Je n'oi talent de repairier,
Ainz m'aprochasse pour le prendre,
Se j'i osasse la main tendre;
Mais chardon agu et poignant
M'en aloient moult esloignant;
Espines trenchans et agues,
Orties et ronces crochues
Ne me laissoient avant traire,
Car je me cremoie mal faire.

Li Dieus d'Amour, qui, l'arc tendu,
Avoit tousjours moult entendu
A moi porsuivre et espier,
S'ert arestés lès un fïer;
Et quant il ot aperceü
Que j'avoie ainsi esleü
Ce bouton qui plus me plaisoit
Que nuls des autres ne faisoit,
Il a tantost pris une floiche,
Et quant la corde fu en coiche,
Il entesa jusqu'à l'oreille
L'arc, qui estoit fors à merveille,
Et traist à moi par tel devise
Que par mi l'ueil m'a ou cuer mise
La saiete par grant roidor. ...

it filled the air around, and when I smelt its perfume I had no thought of going back, but would have come close to pluck it if I had dared to stretch out my hand; but sharp and piercing thistles kept me far away from it, and keen-cutting thorns, nettles, and clutching brambles prevented me from going any farther, for I was afraid of hurting myself.

The God of Love who, with bended bow, had been constantly intent on following and watching me, had stopped beside a fig tree, and when he had perceived how my choice had fallen on this bud, which pleased me more than any other, he straightway took an arrow and, when the string was in the notch, the drew it back to his ear and loosed the arrow from his mighty bow with such skill that he shot it fiercely through my eye and lodged it in my heart. ...

THIBAUT IV DE CHAMPAGNE, ROI DE NAVARRE

Chanson d' Amour

CHANTER m'estuet, que ne m'en puis tenir,
Et si n'ai je fors qu'ennui et pesance;
Mais tout adès se fait bon resjoïr,
Qu'en faire duel nuls du mont ne s'avance.
Je ne chant pas com hom qui soit amés,
Mais com destroiz, pensis et esgarés;
Que je n'ai mais de bien nule esperance,
Ainz sui touz jours à parole menés.

Je vous dis bien une rien sans mentir:
Qu'en Amour a eür et grant chëance.
Se je de li me poïsse partir,
Mieuz me venist qu'estre sire de France.
Or ai je dit com fous desesperés:
Mieuz aim morir recordant ses beautés
Et son grant sens et sa douce acointance
Qu'estre sire de tout le mont clamés.

Love Song

SING I must, for I cannot keep myself from singing, and yet I am
full of grief and sorrow; but it is always a good thing to rejoice, for
no one in the world profits by lamenting. I sing not as one who is
loved, but as one distressed, cast down, and forlorn; for I have no
longer any hope of happiness, but am always deluded by words.

One thing I will tell you truly: in love, much depends on chance
and fortune. If I could cease from loving her, it would be a better
thing for me than to be lord of France. Now I have spoken like a
raving madman: I would rather die remembering her beauties, her
wisdom, and her gentle friendship than be called lord of the whole
world.

Ja n'avrai bien, jel sai à escient,
Qu'Amour me het et ma dame m'oublie,
S'est il raison, qui à amer entent,
Qu'il ne dout mort ne paine ne folie.
Puis que me sui à ma dame donés,
Amour le veut, et quant il est ses grés,
Ou je morrai, ou je ravrai m'amie,
Ou ma vie n'ert mie ma santés.

Li Fenix quiert la busche et le sarment
En quoi et s'art et jete fors de vie.
Aussi quis je ma mort et mon torment,
Quant je la vi, se pitié ne m'aïe.
Dieus! tant me fu li veoirs savorés
Dont j'avrai puis tant de maus endurés!
Li souvenirs me fait morir d'envie
Et li desirs et la granz volentés.

Moult est Amour de merveilleus pouoir,
Qui bien et mal fait tant com li agree.
Moi fait ele trop longuement doloir.
Raison me dit que j'en ost ma pensee,
Mais j'ai un cuer ainz tels ne fu trouvés:

I shall never know happiness, I am certain of that, for Love hates
me and my lady forgets me. And yet it is reasonable for a man who
means to love not to fear death or suffering or madness. Since I
have given myself to my lady, it is Love's will; and since it is his
will either I shall die, or I shall have my lady again, or my life will
never be whole.

The Phoenix seeks out the wood and the vine-shoots on which
it burns itself to death. In the same way I sought my own death and
my own torment when first I saw her – unless Pity comes to my aid.
Oh! God, how delightful was that first sight, which was to bring
so many ills upon me! The memory kills me with longing, and my
desire and my great need for her.

Wonderful indeed is the power of Love, for he gives joy and
sorrow just as he pleases. Me he keeps too long in sadness. Reason
tells me to think of other things, but I have a heart – never such a

Tousjours me dit: «Amez! amez! amez!»
N'autre raison n'ert ja par lui mostree,
Et j'amerai, n'en puis estre tornés.

Dame, merci! qui touz les biens savez;
Toutes valors et toutes granz bontez
Sont plus en vous qu'en dame qui soit nee.
Secourez moi, que faire le poez!

Chançon! Phelipe, à mon ami, courez!
Puis que il s'est dedans la cort boutez,
Bien est s'amour en haïne tornee;
A paine ert ja de bele dame amez.

Chanson

«DAME, merci! une rien vous demant,
Dites m'en voir, se Dieus vous beneïe:
Quant vous mourrez et je – mais c'ert avant,
Car après vous ne vivroie je mie –
Que devendra Amour, cele esbanie?

one was found – always telling me: 'Love! love! love!' – no other argument will it expound. And I shall love, I cannot be turned away from it.

Lady, have mercy, you who know all good things; all worth and all great goodness is in you more than in any woman on earth; come to my help, for you can do so.

My song, hasten to Philip my friend; since he has thrust himself into the life of the Court, his love has turned to hatred; hardly will he be loved by any fair lady.

Song

'MY lady, I beg you, one thing I would ask; answer me truly, as God may bless you: when you are dead, and I – but that will be before, for I could never live after you – what will become of Love, left all forlorn? For you have such wisdom and such worth, and I

Que tant avez sens, valor, et j'aim tant
Que ja croi bien qu'après nous ert faillie.»

«Par Dieu, Thibaut, selon mon escïent
Amour n'ert ja pour nule mort perie,
Ne je ne sai se vous m'alez guilant,
Que trop megres n'estes encore mie.
Quant nous mourrons (Dieus nous dont bone vie!)
Bien croi qu'Amour damage i avra grant,
Mais tousjours ert valor d'Amour complie.»

«Dame, certes ne devez pas cuidier,
Mais bien savoir que trop vous ai amee.
De la joie m'en aim mieuz et tieng chier
Et pour ce ai ma graisse recouvree;
Qu'ainz Dieus ne fist si tres bele rien nee
Com vous, mais ce me fait trop esmaier,
Quant nous mourrons qu'Amour sera finee.»

«Thibaut, taisiez! Nuls ne doit commencier
Raison qui soit de tous drois desevree.

so great a love, that I truly think when we are dead then Love will be no more.'

'In God's name, Thibaud, as I should judge it, Love will never perish for anyone's death, and I do not know whether you mean to mock me; for you are not much wasted away as yet. When we die (God grant us long life!) I think indeed that Love will suffer a great loss, but Love's true worth can never be diminished.'

'Lady, indeed, you must not merely think, but truly know that I have loved you very deeply. The joy of loving you has made me dearer to myself, and that is why I have put on flesh again; for God never made so lovely a creature as you, but this makes me greatly fear that when we die it will be the end of Love.'

'Thibaud, no more of this! No one should embark on a topic divorced from all reason. You say it to soften my heart towards

Vous le dites pour moi amoloier
Encontre vous, que tant avez guilee.
Je ne di pas, certes, que je vous hee,
Mais, se d'Amour me covenoit jugier,
Ele seroit servie et honoree.»

«Dame, Dieus dont que vous jugiez à droit
Et connoissiez les maus qui me font plaindre;
Que je sai bien, quels li jugemenz soit,
Se je i muir, Amour covient à faindre,
Se vous, Dame, ne la faites remaindre
Dedans son lieu arriers où ele estoit;
Qu'à vostre sens ne pourroit nuls ataindre.»

«Thibaut, s'Amour vous fait pour moi destraindre,
Ne vous griet pas, que, s'amer m'estouvoit,
J'ai bien un cuer qui ne se savroit faindre.»

Chanson

Tant ai amours servies longuement
Que desormais ne m'en doit nuls reprendre
Se je m'en part. Or à Dieu les commant,
Qu'on ne doit pas touzjours folie emprendre;

you, when you have already so beguiled me. Indeed, I do not say that I hate you; but if I have to pronounce the fate of Love, he still would be both served and honoured.'

'Lady, God grant that you judge rightly, and that you recognize the ills that make me suffer. For well I know, whatever the judgement may be, that if I die of love, Love will be bound to fade away if you, my Lady, do not maintain him in the place he has always occupied; for no one else can aspire to your wisdom.'

'Thibaut, if Love is making you suffer for my sake, do not regret it, for if I were to love, mine is a heart that would not love by halves.'

Song

I HAVE served love so long that from now on no man should blame me if I forsake it. Now I say, 'Farewell, Love,' for a man should not give all his life to folly, and he is a fool who cannot protect himself

Et cil est fous qui ne s'en set deffendre
Ne n'i connoist son mal ne son torment.
On me tendroit desormais por enfant,
Car chascuns tens doit sa saison atendre.

Je ne sui pas si com cele autre gent
Qui ont amé, puis i veulent contendre,
Et dient mal par vilain mautalent:
On ne doit pas seigneur servise vendre
Ne vers Amour mesdire ne mesprendre;
Mais qui s'en part, parte s'en bonement.
Endroit de moi, vueil je que tuit amant
Aient grant bien, quant je plus n'i puis prendre.

Amour m'a fait grant bien enjusqu'ici,
Qu'ele m'a fait amer sans vilanie
La plus tres bele et la meilleur aussi,
Au mien cuidier, qui onques fust choisie.
Amour le veut et ma dame m'en prie
Que je m'en parte, et je moult l'en merci:
Quant par le gré ma dame m'en chasti,
Meilleur raison ne quier à ma partie.

from it, and does not recognize in it his misfortune and his suffering. Henceforth I should be considered childish [to continue], for
every weather must await its season.

I am not like those other men who, having loved, then seek to
decry love, and speak ill of it with boorish spite. A man should not
sell his service to his lord, nor should he slander love, nor turn
against it; but let whoever gives it up do so without ill feeling. For
my part, I wish all lovers the greatest happiness, now that I myself
can get no more from Love.

Love has been very good to me till now, for he has made me love
the loveliest of women and the best, I think, that ever has been seen.
It is Love's will and my lady's request that I should leave off loving,
and I thank her much for this: since I abandon Love to please my
lady, I seek no better reason to forsake him.

Autre chose ne m'a Amour meri
De tant com j'ai esté en sa baillie;
Mais bien m'a Dieus par sa pitié gari,
Quant delivré m'a de sa seignorie.
Quant eschapés li sui sans perdre vie,
Ainz de mes yeux si bone heure ne vi,
Si cuit bien faire encore maint jeu parti
Et maint sonet et mainte raverdie.

Au commencier se doit on bien garder
D'entreprendre chose desmesuree,
Mais bone amour ne lait homme apenser
Ne bien choisir où mete sa pensee.
Plus tost aime on en estrange contree,
Où on ne peut ne venir ne aler,
Qu'on ne fait ce qu'on peut touzjours trouver;
Ainsi est bien la folie esprouvee.

Or me gart Dieus et d'amour et d'amer
Fors de Celi cui on doit aourer,
Où on ne peut faillir à grant soudee.

I have had no other reward from Love all the time I have been in
his service, but God in his pity has saved me and released me from
Love's power. Since I have escaped with my life, this is the most
fortunate hour my eyes have seen; and I am sure that I shall still
write many a *jeu-parti*, many a song, and many a *raverdie*.

A man should beware at the outset of aiming too high; but Love
does not let us deliberate or choose the object of our thoughts. We
fall more readily in love with someone far away, in a place where
we cannot easily come and go, than with someone who is always
close at hand; in this Love's folly is most clearly shown.

Now may God save me both from love and from loving except
for Her whom all men should adore, whose service cannot fail to
bring its great reward.

JACQUES D'AUTUN

Chanson d' Amour

Douce dame, simple et plaisant,
De vous me covient dessevrer,
Mais j'en ai plus mon cuer dolant
Que nuls hom ne pourroit penser;
Si nel di pas pour vous guiler,
Car il est bien aparissant
Tout i ai mis, cors et argent,
Peine de venir et d'aler,
Pour desevrement destourner.

Mout fui herbergiés hautement
La nuit que jui lès vo costel.
Ainc sainz Juliens, qui peut tant,
Ne fist à nul home mortel
Si beau, si bon, si riche hostel.
He las! chaitis, he las! coment
Vivrai mais touz jourz languissant,
S'encore ne l'ai autretel,
Car nuit et jour ne pens à el?

Love Song

Sweet lady, artless and enchanting, I must part from you, but it
is with a heavier heart than any man could imagine; and I do not
say this to deceive you, for it is clear to see that I have put in my all,
my self, my money, my travail of coming and going, so as to avoid
this separation.

Very nobly was I lodged, the night I lay by your side; never did
St Julian, with all his power, give any mortal man so fair, so good,
so rich a lodging. Alas! unfortunate, alas! how shall I live henceforth, for ever languishing, if I have never such another? for night
and day I think of nothing else.

Moult fist Amour à mon talent
Quant de moi fist vostre mari.
Mais joie m'eüst fait plus grant
S'ele m'eüst fait vostre ami.
Or n'i atent fors que merci:
A vous et à amour me rent,
Et se pitié ne vous en prent,
Par tens en plourront mi ami,
Car longues ne puis vivre ainsi.

Mal vous diront vostre parent
Et felon mesdisant de moi;
Mais sage estes et connoissant,
Si nes en croirez pas, ce croi;
Et je vous aim en bone foi,
Car je sui vostre ligement,
Et le serai tout mon vivant,
Certes, que bien faire le doi,
Car il i a assez de quoi.

Dame, je n'ai confortement
Qu'en vostre debonaireté
Et en un seul petit enfant
Qu'en vos beaus costés engendrai.

Love did exactly what I wished when he made me your husband,
but he would have given me even greater joy had he made me your
lover. Now I can only hope for mercy from him: I surrender myself
to you and to love, and if you do not take pity on me, my friends
will soon be weeping for me, for I cannot long survive like this.

Ill will they speak to you of me, your kinsmen and the cruel slanderers, but you are wise and discerning, and you will not believe
them, this I trust; and I love you in good faith, for I am entirely
yours and shall be so all my life, as I am bound to be, indeed, for
there is cause enough.

Lady, I have nothing to comfort me except the goodness of your
heart, and one little child whom I begot in your fair body. I thank

Graces en rent à Damedé
Quant il de vous m'a laissié tant;
Nourrir le ferai doucement
Et mout bien l'edefierai,
Pour ce que vous l'avez porté.

Ma douce dame, à Dieu commant
Vostre sens et vostre bonté
Et vostre gent cors avenant
Et vos yeus pleins de simpleté:
La compagnie où j'ai esté,
A qui nule autre ne se prent.
Douce dame, proz et vaillant,
De cuer dolant et abosmé
Vous commant à la mere Dé.

COLIN MUSET

Chanson

SIRE cuens, j'ai vielé
Devant vous en vostre ostel,
Si ne m'avez rien doné
Ne mes gages aquité:
C'est vilanie!

the Lord God that He has left me so much of you; I shall have him
gently tended and educated nobly, for your sake who have born
him.

My sweet lady, I give into God's keeping your wisdom and your
goodness and your sweet lovely self and your eyes so full of can-
dour: the company that once was mine, to which none other can
compare. Sweet lady, true and virtuous, with a heavy and despairing heart I commend you to the Mother of God.

Song

SIR count, I have played the viol before you in your house, and
you have given me nothing, nor have you paid my expenses: it's

Foi que doi sainte Marie,
Ainsi ne vous sivrai mie.
M'aumosniere est mal garnie
Et ma bourse mal farsie.

Sire cuens, car comandez
De moi vostre volenté.
Sire, s'il vous vient à gré,
Un beau don car me donez
       Par courtoisie!
Talent ai, n'en doutez mie,
De raler à ma mesnie.
Quant j'i vois bourse esgarnie,
Ma feme ne me rit mie,

Ainz me dit: « Sire Engelé,
En quel terre avez esté,
Qui n'avez rien conquesté?
. . . .
       Aval la ville.
Vez com vostre male plie!
Ele est bien de vent farsie.
Honis soit qui a envie
D'estre en vostre compaignie!»

a vile trick. By the faith I owe St Mary, I'll follow you no longer on these terms. My wallet is ill furnished and my purse is poorly stuffed.

Sir count, now give your orders about me. Sire, if it pleases you, now give me a fine present of your courtesy. I would dearly love, you may be sure, to go back to my home. But when I go with an empty purse, my wife gives me never a smile.

But she says: 'Sir Fool, what country have you been in, that you have brought nothing back with you ... from down the town. Look how your bag falls into folds: it's packed with nothing but wind. A curse on anyone who wants to keep company with you!'

Quant je vieng à mon ostel
Et ma feme a regardé
Derrier moi le sac enflé,
Et je qui sui bien paré
      De robe grise,
Sachiez qu'ele a tost jus mise
La quenoille sans faintise;
Ele me rit par franchise,
Ses deus bras au col me plie.

Ma feme va destrousser
Ma male sans demorer;
Mon garçon va abuvrer
Mon cheval et conreer;
Ma pucele va tuer
Deus chapons pour deporter
      A la janse alie;
Ma fille m'aporte un pigne
En sa main par cortoisie.
Lors sui de mon ostel sire
A moult grant joie sans ire
Plus que nuls ne porroit dire.

When I come home and my wife sees my sack well filled out behind me, and me well dressed in a miniver robe, be sure she soon lays aside her spindle willingly; she smiles brightly at me and throws both her arms round my neck.

My wife goes off to unpack my bag without delay, my servant to water my horse and groom him, my maid to kill two capons to make a feast with garlic sauce; my daughter brings me a comb in her hand, very prettily. Then I am master of my house, in undiluted happiness greater than any man could tell.

Chanson

QUANT je le tens refroidier
       Voi, et geler,
Et ces arbres despoillier
       Et iverner,
Adonc me vueil aaisier
       Et sejorner
A bon feu, lès le brasier,
       Et à vin cler,
   En chaude maison,
   Por le tens felon.
   Ja n'ait il pardon
Qui n'aime sa garison!

Je ne vueil pas chevauchier
       Et feu bouter,
Et si haz mout guerroier
       Et cris lever,
Et grans proies acoillir,
       Et gent rober;

Song

WHEN I see the weather growing cold, and frost coming, and the
trees losing their leaves and growing wintry, then I want to take
my ease and stay in front of a good fire, beside the glowing char-
coal, with clear wine, in a warm house, because of the bad weather.
May he never be forgiven who does not care for his own comfort.
   I have no wish to ride about setting fire to things, and I detest
waging war, and shouting, and gathering great booty and robbing

Assez i a fol mestier
    A tout gaster.
A peu d'ochoison
Se prennent baron;
Par conseil bricon
Meuvent guerres et tençon.

Assez vaut mieuz tornoier,
    Et behorder,
Et grosses lances brisier
    Et bel joster,
Et joie recommencier,
    Et tout doner,
Et despendre sans dangier,
    Et fors geter.
Avoirs en prison
Ne vaut un boton;
Quant plus a prodon,
Plus vient avoirs à foison.

Quant je sui lès le brasier,
    Et j'oi venter,
Et je voi plein le hastier
    A feu torner
Et le bon vin du celier
    Amont porter,

people. It is indeed a foolish business to lay waste everything. These nobles quarrel on the slightest pretext; by treacherous counsel they stir up war and strife.

It is much better to tourney and tilt and break great lances at fine jousts, renewing joy, giving freely, spending without reluctance, scattering good things. Wealth in prison is not worth a button. The more a worthy man has, the more freely does wealth come to him.

When I am beside the brasier and I hear the wind blowing and see the full spit turning before the fire and the good wine brought

Adonc vueil boivre et mangier
Et reposer
A feu de charbon.
Se j'ai gras chapon,
N'ai pas cusançon
D'assaillier à un donjon.

Nen à un plonjon
Tendu sus glaison
N'avrai garison
Par ceste froide saison.

A Sailli, Guion
Qui entent raison
Envoi ma chanson,
Voir se je fais bien ou non.

RUTEBEUF

La Complainte d'Outremer

EMPEREOUR et roi et conte
Et duc et prince, à qui on conte
Romans divers, pour vous esbatre,
De ceus qui se seulent combatre
Ça en arrier pour sainte Eglise,

up from the cellar, then I want to eat and drink and rest beside a coal fire. If I have a fat capon, I feel no itch to attack a tower.

Not under a stook set up on a clod shall I find comfort in this cold season.

To Sailly, to Guy who understands reason, I send my song, to see if I do well or not.

The Lament of the Holy Land

EMPERORS and kings and counts and dukes to whom are told many tales, for your delight, of those who used to fight in the olden days for Holy Church, now tell me on what deeds of yours you

Car me dites par quel servise
Vous cuidiez avoir paradis.

Cil le gaaignerent jadis
Dont vous oez ces romans lire,
Par la peine, par le martire
Que li cors souffrirent sur terre.
Vez ci le tens, Dieus vous vient querre,
Bras estendus, de son sanc teins,
Par qui li feus vous ert esteins
Et d'enfer et de purgatoire.
Recommenciez nouvele estoire!
Servez Dieu de fin cuer entier,
Car Dieu vous mostre le sentier
De son pays et de sa marche
Que on sans raison li sormarche.
Pour ce si devriez entendre
A revengier et à deffendre
La Terre de Promission,
Qui est en tribulacion
Et perdue se Dieus n'en pense,
Se prochainement n'a deffense.

base your hopes of Heaven. These men of old, whose stories you hear read to you, earned Paradise by the suffering and martyrdom their bodies endured on earth. Now is the time, God comes to seek you, his outstretched arms stained with the blood which quenched for you the fires of Hell and Purgatory! Start now to create a new story: serve God with undivided hearts, for God is showing you the way to his own country and his province which is being wantonly trampled underfoot. Therefore you ought to do all in your power to win back and to defend the Land of Promise, which is in tribulation, and lost, if God does not come to its help and if it is not speedily defended.

Soveigne vous de Dieu le Pere
Qui pour souffrir la mort amere
Envoia en terre son Fil.
Or est la terre en grant peril
Là où il fut et mors et vis.
Je ne sai que plus vous devis:
Qui n'aidera à ceste empointe,
Qui ci fera le mesacointe,
Peu priserai tout l'autre afaire,
Tant sache le papelart faire;
Ainz dirai mais et jour et nuit:
«N'est pas tout ors quanque reluit.»

Ha! rois de France, rois de France!
La loi, la foi et la creance
Va presque toute chancelant.
Que vous iroie plus celant?
Secourez la, qu'or est mestiers,
Et vous et li cuens de Poitiers
Et li autre baron ensemble.
N'atendez pas tant que vous emble
La mort l'ame, por Dieu, seigneur;
Mais qui voudra avoir honeur
En paradis, si le deserve. ...

Remember God the Father who, to suffer bitter death, sent down his Son to Earth. Now is the land in great peril where He died and where He lived. I do not know why I should say more to you. If a man will not help in such a case and pretends that it does not concern him I shall value him little for any other quality, whatever hypocritical airs he may give himself, but I shall maintain both day and night that all that glitters is not gold.

Ah! king of France, king of France, law, faith and belief are on the point of collapse. Why should I not speak out? Come to their help, for now you must, you and the count of Poitiers and the other barons all together. Do not delay till Death snatches your souls from you, for God's sake, my lords, but let him who would have honour in Heaven seek now to deserve it. ...

La Complainte Rutebeuf

... D IEUS m'a fait compagnon à Job,
Qu'il m'a tolu à un seul cop
    Quanques j'avoie.
De l'ueil destre, dont mieus veoie,
Ne voi je pas aler la voie
    Ne moi conduire:
A ci dolour dolente et dure,
Qu'à miedi m'est nuiz obscure
    De celui ueil.
Or n'ai je pas quanques je vueil,
Ainz sui dolenz et si me dueil
    Parfondement;
Qu'or sui en grant afondement
Se par ceus n'ai relevement
    Qui jusque ci
M'ont secouru, la lor merci.
Le cuer en ai triste et noirci
    De cest mehain,
Car je n'i voi pas mon gaain.
Or n'ai je pas quanques je ain,
    C'est mes domages.

Rutebeuf's Complaint

... G OD has made me a fit companion for Job, for he has taken from me at one blow all that I had. With my right eye, which used to be my best, I can no longer see enough to find my way about. This is a dreadful grief to me, for it is dark night at midday for that eye. Now I cannot have anything I want and I am sunk in grief, for here I must stay in the depths of despair, unless I am raised up by those who have been so good as to help me in the past. My heart is heavy and cast down because of this infirmity, for I do not see how I can earn my living, and now I have nothing of what gives me pleasure, that is my sad case. I do not know whether this is the re-

Ne sai se ç'a fait mes outrages;
Or devendrai sobres et sages
    Après le fait,
Et me garderai de forfait.
Mais ce que vaut? Ce est ja fait;
    Tart sui meüs,
A tart me sui aperceüs
Quant je sui en mes las cheüs.
    Cest premier an
Me gart cil Dieus en mon droit san
Qui pour nous ot paine et ahan,
    Et me gart l'ame.
Or a d'enfant geü ma fame;
Mes chevaus a brisié la jame
    A une lice;
Or veut de l'argent ma norrice
Qui me destraint et me pelice
    Pour l'enfant paistre,
Ou il revendra braire en l'estre.
Cil Damedieus qui le fist naistre
    Li doint chevance,
Et li envoit sa sostenance,
Et me doint encore alejance
    Qu'aidier li puisse,

sult of my own excesses; I shall become sober and wise now, after the event, and keep myself from doing wrong. But what is the good? The harm is done, I have changed too late. Too late I see the danger, when I have fallen into the trap. In this coming year, may God, who suffered and sorrowed for us all, keep me in my right mind and save my soul. Now my wife has given birth to a child, my horse has broken his leg on a fence, and the nurse is asking for money, and pestering me and fleecing me for the child's keep, or else he'll be brought back to yell here in the house. May the Lord God, that caused him to be born, send him enough to live on and give him sustenance, and lighten my lot, too, so that I can help him and earn a better living for him, and manage my affairs better

Et que mieus son vivre li truisse
Et que mieus mon ostel conduise
Que je ne fais.
Se je m'esmai je n'en puis mais,
Car je n'ai dozaine ne fais
En ma maison
De busche pour ceste saison.
Si esbahi ne fu mais hom
Com je sui, voir,
Qu'onques ne fui à meins d'avoir.
Mes ostes veut l'argent avoir
De son osté,
Et j'en ai presque tout osté;
Et si me sont nu li costé
Contre l'hiver.
Cist mal me sont dur et divers,
Dont moult me sont changié li vers
Envers antan. ...

Li mal ne sevent seul venir;
Tout ce m'estoit à avenir,
S'est avenu.
Que sont mi ami devenu
Que j'avoie si pres tenu
Et tant amé?
Je cuit qu'il sont trop cler semé:

than I do now. I can't help feeling dismayed to think that I have
not even a dozen logs, not a single bundle of firewood in the house
for the winter. Never was a man so much at his wits' end as I am,
truly, for I was never before so short of money. My landlord is de-
manding the rent for his house and I have taken almost everything
out of it, and I have hardly a rag to my back to keep out the cold.
These troubles are hard and cruel to bear, so that my verses are
very different from what they used to be. ...

Misfortunes never come singly; all this had to come upon me and
it has come. What has become of my friends that I used to keep so
near me and love so well? I think they were sown too far apart; they

Il ne furent pas bien femé,
        Si sont failli.
Itel ami m'ont mal bailli,
Qu'onques tant com Dieus m'assailli
        En maint costé
N'en vi un seul en mon osté.
Je cuit li venz les m'a osté.
        L'amors est morte:
Ce sont ami que venz emporte,
Et il ventoit devant ma porte,
        Ses emporta,
Qu'onques nuls ne m'en conforta
Ne du sien rien ne m'aporta.
        Ice m'aprent:
Qui auques a, privé le prent;
Et cil trop à tart se repent
        Qui trop a mis
De son avoir pour faire amis,
Qu'il nes treuve entiers ne demis
        A lui secourre. ...

were not well manured, and they have wilted. Friends like these
have not done me much good, for never, since God rained these
blows on me from every side, have I seen one of them in my house.
I think the wind has carried them away from me. Friendship is
dead: these are the sort of friends that go with the wind, and when
the wind blew before my door it bore them off, for never one of
them gave me either sympathy or help. This teaches me that those
who have money keep it for themselves, and he repents too late
who has wasted his money on making friends; for he doesn't find
them true (or even half-true!) when he needs their help. ...

ANONYMOUS

Chanson bachique

CHANTER me fait bons vins et resjoïr;
Quant plus le boi et je plus le desir,
Car li bons vins me fait souef dormir;
Quant je nel boi, pour rien n'i dormiroie;
Au resveillier volentiers beveroie.

En bon vin a soulas et grant deport;
Quant plus le boi et je plus m'i acort,
Car de bon vin peut on revivre mort;
Religion s'i assent et otroie,
Et le bon vin doit on boire à grant joie.

Ne sai qui a seignourie plus fort,
Ou vins ou rois ou d'Amour le deport;
Sur toute rien au riche vin m'acort:
Vins justise tout le monde et aloie,
Vins vaint Amour et justise et mestroie.

Drinking Song

GOOD wine makes me rejoice and sing; the more I drink, the more
I want; for good wine gives me peaceful sleep: when I drink none,
I cannot sleep for anything; and when I wake I gladly drink again.

In good wine is solace and pleasant pastime; the more I drink,
the better I like it, for good wine will bring the dead to life; the
monastic rule accepts it and allows it; and good wine should be
drunk with great joy.

I do not know which has the greater sovereignty, wine or the
king or the sport of love. I put the claim of noble wine above all
others: wine dominates and governs everyone, wine conquers love
and tames and masters it.

Tous jours doit on sivre bon vin de près.
D'ore en avant de bonne amour me tais,
Qu'Amour tous jours est tournee aus mauvais;
Communaus est à ceus qui ont monnoie;
D'amours venaus pour rien bien ne diroie.

Chançon, va t'en, au bon vin mant salus.
Maint homme a fait tumer en la palus,
Et maint en fait gesir la nuit vestus,
Et maint en fait cheoir en belle voie.
Bien met l'argent qui en bon vin l'emploie.

JEAN DE MEUNG

Le Roman de la Rose (Second Part)

... Et s'il est tel qu'il ne veut mie
Loiauté porter à s'amie,
Si ne la voudrait il pas perdre,
Mais à autre se veut aerdre,
S'il veut à s'amie nouvele
Donner couvrechief ou toele,
Chapel, anel, fermail, ceinture,

A man should always follow after good wine. Henceforth I shall be silent on the subject of true love: for love is always turned to the profit of the wicked, it is the common property of those with money, and nothing shall make me speak well of venal love.

Go, my song, and bear my greetings to good wine; many a man it tumbles in the swamp and many another it sends to bed in his clothes, and trips up many another on the smoothest path. A man employs his money well who spends it on good wine.

The Romance of the Rose (Second Part)

... And if he is the sort who does not want to be true to his mistress, and yet does not wish to lose her, but wants to attach himself to another, should he wish to give his new friend a kerchief or shawl, a hat, a ring, a clasp, a belt, or a jewel of any kind, let him

Ou joyau de quelque faiture,
Gart que l'autres ne les connoisse;
Car trop avroit au cuer angoisse
Quant el les li verrait porter:
Rien ne l'en pourrait conforter.
Et gart que venir ne la face
En icele meïsme place
Où venait à lui la premiere,
Qui de venir est coutumiere;
Car s'ele y vient, pour qu'el la truisse,
N'est rien qui conseil metre y puisse.
Car nul vieuz sanglers hericiés,
Quant des chiens est bien aticiés,
N'est si crueus, ni lionesse
Si triste ne si felonesse,
Quant li venerres qui l'assaut
Li renforce en ce point l'assaut
Quant ele alaite ses chaiaus,
Ne nuls serpens si desloiaus
Quant on li marche sur la queue,
Qui du marchier pas ne se jeue,
Comme est feme quant ele treuve
O son ami s'amie neuve:

take care that the first one does not know them, for she would be
grieved to the heart to see her wearing them; nothing would console her for it. And let him take care never to get the new one to
meet him in the same place where the other used to come to him
and where she is in the habit of coming; for if she should come and
find her rival there, nothing in the whole world would set that to
rights! For no old bristly boar is so fierce, when the dogs are worry-
ing him, nor is the lioness so cruel, so desperate, or so deadly when
the hunter attacks her at the moment when she is feeding her cubs,
nor is a snake so much to be feared when you tread on its tail and it
doesn't consider it a joke, as is a woman when she finds a new mis-

El jette partout feu et flame,
Preste de perdre cors et ame.

Et s'el n'a pas prise prouvee
D'eus deus ensemble la couvee,
Mais bien en chiet en jalousie,
Qu'el set ou cuide estre acoupie,
Coment qu'il aut, ou sache ou croie,
Gart soi cil que ja ne recroie
De li nier tout pleinement
Ce qu'ele set certainement,
Et ne soit pas lent de jurer.
Tantost li reface endurer
En la place le jeu d'amours:
Lors ert quites de ses clamours.

Et si tant l'assaut et angoisse
Qu'il convient qu'il li reconnoisse,
Qu'il ne s'en set espeir defendre,
A ce doit lores, s'il peut, tendre
Qu'il li face à force entendant
Qu'il le fist sur soi defendant;

tress with her lover. She throws out fire and flame in all directions,
ready to put both life and soul in peril.

And if she hasn't actually any real proof of what is going on between them, but still becomes suspicious of it, because she knows
or thinks herself forsaken, however it may be, whether she really
knows anything, or just suspects, let him never budge from a position of complete denial even of what she knows to be true, and let
him not hesitate to swear it. Let him hasten to make love to her on
the spot, then he will put a stop to her reproaches.

And if she worries and attacks him until he has to admit it, perhaps because it can't be denied, he must then, if he can, try to
compel her to believe that he did it against his will, because the

Car cele si court le tenait
Et si malement le menait
Qu'onques eschaper ne li pot
Jusqu'il orent fait ce tripot,
N'onc ne li avint fois fors cette.

Lors jure et fiance et promette
Que jamais ne li avendra:
Si loiaument se contendra
Que s'ele en ot jamais parole,
Bien veut qu'el le tut ou afole;
Car mieus voudrait qu'el fust noiee,
La desloiaus, la renoiee,
Qu'il jamais en place venist
Où cele en tel point le tenist;
Car s'il avient qu'ele le mant
N'ira mais à son mandement,
N'il ne souferra qu'ele viegne,
S'il peut, en lieu où el le tiegne.
Lors doit cele estroit embracier,
Baisier, blandir, et soulacier,
Et crier merci du mesfait,
Puis qu'il ne sera ja mais fait;

other woman had got him in her clutches and was persecuting him so that he simply could not get away from her without going to bed with her, and that it had never happened except this once.

Then let him take his oath, and swear and promise that it will never happen again; he will be so true to her that if she ever hears a word of such a thing he gives her full leave to kill or injure him, for he would see that other woman drowned, the shameless baggage, before he would go anywhere where she could put him in such a position again; if she should send for him, he will never go to her, nor will he allow her to come, as far as he can help it, to any place where she can get hold of him. Then let him take the other tightly in his arms and kiss, flatter, and caress her, and beg her to forgive

Qu'il est en vraie repentance
Pres de faire en tel penitance
Com cele enjoindre li savra
Puis que pardonné li avra.
Lors face d'Amour la besoigne,
S'il veut que ele li pardoigne.

Et gart que de li ne se vante,
Qu'ele en pourrait estre dolente.
Si se sont maint vanté de maintes,
Par paroles fausses et feintes,
Dont les cors avoir ne pouvaient;
Les noms à grant tort diffamaient,
Mais à ceus sont bien cuer faillant;
Ne sont pas courtois ne vaillant.
Vanterie est trop vilains vices.
Qui s'en vante il fait trop que nices,
Car, ja soit ce que fait l'eüssent,
Toutefois celer le deüssent.
Amour veut celer ses joyaus,
Se n'est à compagnons loyaus
Qui les veuillent taire et celer:
Là les peut on bien reveler.

him for this injury, since it will never be repeated, for he is truly sorry, ready to perform any penance she can lay upon him, once she has forgiven him. Then let him set about love's work if he wants her forgiveness.

And let him take care never to boast about his mistress, for she could be furious about that; and many men have boasted in false misleading words of many women they could never win, and wickedly slandered their names. But such men are a cowardly lot, neither courteous nor gallant. Boasting is the lowest of vices; a man who boasts is making a fool of himself, for even if he has really done what he says, he ought to keep it secret anyway. Love wills that his delights should be concealed, except from true friends who are willing to keep quiet about them and hide them; to such they can properly be revealed.

Et s'ele chiet en maladie,
Droit est, s'il peut, qu'il s'estudie
En estre li moult serviables
Pour estre après plus agreables.
Gart que nuls ennuis ne le tiegne
De la maladie lointiegne;
Lès li le voie demourant,
Et la doit baisier en plourant,
Et se doit vouer, s'il est sages,
En mains lointains pelerinages,
Mais que cele les veus entende.
Viande pas ne li defende,
Chose amere ne li doit tendre
Ne riens qui ne soit douz et tendre.
Si li doit feindre nouveaus songes,
Tous farsis de plaisans mensonges:
Que quant vient au soir qu'il se couche
Tout seul en sa chambre en sa couche,
Avis li est, quant il sommeille, –
Car peu i dort et moult i veille, –
Qu'il l'ait entre ses bras tenue
Trestoute nuit trestoute nue,

And if his mistress falls ill, he should, if possible, do everything he can to be of help to her, so as to be more pleasing to her afterwards. Let him take care not to be kept away from her sick-bed because he finds it tiresome. Let her see him always at her side; he should kiss her with tears in his eyes, and if he is wise he will vow himself to many a distant pilgrimage – but let him make sure she hears his vows! He must never withhold her food from her, or give her any bitter thing she has to take, or anything that is not tasty and tender. And he should make up new dreams for her benefit, all full of flattering lies: that when night comes and he lies down in his bedroom on his lonely bed, he imagines, when he does drop off (for he sleeps very little and lies awake a lot), that he holds her in his arms, all naked, all night long, in pleasure and in love, quite well

Par soulas et par druerie,
Toute saine et toute guerie,
Et par jour en lieus delitables.
Tels fables li cont, ou semblables. ...

Femes n'ont cure de chasti,
Ainz ont si leur engin basti
Qu'il leur est vis qu'els n'ont mestier
D'estre aprises de leur mestier;
Ne nul, s'il ne leur veut desplaire,
Ne deslot rien qu'els veuillent faire.
Si com li chas set par nature
La science de surgeüre,
Ne n'en peut estre destournés,
Qu'il est o tel sen tousjours nés
N'onques n'en fu mis à escole,
Ainsi set feme, tant est fole,
Par son naturel jugement,
De quanqu'el fait outreement,
Soit bien, soit maus, soit tors ou droiz,
Ou de tout quanque vous voudroiz,
Qu'el ne fait chose qu'el ne doie;
Si het quiconques la chastoie;

and strong again – and by day as well in many a lovely spot. Let him tell her these stories or others like them. ...

Women do not like to be corrected, but their minds are so formed that they think they know their own business without being taught, and let no one who doesn't want to annoy them take exception to anything they do. Just as the cat knows by nature all about catching mice, and can't be stopped from doing it, for it is born with that instinct, and never had to learn; in the same way, a woman, however stupid, has an inner conviction that whatever she may do, good or bad, wrong or right, absolutely anything you like, she is never doing anything but what she ought to do, so she hates

N'el ne tient pas ce sens de maistre,
Ainz l'a dès lors qu'ele pot naistre
Si n'en peut estre destournee;
Qu'ele est o tel sens tousjours nee
Que qui chastier la voudrait
Jamais de s'amour ne jourrait. ...

... TROP ere lors de grant renon.
Partout courait la renomee
De ma grant beauté renomee;
Tele ale avait en ma maison
Qu'onques tele ne vit mais on;
Moult ert mes uis la nuit hurtés;
Trop leur faisaie de durtés
Quant leur faillaie de couvent,
Et ce m'avenait trop souvent,
Car j'avaie autre compagnie.
Faite en estait mainte folie,
Dont j'avaie courrous assez.
Souvent en ert mes uis cassés
Et faites maintes tels mellees
Qu'anceis qu'els fussent desmellees
Membres i perdaient et vies
Par haïnes et par envies. ...

anyone who finds fault with her; and she hasn't learnt this conviction, but she has it from the moment of her birth and can't be turned
from it; for a woman is born so sure of herself that if anyone tries
to put her right he will never have her love. ...

... I WAS very well known in those days; the fame of my renowned
beauty ran everywhere; there was such coming and going in my
house as no one ever saw: much knocking on my door at night;
I played them many a cruel trick when I failed to keep appoint-
ments – which happened very often, because I had other company.
Many a folly came of it and got me into trouble enough; my door
was often broken down, and there was many a fight where limbs
and even lives were lost in hatred and in envy before the scores
were settled. ...

Lors ert mes cors fors et delivres;
J'eüsse or plus vaillant mil livres
De blans esterlins que je n'ai,
Mais trop nicement me menai.
Bele ere et jeune et nice et fole,
N'onc ne fui d'Amours à escole
Où l'on leüst la theorique,
Mais je sai tout par la pratique:
Esperiment m'en ont fait sage,
Que j'ai hantés tout mon eage. ...

Et puis que j'oi sen et usage,
(Que je n'oi pas sans grant domage)
Maint vaillant homme ai deceü
Quant en mes las le tin cheü;
Mais ainz fui par mains deceüe
Que je me fusse aperceüe.
Ce fu trop tart, lasse dolente!
J'ere ja hors de ma jouvente;
Mes uis, qui ja souvent ouvrait,
— Car par nuit et par jour ouvrait —
Se tint adès près du lintier:
«Nuls n'i vint ui, nuls n'i vint hier,
Pensaie je, lasse chaitive!

In those days I was strong and supple; I should have had a
thousand pounds' worth more in silver sterling now than I have, if
I had not behaved so stupidly. Beautiful and young I was, and
simple and foolish, and I had never been schooled in the theory of
love, but I learnt all about it by practice: a lifetime of experience
has brought me wisdom. ...

And since I achieved wisdom and experience, which I didn't get
without great losses, I have tricked many a rich man when I have
had him in my toils, but I was tricked myself by many before my eyes
were opened. That came too late for me, alas! I was already past my
youth; my door, which formerly opened so often — for it was at
work both night and day — stayed henceforth close to the lintel.
'No one came today and no one yesterday,' I used to think, 'poor
wretched me! I must live my life in sadness.' My heart was fit to

En tristeur estuet que je vive.»
De deul me dut li cuers partir.
Lors me vos du païs partir
Quant vi mon uis en tel repos,
Et je meïsmes me repos,
Car ne poi la honte endurer.
Coment poïsse je durer,
Quant cil joli vallet venaient
Qui ja si chiere me tenaient
Qu'il ne s'en poaient lasser,
Et jes voaie trespasser,
Qu'il me regardaient de coste,
Et jadis furent mi chier oste?
Lès moi s'en alaient saillant
Sans moi prisier un euf vaillant,
Nes cil qui plus jadis m'amaient;
«Vieille ridee» me clamaient;
Et pis disait chascuns assez
Ainz qu'il s'en fust outre passez.

break for sorrow. Then I wanted to leave the district when I saw my door so much at peace; and I myself hid away, for I could not endure the shame of it. How could I bear it when those elegant young men came along who used to hold me so dear that they could not weary of me, and now I saw them going by without giving me more than a passing glance – those who had been my dearest guests? They went pushing past me without considering me worth an egg, even those who used to love me most; they called me a wrinkled old woman, and every one of them said things much worse than that before he had passed by.

D'autre part, mes enfes gentis,
Nuls, se trop n'ert bien ententis,
Ou grans deaus essaiés n'avrait,
Ne penserait ne ne savrait
Quel douleur au cuer me tenait
Quant en pensant me souvenait
Des beaus dis, des dous aaisiers,
Des dous deduis, des dous baisiers,
Et des tres douces acolees
Qui s'en erent si tost volees.
Volees? Voire, et sans retour.
Mieus me venist en une tour
Estre à toujours emprisonee
Que d'avoir esté si tost nee.
Dieus! en quel soussi me metaient
Li beau don qui failli m'estaient!
Et ce qui remés leur estait
En quel torment me remetait! ...

And on the other hand, my noble youth, no one, unless he gave the thing deep thought, or had suffered great grief himself, could imagine or conceive the sorrow I felt in my heart when in my thoughts I recalled the fine speeches, the sweet comforts, the sweet delights, the sweet kisses, and the very sweet embraces which had all flown away so soon. Flown away? Ah! yes, indeed, and never to return. It would have been better for me to have been shut up for ever in a tower than to have been born so soon. God! what torment I suffered to think of the rich gifts which came my way no longer; and the thought that the men were able to keep their money tormented me just as much! ...

... Sans faille toutes bestes mues,
D'entendement vuides et nues,
Se mesconoissent par nature;
Car, s'els eüssent parleüre
Et raison pour els entr'entendre,
Qu'els s'entrepeüssent aprendre,
Mal fust aus homes avenu.
Jamais li bel destrier crenu
Ne se laisseraient donter,
Ne chevaliers sur eus monter;
Jamais beus sa teste cornue
Ne metrait à jou de charrue;
Asne, mulet, chamel pour homme
Jamais ne porteraient somme:
Nel priseraient un gastel;
Jamais ne porterait chastel
Olifanz sur sa haute eschine,
Qui de son nés trompe et boisine,
Et s'en paist à soir et à main,
Si com uns hom fait de sa main;
Ja chien ne chat nel serviraient,
Car sans homme bien cheviraient;
Ours, lou, lion, lepart, sangler,

... Certainly all dumb beasts, empty and bare of understanding, are by nature unaware of themselves. For if they had speech and reason so that they could understand each other, and could learn from each other, it would be a bad thing for men. Never would handsome chargers with their flowing manes let themselves be tamed or allow knights to mount them; never would the ox put his horned head into the yoke for the plough; neither donkeys, mules, nor camels would bear burdens for man: they would not care a fig for him. Never would the elephant carry a castle on his lofty spine, he who trumpets and clarions through his nose, and feeds himself with it too, both evening and morning, just as a man does with his hands; nor would cats or dogs serve man, for they can get on very well without him; bears, wolves, lions, leopards, wild boars would

Tuit voudraient home estrangler;
Li raz neïs l'estranglerait
Quant au berceul petiz serait;
Jamais oiseaus pour nul apel
Ne metrait en peril sa pel,
Ainz pourrait moult home grever
En dormant, par les eus crever.
Et s'il voulait à ce respondre
Qu'il les cuiderait tous confondre,
Pour ce qu'il set faire armeüres,
Heaumes, hauberz, espees dures,
Et set faire ars et arbalestes:
Aussi feraient autres bestes.
Ne ront il singes et marmotes,
Qui leur feraient bones cotes
De cuir, de fer, voire pourpoinz?
Il ne demourrait ja pour poinz,
Car cist ouvreraient de mains,
Si n'en vaudraient mie meins;
Et pourraient estre escrivain.
Il ne seraient ja si vain
Que trestuit ne s'assoutillassent
Coment aus armes contrestassent;

all seek to destroy man; even the rat would destroy him when he
was a baby in his cradle. Never a bird for any call would put his
skin in danger; indeed, he could harm man by pecking out his eyes
as he lay asleep. And if man should reply to this that he would be
sure to confound them all because he can make armour, helmets,
hauberks, keen swords, and can make longbows and crossbows,
beasts in their turn could do the same. Have they not apes and
monkeys too who would make them good tunics of leather or of
iron, and indeed doublets too? They would not be held up for
stitches, for these could work with their hands and be just as good at
it, and could be scribes too. They would never be so foolish as not
to become, all of them, skilful in resisting armed attack; and they

Et quelques engins referaient
Dont moult aus homes greveraient.
Neïs puces et oreilliees,
S'eles s'erent entortilliees
En dormant dedans leur oreilles,
Les greveraient à merveilles.
Peoil neïs, siron et lentes
Tant leur livrent souvent ententes
Qu'il leur font leur euvres laissier
Et eus flechir et abaissier,
Ganchir, tourner, saillir, triper,
Et degrater et defriper,
Et despoillier et deschaucier,
Tant les peuent il enchaucier.
Mousches neïs à leur mangier
Leur meinent souvent grant dangier
Et les assaillent es visages;
Ne leur chaut s'il sont rois ou pages.
Fourmiz et petites vermines
Leur feraient trop d'ataïnes,
S'il ravaient d'eus conoissance.
Mais voir est que cette ignorance
Leur vient de leur propre nature. ...

would also make for themselves engines of war of some kind with which they would do great damage to men. Even fleas and earwigs, if they had worked their way into men's ears when they were asleep, could do them very great damage. Lice even, bugs and nits, often make such attacks upon men that they make them leave what they are doing and bend and stoop, dodge, twist, jump, leap about, and scratch and wriggle, throw off their clothes, and pull off their shoes, so greatly can these creatures harry them. Even flies often annoy them greatly when they are eating, and often attack their faces, not caring whether they are kings or pages. Ants and small insects could cause them very great vexation if they, too, realized their own powers. But in truth this ignorance comes to them from their very natures. ...

... Vers les cieus arrier m'en retour,
Qui bien font quanque faire doivent
Aus creatures, qui reçoivent
Les celestiaus influences
Selonc leur diverses substances.
Les venz font il contrarier,
L'air enflamber, braire et crier,
Et esclater en maintes parz
Par toneirres et par esparz,
Qui tabourent, timbrent et trompent
Tant que les nues s'en desrompent
Par les vapeurs qu'il font lever,
Si leur fait les ventres crever
La chaleur et li mouvemenz
Par orribles tournoiemenz,
Et tempester et jeter foudres,
Et par terre eslever les poudres,
Voire tours et clochiers abatre,
Et mains vieus arbres si debatre
Que de terre en sont arachié;
Ja si fort n'erent atachié
Que ja racines rien leur vaillent

... I TURN once more to speak of the stars, which duly perform all
that they ought to do towards all created things, which receive
celestial influences according to their diverse substances. It is because of the stars that the winds strive together and the sky flares up
and roars and wails and splits open in many a place with thunder
and lightning, drumming and rattling and trumpeting until the
clouds are torn by the vapours they give rise to, and their bellies
are ripped open by the heat and the rush of air in dreadful whirl-
winds; and tempests rise up and thunderbolts are hurled, and dust
storms arise over the earth, and even towers and steeples are blown
down, and many old trees so shaken that they are torn out of the
earth; be they attached never so strongly, yet their roots are of no

Que tuit envers à terre n'aillent
Ou que des branches n'aient routes,
Au moins une partie ou toutes.

Si dit l'on que ce font diables
A leur cros et à leur chaables,
A leur ongles, à leur havez,
Mais tels diz ne vaut deus navez,
Qu'il en sont à tort mescrëu,
Car nule rien n'i a nëu
Fors les tempestes et li vent,
Qui si les vont aconsivant;
Ce sont les choses qui leur nuisent,
Cels versent blez et vignes cuisent
Et fleurs et fruiz d'arbres abatent;
Tant les tempestent et debatent
Qu'il ne peuent es rains durer
Tant qu'il se puissent meürer.

Voire plourer à grosses lermes
Refont il l'air en divers termes,
S'en ont si grant pitié les nues
Qu'els s'en despeuillent toutes nues,

avail to prevent their being flung flat on to the ground or having their branches broken, some at least if not all of them.

And people say that this is the work of devils with their crooks and their cables, with their claws and their hooks, but such a saying is not worth two turnips, for they are wrongly suspected of it, for nothing has done the harm except the storms and the winds, which thus rain their blows upon them. These are the things which harm them, these lay the corn and blast the vines and beat down blossom and fruit from the trees; so roughly they blow upon them and knock them about that they cannot cling to the branches long enough to ripen.

Moreover, they (the stars) make the sky weep great tears at different seasons, and the clouds are so full of pity that they cast off

Ne ne prisent lors un festu
Le noir mantel qu'els ont vestu;
Car à tel deul faire s'atirent
Que tout par pieces le descirent.
Si li aïdent à plourer
Com s'on les deüst acourer,
Et pleurent si parfondement,
Si fort et si espessement
Qu'els font les fleuves desriver
Et contre les chans estriver
Et contre les forez voisines
Par leur outrageuses cretines,
Dont il couvient souvent perir
Les blez, et le tens encherir,
Dont li povre qui les labeurent
L'esperance perdue pleurent.
Et quant li fleuve se desrivent,
Li poisson, qui leur fleuve sivent,
(Si come il est droiz et raisons,
Car ce sont leur propres maisons)
S'en vont, comme seigneur et maistre,
Par chans, par prez, par vignes paistre;

all their clothing and they do not then care a straw for the black cloak they are wearing, for they set themselves to make so great a lament that they tear it all into shreds, and help the sky to weep, as though they were about to be put to death; and their bitter tears fall so thick and fast that they make the rivers overflow and hurl themselves upon the fields and upon the neighbouring forests with their unbridled floods, and hence it often comes about that the corn must rot, and living become dear, so that the poor who till the fields must weep for their lost hopes. And when the rivers overflow, the fish, which follow their rivers (as is right and proper, for these are their own homes), go off as lords and masters over fields and meadows and vineyards to find their food; and invade the oaks,

Et s'escoursent contre les chesnes,
Contre les pins, contre les fresnes,
Et tolent aus bestes sauvages
Leur manoirs et leur heritages,
Et vont ainsi par tout nageant;
Dont tuit vif s'en vont enrageant
Bachus, Cerès, Pan, Cybelé,
Quant si s'en vont atroupelé
Li poisson à leur noëures
Par leur delitables pastures.
Et li satirel et les fees
Sont mout dolent en leur pensees
Quant il perdent par tels cretines
Leur delicieuses gaudines;
Les nymphes pleurent leur fontaines
Quant des fleuves les treuvent pleines
Et seurabondanz et couvertes,
Come dolentes de leur pertes;
Et li folet et les dryades
Ront les cueurs de deul si malades
Qu'il se tienent trestuit pour pris
Quant si voient leur bois pourpris,
Et se plaignent des dieus des fleuves

pines, and ashes, and take from the wild animals their dwellings
and their inheritances, and so go swimming on everywhere; and
therefore Bacchus, Ceres, Pan, and Cybele go nearly mad with rage
when they see these fishy troops thus plying their fins above their
own sweet meadows. And the satyrs and fairies are very grieved in
their minds when they lose their pleasant groves by such floods;
the nymphs weep for their fountains when they find them filled up
by the rivers, or overflowing or lost to sight, and they lament their
losses. Goblins and dryads, too, are so sick at heart that they think
themselves all taken captive when they see their woods thus
usurped, and make complaint against the river-gods who do them

Qui leur font vilenies neuves
Tout sans deserte et sans forfait,
Com rien ne leur aient forfait.
Et des prochaines basses viles,
Qu'il treuvent chaitives et viles,
Resont li poisson ostelier:
N'i remaint granche ne celier
Ne lieu si vaillant ne si chier
Que par tout ne s'aillent fichier.
Vont en temples et en eglises
Et tolent aus dieus leur servises,
Et chacent des chambres oscures
Les dieus privés et leur figures.

Et quant revient à chief de piece
Que li beaus tens le lait depiece,
Car aus cieus desplaist et enuie
Tens de tempestes et de pluie,
L'air ostent de trestoute s'ire
Et le font resbaudier et rire;
Et quant les nues raperçoivent
Que l'air si resbaudi reçoivent,
Adonc se resjoïssent eles,
Et, pour estre avenanz et beles,

new injuries most undeservedly, without the least offence on their part, when they have done them no wrong. And in the nearby low-lying towns, which they find easy prey, here too the fish are in occupation: not a barn or a cellar is left, nor any place, however precious or splendid, where they do not install themselves. They go into temples and churches, and rob the gods of their rights and drive the domestic gods and their images from the dark chambers.

And when the time comes, after a while, that good weather scatters the bad, because stormy, rainy weather is unpleasing to the stars, they clear the air of all its anger and make it rejoice and laugh; and when the clouds once more perceive that the air around them is so joyous, then they are glad, and in order to be comely and beautiful

Font robes, après leur douleurs,
De toutes leur beles couleurs;
Et metent leur toisons sechier
Au bel soleil plaisant et chier,
Et les vont par l'air charpissant
Au tens cler et resplendissant;
Puis filent, et quant ont filé,
Si font voler de leur filé
Granz aguilliees de fil blanches,
Aussi com pour coudre leur manches.

Et quant il leur reprent courage
D'aler loin en pelerinage,
Si font ateler leur chevaus,
Montent et passent monz et vaus,
Et s'en fuient come desvanz;
Car Eolus, li dieus des venz
(Ainsi est cil dieus apelés)
Quant il les a bien atelés
Car els n'ont autre charretier
Qui sache leur chevaus traitier,
Leur met es piés si bones eles
Que nus oiseaus n'ot onques teles. ...

they make dresses, now their grief is past, of all their lovely colours, and put out their fleeces to dry in the fair, sweet, beloved sunlight, and then go drawing them out through the air in the clear and brilliant weather, then spin them, and when they have spun them they let fly from their spinning great needlefuls of white thread, as if to sew up their sleeves.

And when the wish comes to them once more to go on far pilgrimages, then they have their horses harnessed, and mount and drive over mountains and valleys, fleeing like mad things, for Eolus, the god of the winds (thus is their god called), when he has harnessed them well – for they have no other charioteer who can manage their horses – puts such good wings to their feet as no bird ever had. ...

ADAM DE LA HALLE

Chanson d' Amour

GRANT deduit a et savoreuse vie
En bone amour honorer et servir,
Qui le maintient, si qu'il doit, sans boidie;
Qu'amour rent plus qu'on ne puist deservir.
Pour ce le serf, mieus faire ne pourroie.
  Et se ja merci n'avoie
  Quant tant averai servi,
Si me plaist il user ma vie ainsi.

Car je le fais pour la mieus enseignie
Qu'on puist de cuer penser ne d'yeus veïr;
Et tant apert à tous sa seignorie
Qu'il est tous liés qui la puet conjouir.
E! las, et je ne m'os metre en sa voie;
  Car peu parans i seroie;
  Si n'ai qui là soit pour mi,
S'amour n'i est et pitiés que j'en pri.

Love Song

THERE is great pleasure and a delectable life in honouring and
serving Love, if a man will pursue it, as he should, without deceit;
for Love gives back more than any man can deserve. Therefore I
serve Love, I could do nothing better. And even if I were never to
be rewarded, when I have served so well, still I am glad to wear my
life out thus.

For I do it for the most accomplished lady that heart could
imagine or eye could see, and her peerlessness is so clear to all that
he is a happy man who can enjoy her company. But alas! I dare not
put myself in her way, for I should make but a poor showing there,
and I have none to take my part there, unless it be Love and Pity,
whom I beg to do so.

Ainc de si lonc de moi ne fu choisie,
Qu'à ses dous yeus amoreus entr'ouvrir
Ne fusse espris de joie raemplie,
De loiauté, d'amour et de desir.
Et, quant d'un seul veoir ai si grant joie,
      Que ce seroit, se j'ooie
      Qu'ele m'apelast ami?
Dieus, je ne vous demant autre merci.

J'ai mainte fois laissié la compaignie,
Quant bone amours m'en donoit souvenir
Pour deliter en pensee envesie,
En remembrant sa valour à loisir.
Et lors qu'estoie esseulés, m'enfermoie;
      Lors par semblant me cuidoie
      Delès li tout esbaubi.
Ainsi mes maus à la fois entr'oubli.

I never caught sight of her, however far away, but at the sweet half glance from her lovely eyes I was alight with teeming joy, with loyalty, with love, and with desire. And since a single glimpse of her gives me such great joy, what would it be if I should hear her call me her love? Oh! God, I ask of you no other mercy.

I have many a time left my companions when true love brought her image to my mind, to delight in glad thoughts by recalling her excellence at leisure. And when I was alone, I locked my door; then in my fancy thought myself at her side, all ravished with delight. So for a time I half forget my pain.

Se m'osasse retourner à la fie,
Quant je l'encontre en la voie au venir,
Tant qu'ele fust de mes yeus convoïe
Avec mon cuer qu'ele a sans departir,
Trop doucement à paiés m'en tendroie.
    Mais pour rien je n'oseroie
    Avoir le cuer si hardi,
Tant l'aim et crien et vueil l'honour de li.

Chanson d' Amour

Pour ce, se je n'ai esté
    Chantans et jolis,
N'ai je mie meins amé;
    Ains sui plus espris
Qu'onques mais, et plus sourpris;
Car behours, robe envesie,
Beaus chanters, langue polie,
    Ne souliers agus,
L'amour pas ne senefie,
Mais fins cuers loiaus, repus,
    Qu'on n'en mesdie.

If I dared to turn round sometimes when I meet her coming along the road, so that my eyes should go with her as well as my heart, which she has always with her, how sweetly I should think myself rewarded; but not for anything would I dare to behave so rashly, so much I love and fear her and hold her honour dear.

Love Song

Because I have not gone about singing and full of finery, I have not loved the less, but am deeper in love and more overwhelmed than ever before. For revelry and a gay robe, sweet song and polished speech, and pointed shoes do not show love, but a true loyal heart so hidden as to cause no scandal.

De tel cuer ait on pité,
    Nient des soursalis.
On voit tant homme effronté
    En fais et en dis,
En regars et en faus ris,
Et tante femme honie;
Par quoi cele qui n'a mie
    Lor assaus eüs,
Doit estre bien chastoïe:
On doit dire: «Levez sus»
    A tel mainie.

Li mesdisant ont parlé
    Sur aucuns amis,
Que, s'il se fussent mené
    En simples habis,
Ja n'en fust issus mesdis;
Mais par leur cointe veulie
Font sage autrui de lor vie,
    Tant qu'on leur met sus.
Mais cors qui desire amie
Doit estre com cos emplius,
    Et li cuers rie.

Women should have compassion on such a heart, and not on those of the swaggerers; we see so many men brazen in word and deed, in glances and deceiving smiles, and so many women brought to shame; therefore any girl who has not yet come under their attack ought to be well warned. Women should say, 'Away with you' to such a crew.

Scandal has gone abroad about some lovers who would never have given rise to it if they had gone simply dressed; but by their gilded dalliance they betray their secret to others and get it talked about. But if a man wishes to have a lover, he should go about looking like a cock in the rain – and laughing in his heart.

Motet

DIEUS! comment pourroie
Trouver voie
D'aler à celui
Cui amiete je sui?
Ceinturele, va i en lieu de mi,
Car tu fus soue aussi:
Si m'en conquerra mieus.
Mais comment serai sans ti, Dieus?
Ceinturele, mar vous vi:
Au desceindre m'ociés.
De mes grietés
A vous me confortoie,
Quant je vous sentoie
(Aymi!)
A la savour de mon ami.
Nepourquant
D'autres en ai à clous d'argent
Et de soie pour mon user.
Moi lasse! comment
Pourroie sans cele durer
Qui me tient en joie?
Ceinturele, ce li proie,
Qui la m'envoia,

Motet

GOD! how can I find a way to go to him whose darling I am?
Little girdle, go to him in my place, for in fact you once belonged
to him, and you will make him love me better. But oh God! how
shall I do without you? Little girdle, what grief you bring me: it
kills me to unclasp you, for you were my comforter in my sorrows,
when I used to feel in you, alas, the very essence of my lover. Yet I
have other girdles, studded with silver and fashioned of silk for me
to wear; alas, how can I live without the one that preserves my
happiness? Little girdle, beg him who sent you to me, since I

Puis que je ne puis aler là,
Qu'il en viegne anuit ci
Droit au jour failli,
Pour faire tous ses bons, et il m'avra,
Quant ert poinz de chanter à haute vois:
«Par ci va la mignotise,
Par ci où je vois.»

ANONYMOUS MOTETS

Je sui joliete,
Sadete, plaisans,
Jeune pucelete;
N'ai pas quinze ans;
Point mamelete
Selonc le tans;
Si deüsse aprendre
D'amors, et entendre
Les semblans
Deduisans.
Mais je sui mise en prison.

cannot go to him, that he will come here tonight, as soon as it is dark, to do all his will; and I shall be his, and then will be the time to sing aloud, 'This way goes love's delight, this way go I.'

I AM a young girl, gay and graceful and attractive. I am not yet quite fifteen, at the age when my young breasts are swelling; and I ought to be learning of love and turning my mind to its delightful signs. But I am put in prison: may God's curse be on him who put

De Dieu ait maleïçon
        Qui m'i mist!
Mal et vilanie
      Et pechié fist
De tel pucelete
    Rendre en abiete.
Trop i mesfist, par ma foi;
En religion vif en grant anoi,
    Dieus! car trop sui jonete.
Je sens les dous maus desous ma ceinturete:
Honis soit de Dieu qui me fist nonnete.

    En mai quant naist la rosee,
    Que gelee s'en reva,
    Garis est qui amie a,
    Car sa joie en est doublee.
    Hé Dieus! mes cuers que fera?
    Comment tenir se pourra?
    Tant est ma joie doublee
    Quant cele qui mon cuer a,
    Que lonc tens ai deservie,
    Cele m'a s'amour donee
    Qui mon cuer et mon cors a.

me there. Evil and villainy and sin he did to give up a girl like me
to a nunnery. It was a wicked thing to do, by my faith; the life of
a convent is wretched to me, my God! for I am far too young.

    I feel the sweet trouble beneath my girdle; God's curse on him
who made me a nun.

In May, when dew begins to fall and frost goes away, happy is
the man who has a lover, for his joy is doubled. Ah God! What is
my heart to do? How can it contain itself? Now my joy is doubled,
since she who has my heart, whose love I have earned by my long
devotion, she has given me her love, who has my heart and my
body.

BEAUS douz amis, or ne vous enuit mie
Se d'estre ensemble faisons tel demouree,
Car on dit: «Qui bien aime à tart oublie.»
Pour ce n'ert ja nostre amour desevree,
Ne n'ai aillors ne desir ne pensee
Fors seulement qu'ensemble estre puissomes.
Hé! beau cuers douz, je vous aim sur tous homes:
Aiez pitié de vo loial amie,
Et si pensez que par tens i soiomes,
Pour mener joie, com amans à celee.
            Dieus! car nous herberjomes.

    AMIS, dont est engendree
    En vo cuer tel volentez
    Qu'estre cuidiez refusez,
    Pour ce que vous ai monstree
    Chiere autre que ne voulez?

FAIR sweet love, now do not let it grieve you if we have to wait so long to be together; for they say, 'He who loves well is slow to forget.' Therefore our love will not soon be ended, and I have not a single wish or thought except only to be with you. Oh fair sweet heart, I love you above all men. Take pity on your true love and find some way for us soon to be alone as lovers for our delight. In God's name, let us find some place to be together.

MY love, how has your heart conceived such an idea as to think yourself rejected because I did not receive you exactly as you wished?

Mais se bien saviez
Comment on doit retenir
Amant qu'on crient departir,
Entendre porriez
Que le fis par tel desir
Qu'enaigrir
Vous feïsse en moi amer.
Fins cuers, ne veuilliez cesser,
Car aillours que vous chierir
Ne puis penser.

Tout li cuers me rit de joie
De vostre beauté veïr;
Mais ce qu'il m'estuet partir
De vous, plaisant, simple et coie,
Et aler estrange voie,
Fait ma joie en duel vertir;
Ne ja ne m'en puis souffrir
Que je ne voise; si vous proi
Pour Dieu ne m'oubliez mie,
Se plus souvent ne vous voi.
Las! je m'en vois, ma douce amie,
Si vous lais, ce poise moi.

But if you knew how a woman has to hold a lover whom she
dreads to lose, you could understand that I did it in the hope that
I should sharpen your love for me.

Sweet heart, do not cease to love me, for I cannot set my heart
on anything but loving you.

My whole heart laughs for joy to see your beauty; but to have to
leave you, so sweet, so loyal, so serene, and take an unknown road –
this turns my joy to mourning, and I cannot help but go; and so I
beg you for God's sake not to forget me if I can no longer see
you often. Alas! I must go, my sweet love and leave you; how it
grieves me.

El mois d'avril qu'hiver va departant,
Que cil oisel recommencent leur chant,
Par un matin lès un bois chevauchant
M'en alai;
En une sente pensant m'en entrai.

Que qu'estoie d'amours en tel pensé,
Lors ne sai quel part fus torné.
Et quant en moi regardai
Et fus apercevant,
En un vergier lors m'en entrai,
Qui tant estoit deduisant
Que d'une part chante li rossignol,
D'autre part li mauvis,
Qu'il n'est nus cuers tant durs ne fust resbaudis.
L'esproön et l'aloe chantent si doucement,
La chalandre s'i renvoise ensement;
Que vous diroie je les noms de tous ceaus?
Illuec estoit tous li deduis d'oiseaus.

In the month of April, when winter goes on his way, when the birds begin their song again, one morning I went out riding beside a wood; deep in thought, I turned along a path.

While I was thus thinking of love, I had ridden on I know not where, and when I came to myself and looked about me, I went into an orchard, which was such a delightful place that on one side the nightingale was singing, on the other side the thrush, so that there was no heart so hard that it would not have been made glad. The starling and the skylark sang so sweetly, and the *chalandre* [a species of lark] rejoiced also. Why should I tell you the names of all of them? In that place was the whole delight of birds.

Entré qu'estoie illueques, si oï
Une pucelle qui chante à haut cri:
«Amours novelles font fins amans jolis.»
Tant ert plaisant
Et de bele faiture
Qu'à icel tens
N'avoit onques Nature
Mieuz pensé
A si grant beauté.
Fraiche ot la couleur,
Blanche com fleur,
Ieuz vairs rians,
Vis a point coloré,
Chief blont luisant
Menu recercelé,
Bouche vermeille, dens petis
Druz semés,
Bien ordenés,
Sorcis
Voutis,
Brunés
Et bien formés.
Sa grant beauté raconter
Ne peut bouche, ne cuer penser.

When I had entered there, I heard a girl singing aloud, 'New love makes true lovers joyful.' She was so charming and lovely that until that time Nature had never better conceived such beauty. She had fresh colour, skin white as a flower, laughing grey eyes, cheeks perfect in colour, shining fair hair in little curls, red lips, small teeth close together and regular, eyebrows arched, dark, and well shaped. No mouth can tell her great beauty, nor can heart think it.

S'amour li pri;
Sospirant respondi:
«Aïmi!
Ja ne m'en partirai,
Car loial l'ai,
L'ami.»

JE gart le bois,
Que nuls n'en port
Flourete ne verdure,
Et que nul confort
N'en ait, qui d'amours n'a cure.
Dieus! j'aim si loiaument
Que nul mal ne sent,
Chaleur ne froidure.
Ainsi gart la raime
Et la fleur du bois,
Si que nuls n'en port
Chapeau de fleurs, s'il n'aime.

VIERGE pucelle honoree,
Vierge munde et pure,
Par vous est reconfortee
Humaine nature;
Par vous est enluminee
Toute creature.

I asked her for her love; sighing she replied, 'Ah me! I will never leave him, for he is true to me, my lover.'

I GUARD the wood, that none may take away floweret or green branch, or find any pleasure here, if he cares nothing for love. God! I love so truly that I feel no ill, or heat or cold. Thus I guard the branches and the flowers of the wood, so that none may take away a garland of flowers unless he is in love.

VIRGIN, honoured maiden, virgin chaste and pure, by you is humanity comforted, by you is every creature illumined.

Vierge pucelle Marie,
Fleur de lis, rose florie
En mai,
Fleur de glai,
Fleur espanie,
Pucelle en qui j'ai
Esperance et bonne foi,
Otroiez moi vostre aïe,
Mere au puissant roi.

A LA clarté qui tout enlumina
Nostre grant tenebrour,
A la dame qui si grant mecine a
Contre toute doulour,
Doivent venir trestuit li pecheour
Et devenir si serjant nuit et jour;
N'autrui ne doit nul donner
Son cuer, son cors ne s'amour
Fors à la douce mere au Creatour,
Vierge pucelle et de si sainte atour;
Rose est novelle et des dames la flour.

Virgin, maiden Mary, lily flower, rose flowering in May, flower of the iris, flower in full bloom, maiden in whom I have hope and firm faith, grant me your help, oh! mother of the mighty King.

To the light which has illumined our great darkness, to the lady who has such balm for every sorrow, all sinners should come, to be her servants night and day. And to none other should any man give his heart, his body, or his love, but only to the gentle Mother of God, virgin, maid, clothed in such holiness. She is the rose newly opened and the flower of all women.

A LA cheminee
El froit mois de janvier,
    Vueil la char salee,
Les chapons gras mangier;
    Dame bien paree,
Chanter et renvoisier,
    C'est ce qui m'agree:
Bon vin à remuer,
    Cler feu sans fumee,
Les des et le tablier
            Sans tencier.

BONE compaignie,
    Quant ele est bien privee,
Maint jeu, mainte druerie
    Fait faire à celee.
Mais quant chascun tient s'amie
    Cointe et bien paree,
Lors a par droit bone vie
    Chascun d'eus trovee.

Li mangiers est atornez
    Et la table aprestee:
De bons vins i a assez
    Par quoi joie est menee.

By the fireside, in the cold month of January, I like to eat salt meat
and fat capons; a well-dressed lady, and singing and merrymaking,
that is what pleases me, with good wine in plenty, a bright fire that
does not smoke, dice and a board, and no quarrelling.

GOOD company, among intimate friends, gives rise to many a
game and much jollity of a homely kind. But when every man has
his love at his side, elegant and beautifully dressed, then each of
them can truly say that life is good.
    The food is prepared and the table is laid; there are plenty of
good wines to make them merry. After dinner, they have the dice

Après mangier font les dez
Venir en l'assemblee
Sour la table lee.
Et si ai souvent trové
Maint clerc, la chape ostee,
Qui n'ont cure que là soit logique desputee.
Li hostes est par delez,
Qui dit: «Bevez!
Et quant vins faut, si criez:
Ci nous faut un tour de vin!
Dieus, car le nous donez.»

ON parole de batre et de vanner
Et de foïr et de hanner;
Mais ces deduis trop me desplaisent,
Car il n'est si bone vie que d'estre à aise
De bon cler vin et de chapons,
Et d'estre avec bons compaignons,
Liés et joians,
Chantans,
Truffans
Et amorous; et d'avoir quant qu'on a mestier
Pour solacier,
Beles dames à devis;
Et tout ce treuve on à Paris.

set out for the company on the broad table. And I have often found
many a cleric there, his cowl cast off, happy to dispense with logical
disputation. The host is at their side saying, 'Drink up, and when
the wine runs out, call out, "We need a round of wine here, now for
God's sake let us have it!"'

SOME talk of threshing and winnowing, digging and ploughing,
but I care nothing for these sports; for there is no life so good as
to be well supplied with good clear wine and capons, and to be
with good companions, happy and joyous, singing, joking, and
making love, and to have whatever you need for your pleasure, and
fair ladies to your liking. And all this can be found in Paris.

Lès un bosket
Vi Robechon.
Moult i ot joli vallet;
Houseaus ot
Oins et chapeau vert, sourcot
Griset
Et chaperon.
Il n'estoit pas sans son chienet;
Fretel,
Coutel
Ot et baston;
Sonete avoit,
Son flajol ot, si flajoloit.
Marote saut
Quant ele l'ot,
Et Emmelos
La bele.
Or renouvele
Li dorenlos,
Li dorenlos
En la praele,
Quant chascune pastourele
Aveques li son ami ot.

BESIDE a little wood I saw young Robin, and very smart he looked. He had boots of soft leather, a green garland for his head, and a grey surcoat and hood. He was not without his dog; he had his pipes and his knife and his staff; he had a bell, and he had his flute and was fluting. Marian dances when she hears it, and so does the fair Emily. Now the refrain, the refrain begins again, in the little meadow when every shepherdess has her lover by her side.

ANONYMOUS RONDEAUX

Est il paradis, amie,
Est il paradis qu'amer?
Nenil voir, ma douce amie.
Est il paradis, amie?
Cil qui dort es bras s'amie
A bien paradis trouvé.
Est il paradis, amie,
Est il paradis qu'amer?

Toute seule passerai le vert boscage,
Puis que compagnie n'ai;
Se j'ai perdu mon ami par mon outrage,
Toute seule passerai le vert boscage.
Je li ferai à savoir par un message
Que je li amenderai.
Toute seule passerai le vert boscage,
Puis que compagnie n'ai.

Is there any Heaven, my darling, is there any Heaven but loving?
No, indeed, my sweet darling.
  Is there any Heaven, my darling?
  He who sleeps in his love's arms has found Heaven indeed.
  Is there any Heaven, my darling, is there any Heaven but loving?

I will walk through the greenwood alone, for I have no one to go with me. If I have lost my love through my own fault, I will walk through the greenwood alone. I will send a message to let him know that I will make him amends. I will walk through the greenwood alone, for I have no one to go with me.

Encore un chapelet ai
Qui fut m'amie;
Donnés me fut de cuer gai.
Encore un chapelet ai;
Pour s'amour le garderai
Toute ma vie;
Encore un chapelet ai
Qui fut m'amie.

Trop me regardez, amie, souvent;
Vostre doux regart trahissent la gent.
Cuers qui veut amer jolietement
– Trop me regardez, amie, souvent –
Ne se doit vanter pardevant la gent,
Ainz se doit garder pour les mesdisant.
Trop me regardez, amie, souvent;
Vostre douz regart trahissent la gent.

Fines amouretes ai;
Dieus,
Si ne sai quant les verrai.

I still have a garland that belonged to my love. It was given to me with a joyful heart. I still have a garland; for her sake I shall keep it all my life. I still have a garland that belonged to my love.

You look at me too often, darling; others are intercepting your sweet glances. A heart that would love happily – you look at me too often, darling – should not boast its love in public, but should keep on its guard because of the gossips. You look at me too often, darling; others are intercepting your sweet glances.

I have a true love, but oh! God, I do not know when I shall see her.

Or manderai m'amiete,
Qui est cointe et joliete
Et s'est si saverousete
Qu'abstenir ne m'en pourrai.
Fines amouretes ai;
       Dieus,
Si ne sai quant les verrai.

Et s'ele est de moi enceinte,
Tost devendra pale et tainte;
S'il en est esclandle et plainte,
Deshonneree l'avrai.
Fines amouretes ai;
       Dieus,
Si ne sai quant les verrai.

Mieux vaut que je m'en abstiegne
Et pour li joli me tiegne
Et que de li me souviegne,
Car s'honour li garderai.
Fines amouretes ai;
       Dieus,
Si ne sai quant les verrai.

Now I will send a message to my darling who is gay and lovely and so very sweet that I cannot forbear from loving her. I have a true love, but oh! God, I do not know when I shall see her.

And if she should be pregnant by me, she will soon be pale and wan; and if scandal and blame should arise, I shall have disgraced her. I have a true love, but oh! God, I do not know when I shall see her.

It is better that I should forbear, and be glad for her sake, and never forget her, for thus I shall safeguard her honour. I have a true love, but oh! God, I do not know when I shall see her.

Vous qui amez, je vous fais à savoir:
Donnez dames et à main et au soir,
Et s'i metez cuer et cors et avoir,
      Pendez moi s'elle vous aime,
      Se ce n'est par traïson.
      Mal li veigne et Dieus le dont
      Qui sotte croit ne qui l'aime;
      Qu'elles ne font se mal non.

Or li avez donné un pelisson
Et en après la cotte à recorson:
Encor vous dit qu'il li faut un chausson
      D'escarlate teinte en graine,
      Et soulers à bekillon.
      Mal li veigne et Dieus le dont
      Qui sotte croit ne qui l'aime;
      Qu'elles ne font se mal non.

Encor vous dit qu'il li faut un mantel,
Une aumoniere, une coife, un chapel;
S'avoir pouoit un tronson de vo pel,
      Volentiers i metroit peine,
      Pour orler son pelisson.

You who love, I tell you this: give presents to ladies morning and evening, put your heart into it, and your body and your money, hang me if she loves you, unless it is with a feigned love. May evil come to him and may God send it to him, whoever trusts a foolish woman or loves her; for they do nothing but evil.

Now you have given her a fur-lined mantle, and then the kilted[?] kirtle, and she tells you she'll also need a pair of fine woollen stockings dyed with cochineal and some shoes with pointed toes. May evil come to him and may God send it to him, whoever trusts a foolish woman or loves her; for they do nothing but evil.

Next she tells you she needs a cloak, a purse, a coif, and a hat; if she could have a slice of your skin, she would gladly try to get it to make a border for her mantle. May evil come to him and may

Mal li veigne et Dieus le dont
Qui sotte croit ne qui l'aime;
Qu'elles ne font se mal non.

Qui feme croit, il euvre follement;
Je le vous di à tous comunalment:
Gardez vous en, s'ouvrerez sagement.
     Qui à sotte s'accompagne,
     Il n'i peut se perdre non.
     Mal li veigne et Dieus le dont
     Qui sotte croit ne qui l'aime;
     Qu'elles ne font se mal non.

Quant vous avrez tout le vostre gasté,
Et as dames l'averez tout donné,
Donc vous serez «Povres chaitis» clamé;
La gent diront: «Dieus en soit aoré!
     Cil est pris à la musenne.
     On nel fait se gaber non.»
     Mal li veigne et Dieus le dont
     Qui sotte croit ne qui l'aime;
     Qu'elles ne font se mal non.

God send it, whoever trusts a foolish woman or loves her; for they do nothing but evil.

Whoever trusts a woman behaves like a fool. I say this to all of you: keep away from women and you will be acting wisely. He who goes about with a foolish woman can only lose by it. May evil come to him and may God send it, whoever trusts a foolish woman or loves her; for they do nothing but evil.

When you have squandered everything you have, and given it all to the ladies, then you will be called 'Poor wretch'. People will say: 'Praise be to God, he's been caught in the trap; he's just being made a fool of.' May evil come to him and may God send it to him, whoever trusts a foolish woman or loves her; for they do nothing but evil.

ANONYMOUS

Une Branche d'Armes

Qui est li gentis bachelers?

Qui d'espee fu engendrés
Et parmi le heaume alaitiés,
Et dedans son escu berciés,
Et de char de lion nourris,
Et au grant tonnoire endormis,
Et au visage de dragon,
Ieus de liepart, cuer de lion,
Dens de sengler, isniaus com tigre,
Qui d'un estorbeillon s'enivre,
Et qui fait de son poing maçue
Qui cheval et chevalier rue
Jus à la terre comme foudre;
Qui voit plus cler parmi la poudre
Que faucons ne fait la riviere,
Qui torne ce devant derriere
Un tornoi, pour son cors deduire:
Ne cuide que rien li puist nuire;

Lines on Knighthood

Who is the noble young knight?

He who was engendered of the sword, suckled in the helmet, and cradled in his shield; and fed on lion's flesh, and lulled to sleep by mighty thunder; he with the dragon's face, the leopard's eyes, the lion's heart, the wild boar's fangs; swift as a tiger, drunk with the whirlwind, making a club of his fist to strike down knight and horse like a thunderbolt; who sees more clearly through the dust of battle than the falcon sees the river below her; who reverses the whole fortunes of a tournament for his pleasure, and thinks that no man there can do him injury; who to accomplish adventure leaps

Qui tressaut la mer d'Engleterre
Pour une aventure conquerre,
Si fait il les mons de Mongeu:
Là sont ses festes et si jeu;
Et, s'il vient à une bataille,
Ainsi com li vens fait la paille,
Les fait fuir par devant lui,
Ne ne veut jouster à nului
Fors que du pié hors de l'estrier,
S'abat cheval et chevalier,
Et souvent le crieve par force.
Fer ne fust, platine n'escorce
Ne peut contre ses cops durer;
Et peut tant le heaume endurer
Qu'à dormir ne à sommeillier
Ne li covient autre oreillier;
Ne ne demande autres dragiees
Que pointes d'espees brisiees
Et fers de glaive à la moustarde
(C'est un mes qui forment li tarde)
Et haubers desmailliés au poivre;
Et veut la grant poudriere boivre
Avec l'alaine des chevaus;

across the English sea or over the Alps to Italy. Such are his feasts
and such his sports, and if he comes to a battle, like straw before the
wind he makes them flee before him, and he never wishes to joust
with anyone except with his feet out of the stirrups, and he over-
turns both horse and knight and often kills him by the force of the
blow. Iron nor wood nor metal plates nor hide can stand against his
blows, and he can endure his helmet for so long that for sleep and
for slumber he needs no other pillow; he seeks no better sweetmeat
than shattered swordpoints and lance-heads with mustard (that is a
dish he longs to eat) and hacked chainmail with pepper; and he
would drink battle-dust with the breath of horses; and over hills

Et chace par mons et par vaus
Ours et lions et cers de ruit
Tout à pié: ce sont si deduit.
Et donne tout sans retenir.

Cil doit moult bien terre tenir
Et maintenir chevalerie;
Que cil dont li hiraus s'escrie
Qui ne fu ne puns ne couvés
Mais el fiens des chevaus trouvés,
S'il savoient à quoi ce monte,
Sachiez qu'il li dient grant honte.

PHILIPPE DE VITRY

Franc Gontier

Sous feuille vert, sur herbe delictable,
Lès rui bruiant et pres clere fontaine,
Trouvai fiché une borde portable.
Illec mangeoit Gontier et dame Helaine
Fromage frais, lait, beurre, fromagee,
Cresme, mattons, pomme, nois, prune, poire,

and valleys he hunts bears and lions and rutting stags, and all on foot – such are his pleasures; and he gives away all that he has without reserve.

Such a man well deserves to hold lands and uphold chivalry; for this man whom the heralds announce as 'neither laid nor hatched but found among the horse-dung', if they knew the whole truth, believe me, they do him great injustice.

Franc Gontier

Under the green leaves, on the soft turf beside a chattering brook with a clear spring near at hand, I found a rustic hut set up. Gontier and Dame Helen were dining there, on fresh cheese, milk, butter, cheesecake[?], cream, curds, apples, nuts, plums, pears; they had

Aulx et oignons, eschalogne froiee,
Sur crouste bise, au gros sel, pour mieux boire.

Au gomer burent, et oisillons harpoient
Pour resjouir et le dru et la drue,
Qui par amour après s'entrebaisoient
Et bouche et nés, polie et bien barbue.
Quant orent pris le doux mes de nature,
Tantost Gontier, hache au col, au bois entre;
Et dame Helaine si met toute sa cure
A ce buer qui cueuvre dos et ventre.

J'ouy Gontier, en abattant son arbre,
Dieu mercier de sa vie seüre:
«Ne sai, dit il, que sont pilliers de marbre,
Pommeaux luisans, murs vestus de peinture;
Je n'ai paour de trahison tissue
Sous beau semblant, ne qu'enpoisonné soie
En vaisseau d'or; je n'ai ne teste nue
Devant tyrant ne genoul qui se ploie.

garlic and onions, and crushed shallots, on crusty black bread, with coarse salt to give them a thirst.

They drank from the jug, and the birds made music to cheer the hearts of both lover and lass, who next exchanged their loving kisses on mouth and nose, the smooth face and the bearded. When they had taken the sweet feast of Nature, soon Gontier, axe on shoulder, goes off into the wood, and Dame Helen addresses all her care to washing clothes that cover back and belly.

I heard Gontier, as he chopped down his tree, giving thanks to God for the security of his life: 'I know nothing,' he said, 'of marble pillars, gleaming bosses, walls covered with paintings, but I need not fear a web of treachery behind a smiling face or poison hidden in a golden cup. My head is not bared before a tyrant, nor is my knee bended.

«Verge d'huissier jamais ne me deboute,
Car jusque là ne me prent convoitise,
Ambition, ne lescherie gloute.
Labour me paist en joieuse franchise,
Moult j'aime Helaine, et elle moi, sans faille;
Et c'est assez, de tombel n'avons cure.»
Lors je dis «Las, serf de court ne vaut paille,
Mais franc Gontier vaut en or gemme pure.»

PIERRE D'AILLY

Le Tyran

Un chastel sai sur roche espouvantable,
En lieu venteux et sur eaue perilleuse.
La vi tyrant seant à haute table,
En grant palais, en sale plantureuse,
Avironné de famille pompeuse,
Pleine de fraude, d'envie et de murmure,
Vuide de foi, d'amour, de paix joieuse,
Serve et subjette par convoiteuse ardure.

'I am never thrust back by the usher's rod, for I am never brought within its range by greed, ambition, or foul gluttony. My labour finds my food in happy freedom. I love my Helen dearly and she truly loves me. That is enough; we want no splendid tomb.' Then said I: 'Alas! a court slave is not worth a straw, but honest Gontier is worth a jewel set in gold.'

The Tyrant

I know a castle set upon a fearful precipice, exposed to the winds above perilous waters. There I saw a tyrant seated at his high table in a great palace, in his sumptuous hall, surrounded by his haughty retinue, all full of deceit, envy, and discontent, devoid of loyalty and love and happy peace, slavish and fawning because of their rapacious greed.

Vins et viandes avoit il sans mesure,
Chars et poissons aussi en mainte guise,
Brouets et sauces de diverse taincture
Et entremés par art fais à devise.
Le mal glouton par tout guette et avise
Pour appetit trouver, et quiert maniere
Comme sa bouche, de lescherie esprise,
Son ventre emplisse com bourse pautonniere.

Mais, sac à fiens et puant cimetiere,
Sepulcre à vin, corps bouffi, grasse pance,
Pour tous ses biens en lui n'a lie chiere;
Car ventre saoul en saveur n'a plaisance.
Ne le delite ris, jeu, chanson ne dance;
Car tant convoite, tant quiert et tant desire
Qu'en rien qu'il ait n'a vraie souffisance:
Acquerir veut ou royaume ou empire.

Par avarice sent douloureux martire,
Trahison doute, en nullui ne se fie,
Cuer a felon, enflé d'orgueil et d'ire,
Triste, pensif, plein de melancolie:

Viands and wines he had beyond all measure, and flesh and fish also served in many a fashion, soups and sauces of different colours, and dishes skilfully made up to suit his fancy. The swinish wretch is ever watchful and alert to find an appetite, seeking means by which his mouth, afire with gluttony, can fill his belly like a beggar's pouch.

But this bag of excrement, this stinking cemetery, sepulchre of wine, with body puffed and swollen belly, for all his wealth has yet no gladness in him; for an overful stomach finds no delight in savour; nor can he be pleased by laughter, sport, song, or dance, for he desires and covets and craves so many things that he finds true satisfaction in nothing that he has. He wants to seize a whole kingdom or an empire.

He suffers grievous martyrdom through avarice, he dreads treason, he trusts no man. His heart is cruel, swollen with pride and anger, gloomy, full of care and melancholy. Alas! far better is the

Las, trop mieux vaut de franc Gontier la vie,
Sobre liesse et nette povreté,
Que poursuivir par orde glotonnie
Court de tyrant et riche maleurté.

GUILLAUME DE MACHAUT

Ballade

De toutes fleurs n'avoit, et de tous fruis,
En mon vergier fors une seule rose:
Gasté estoit li surplus et destruis
Par Fortune, qui durement s'oppose
        Contre ceste douce fleur
Pour amatir sa couleur et s'odeur.
Mais se cueillir la voi ou tresbuchier,
Autre après li jamais avoir ne quier.

Ha! Fortune, qui es gouffres et puis
Pour engloutir tout homme qui croire ose
Ta fausse loi, où rien de bien ne truis
Ne de seür, trop est decevans chose:
        Ton ris, ta joie, t'honneur
Ne sont que pleur, tristece et deshonneur.

life of honest Gontier, in sober happiness and cleanly poverty, than
haunting tyrants' courts and wealthy misery to satisfy foul greed.

Ballade

Of all the flowers and all the fruits, there is but a single rose left
in my garden: the rest has all been laid waste and destroyed by
Fortune, who is now setting herself fiercely against this sweet
flower, so as to spoil its colour and its scent. But if I see it plucked
or broken down, after that rose I never want another.

Ah! Fortune, you who are a gulf and a pit to swallow up any
man who dares to trust in your false doctrine, in which I find nothing good or certain, it is so fraudulent a thing; your smile, your joy,

Se ti faus tour font ma rose sechier,
Autre après li jamais avoir ne quier.

Mais vraiement imaginer ne puis
Que la vertu où ma rose est enclose
Viegne par toi et par tes faus conduis,
Ainz est drois dons natureus; si suppose
Que tu n'avras ja vigueur
D'aniantir son pris et sa valeur.
Lai la moi donc, qu'ailleurs n'en mon vergier
Autre après li jamais avoir ne quier.

Ballade

Ne qu'on pourroit les estoiles nombrer,
Quant on les voit luire plus clerement,
Et les goutes de pluie et de la mer,
Et l'araine sur quoi elle s'estent,
Et compasser le tour du firmament,
Ne pourroit on penser ne concevoir
Le grant desir que j'ai de vous veoir.

your honour are only tears and sadness and dishonour. If your false tricks make my rose wither, after that rose I never want another.

But truly, I cannot imagine that the virtue that enwraps my rose comes from you or from your lying ways; rather it is a direct gift of Nature, and I think you will never have the strength to destroy its value and its worth. Leave it to me, then, for whether in my garden or elsewhere, after that rose I never want another.

Ballade

No more than the stars can be counted when they shine at their brightest, or the drops of the rain, or the sea, or the grains of the sand it flows over, or the firmament's girth can be measured, no more can be thought or imagined the great longing that I have to see you.

Et si ne puis par devers vous aller
Pour Fortune qui le vee et deffent,
Dont maint souspir me convient estrangler,
Quant à vous pense et je sui entre gent;
Et quant je sui par moi secretement
Adonc me fait tous meschiés recevoir
Le grant desir que j'ai de vous veoir.

Car il me fait complaindre et dementer
Et regretter vostre viaire gent
Et vo beauté souveraine et sans per
Et la tres grant douceur qui en descent.
Ainsi me fait languir piteusement,
Mon cuer esprent et esteint mon espoir,
Le grant desir que j'ai de vous veoir.

Ballade

J'AIM mieux languir en estrange contree
Et ma douleur complaindre et dolouser
Que pres de vous, douce dame honnoree
Entre les liés triste vie mener;

And yet I cannot come to you because Fortune forbids it and
prevents it, so that I have to strangle many a sigh when I think of
you while I am with other people; and when I am alone and in
secret, then I must suffer every torment, for the great longing that
I have to see you.

For it makes me lament and complain, and sigh for your sweet
face and your sovereign matchless beauty and the marvellous
sweetness that flows from it. Thus I am made to languish wretch-
edly, my heart is set on fire and my hope is quenched by the great
longing that I have to see you.

Ballade

I WOULD rather languish in a foreign land, and weep and lament
for my sorrow there, than by your side, sweet honoured lady, lead

Car se loing souspir et plour
On ne savra la cause de mon plour;
Mais on peut ci veoir legierement
Que je languis pour amer loyaument.

Et s'on connoit que j'ai face esplouree,
Ce poise moi, ne le puis amender,
Car grant douleur ne peut estre celee;
Aussi ne fait grant joie, à droit parler.
      Comment seroit en baudour
Cuer qui languist en peine et en dolour?
Je ne le sai; pour ce pense on souvent
Que je languis pour amer loyaument.

Si vous lairai comme la mieux amee
Qu'onques amans peüst servir n'amer.
Mais au partir mon cuer et ma pensee
Vous lais pour vous servir et honnourer;
      Ne jamais n'avront retour
Par devers moi; et pour ce à Fine Amour
Pri que savoir vous fasse clerement
Que je languis pour amer loyaument.

a life of sadness among those who are happy; for if I sigh and weep far away, no one will know the reason for my tears, but here it can easily be seen that loving truly makes me languish.

And if my face shows signs of weeping, I am sorry, but I cannot help it, for great grief cannot be hidden, nor yet give rise to joy, to tell the truth; how can the heart rejoice that languishes in trouble and in sorrow? I know no way: therefore men often think that loving truly makes me languish.

So I shall leave you, the best beloved that ever a lover served and loved, but when I go my heart and thoughts I leave with you, to serve and honour you, and never will they be recalled to me. And therefore I beseech True Love to make you clearly know that loving truly makes me languish.

Ballade

Se je vous aim de fin loyal courage
Et ai amé et amerai toudis,
Et vous avez pris autre en mariage,
Dois je pour ce de vous estre en sus mis
        Et de tous poins en oubli?
Certes, nennil; car puis que j'ai en mi
Cuer si loyal qu'il ne savroit meffaire,
Vous ne devez vo cuer de moi retraire.

Ainz me devez tenir en vo servage
Comme vo serf qu'avez pris et acquis,
Qui ne vous quiert vilenie n'outrage.
Et si devez amer, j'en suis tous fis,
        Vo mari com vo mari
Et vostre ami com vostre douz ami;
Et quant tout ce pouez par honneur faire,
Vous ne devez vo cuer de moi retraire.

Et s'il avient que cuer aiez volage,
Onques amans ne fu si fort trahis
Com je serai; mais vous estes si sage,

Ballade

If I love you with a true loyal heart, and have loved you, and always shall do so, and you have taken another man in marriage, must I for that be sent away from you and quite forgotten? No, no, indeed, for since I have in me a heart so loyal that it could do no ill, you must not take away your heart from me.

Rather you must keep me in your service, as your slave whom you have captured and bought, who wishes you no wrong or injury. And you must love – I am sure of this – your husband as your husband and your friend as your dear friend. And since you can do all this with honour, you must not take away your heart from me.

And if your heart should turn out to be fickle, never a lover was so cruelly betrayed as I shall be; but you are so wise and your heart

Et s'est vo cuer si gentieument nourris
        Qu'il ne daigneroit ainsi
Moi decevoir pour amer. Et si di:
Puis que sur tout aim vostre douz viaire,
Vous ne devez vo cuer de moi retraire.

Ballade

Se vo grandeur vers moi ne s'humilie,
Tres douz ami, que j'aim sans decevoir,
Povre esperance avoir dois en ma vie;
Car j'ai douleur qui trop me fait douloir,
        Pour vous, où j'ai mon cuer mis,
Si que jamais n'en peut estre partis.
Si ne dois pas toudis à vous penser
Sans vostre amour avoir ou esperer.

En deus amans qui s'aiment, signourie
Estre ne doit, ainçois doivent avoir
Un cuer, une ame et une maladie,
Une pensee, un desir, un vouloir;

is so gently nurtured that it would never stoop to deceive me so as
to love [another]; so I say, since above all I love your lovely face:
you must not take away your heart from me.

Ballade

If your great rank will not stoop down to me, my dearest friend,
whom I most truly love, then there is little hope in life for me, for
I endure most grievous pain for you, on whom I have so set my
heart that it can never be removed. And I ought not to have you
always in my thoughts without your love or any hope of it.

    Between two lovers who love each other, rank should not exist;
rather should they have one heart, one soul, one malady, one

Donc se vo cuer n'est onnis
A mon desir, li miens sera honnis,
Car je ne puis pas longuement durer
Sans vostre amour avoir ou esperer.

Et se des biens de Fortune n'ai mie
Si largement comme autre peut avoir,
S'ai aussi bien vaillant un cuer d'amie,
Comme tele est roïne, à dire voir.
Et bonne amour, ce m'est vis,
Ne demande que le cuer, si qu'amis
Le mien avez; si ne dois demourer
Sans vostre amour avoir ou esperer.

Le Dit du Lion

... Car ceste gent dont ci propos
Furent moult joint et moult poli,
Gent, cointe, faitis et joli,
Si espincié, si crespelet,
Si bien peignié, si blondelet,
Si tressaillant, si tres mignot,

thought, one longing, and one wish; so if your heart is not at one
with my heart's desire, mine will be shamed, for I cannot endure
much longer without your love or any hope of it.

And if I am not so well endowed with Fortune's goods as another woman might be, yet have I, truth to tell, a loving heart as
good as any queen's, and True Love, so I think, asks only for the
heart, as you have mine, my dear. And so I ought not be left without your love or any hope of it.

The Story of the Lion

... These people I am speaking of were very elegant and most
polite, noble, well-dressed, handsome, and gay; so spick and span,
so tightly curled, so neatly combed, so blond, so nimble, so prettily

Si estroit chaucié au lignot,
Si virolé, si envoisié,
Qu'il avoient nom *Frere aisié*;
Et sembloit, ce me dit l'auteur,
Que de la boite à l'enchanteur
Fussent sailli, quant il venoient
En chambres où dames estoient.
Et si vivoient à tous aises;
Ne savoient qu'estoit mesaises;
Onques n'avoient eü fain,
N'esté couchié sus peu d'estrain,
Qu'onques n'avoient mal geü,
Ne point de vin trop chaut beü;
N'il ne doutassent nul preudomme,
Prince, roi, ne pape de Rome,
D'estre bien aise, à pance pleine,
Huit jours ou neuf en la semaine.

Je souhaide que tels gens fussent
En païs où il ne seüssent
Chemin ne voie ne sentier;
Si n'eüssent housel entier,
Gant, mouffle, mitte n'esperon,
Housse, chapeau ne chaperon;

turned out, so tightly yet so smartly shod, in such good trim and such good humour that they were called the Brotherhood of Ease, and, as my author says, they looked as if they had just jumped out of a magician's box when they came into rooms where ladies were. And they led a life of great ease: they did not know what discomfort was. They had never gone hungry or lain down to sleep on a little straw, for they had never slept hard or drunk wine that was too hot for them; and they yielded to no man, prince or king or Pope of Rome, in living well at ease with bellies full, eight or nine days a week.

I wish these gentry were in some land where they did not know path, road, or track, with no sound boots, gloves, muffs, mittens or spurs, horsecloth, or hat or cloak, and it was as cold as it should by

Et si feïst si grant froidure
Comme il doit faire par nature
A Noël, pour veoir la guise;
Et si ventast li vens de bise
Taillans, bruians, fort, roide et sec,
Et l'eüssent enmi le bec,
Par qu'il fussent bien esgroé;
Et que leur cheval ecloé
Fussent tuit d'un pié ou de deus,
Et que tuit li mauvais pié d'eus
Fussent defferré tuit ensemble;
Si n'i eüst chesne ne tremble,
Homme, femme, ami ne parent
Où il treïssent à garant;
Et qu'il fust noire nuit serree,
Pleine de froit et de gelee,
Si ne peüssent chevauchier;
N'il n'eüst ville ne clochier
Près à trois lieues ou à quatre,
Par quoi il s'alassent esbatre;
Et que d'aucune mortel guerre
Fussent espandu par la terre
Tout environ li ennemi,
Et ceste gent fussent enmi. ...

nature be at Christmas, to see what they would look like then. And I wish the north wind would blow, cutting and howling, strong and stiff and dry, and they had it full in their faces, and it gave them a good shaking, and all their horses had one or two lame feet, and all those lame feet cast their shoes at once, and neither oak nor aspen gave them shelter, man, woman, friend, or relation, and it was a thick black night, full of cold and frost, and they could not ride their horses, and there was neither town nor steeple within three or four leagues where they could find comfort; and by some dreadful war their enemies were spread about the country all around, and these men in the midst of them. ...

Et ce pourquoi je leur souhaide
C'est pour ce que c'est chose laide;
Car quant il sont dessus la couche
Tels rages dient de leur bouche
Qu'Artus, Godefroy, Charlemainne
Qui l'empire ot en son demainne,
Hector, Julius, Alixandres,
Qui ne furent de guere mendres,
David, Judas Macabeüs,
Josué, li bons Troïllus,
Gauvains, Tristans, ne Lancelos
Ne valurent, bien dire l'os,
Que cil ne cuident bien valoir
Autant. Mais ne m'en doit chaloir;
Car il sont tuit vaillant et riche
De cuidier; ce n'est pas grant vice;
Et si sevent bien requerir
Les dames et merci querir.
Mais se l'une n'i veut entendre,
Il prient l'autre sans attendre. ...

And the reason I wish them all this is because that is a difficult situation; for when they are lying on their couches, they speak such fiery words that Arthur, Godfrey, Charlemagne who held the Empire under his rule, Hector, Caesar, Alexander, who were hardly less great, David, Judas Maccabeus, Joshua, the valiant Troilus, Gawain, Tristram, or Lancelot were not of such great worth, I dare well say, that these do not consider themselves just as good. But why should I care? For they are all valiant and rich by thinking only – not much wrong in that; and they are very good at begging mercy from the ladies, though if one will not listen, they go straight on to ask her neighbour. ...

JOHN GOWER

Ballade

EL mois de mai la plus joiouse chose
C'est fin amour, mais vous, ma Dame chiere,
Prenez à vous plustost la rouge rose
Pour vo desport, et plus la faites chiere
Que mon amour, o toute la priere
Que vous ai fait maint jour y a passé:
Vous estes franche et je sui fort lié.

Je voi tout plein de flours dans vo parclose
Privé de vous, mais je sui mis deriere:
Ne puis entrer, que l'entree m'est forclose;
Je prens tesmoign de vostre chamberiere,
Qui set et voit trestoute la matiere
De si long temps que je vous ai amé.
Vous estes franche et je sui fort lié.

Ballade

OF all the joys of the month of May, true love is best, but you, my
lady dear, take to yourself rather the red rose for your pleasure,
and hold it dearer than my love and all the prayers that I have
made you now for many a day. You go free while I am tightly
bound.

Plenty of flowers I see within your garden cherished by you
while I am thrust aside. I cannot enter there, for the gate is shut
tight against me. I call your maid to witness, who has known and
seen the whole story as long as I have loved you. You go free while
I am tightly bound.

Quant l'herbe croist et la flour se desclose,
Mai m'a osté de sa blanche baniere,
Dont pense assez plus que je dire n'ose
De vous, ma Dame, qui m'estes si fiere;
A vo merci car se je me refiere,
Vostre danger tantost m'a delaié:
Vous estes franche et je sui fort lié.

En le dous temps ma fortune est amere;
Le mois de mai s'est en hiver mué;
L'ortie truis quant je la rose quiere.
Vous estes franche et je sui fort lié.

Ballade

JE cuide que ma dame de sa main
M'a dans le cuer escrit son propre nom;
Car, quant je puis oïr le chapelain
Sa letanie dire et sa leçon,
Je ne sai nomer autresi le nom;
Car j'ai le cuer de fin amour si plein
Qu'en lui gist toute ma devotion.
Dieu doint que je ne prie pas en vain.

When the grass grows and the flower opens, May has rejected me from among the followers of her white banner, and therefore I think, much more than I dare say, of you, my lady, who are so cruel to me; for if I cast myself once more upon your mercy, your disdain thrusts me back immediately. You go free while I am tightly bound.

In the sweet season my fate is bitter; the month of May is turned into winter; I find the nettle when I seek the rose. You go free while I am tightly bound.

Ballade

I THINK my Lady's own hand has inscribed her name within my heart; for when I hear the chaplain read his litany and lesson, no other name but hers can I invoke, for my heart is so full of true love that all my devotion is fixed on her. God grant my prayer is not in vain.

Pour penser les amours de temps lointain,
Com la priere de Pygmalion
Faisoit miracle et l'image au derrain
De pierre en char mua de s'oraison,
J'ai grant espoir de la comparison
Que par souvent prier serai certain
De grace; et pour si noble reguerdon
Dieu doint que je ne prie pas en vain.

Com cil qui songe et est en noncertain,
Ainz semble à lui qu'il va tout environ
Et fait et dit, ainsi, quant sui soulain,
A moi parlant je fais maint question,
Despute et puis respond à ma raison;
Ne sai se je sui faie ou chose humain,
Tel est d'amour ma contemplation.
Dieu doint que je ne prie pas en vain.

A vous qui m'avez en subjection,
Seule après Dieu, si m'estes souverain,
Envoie ceste supplication:
Dieu doint que je ne prie pas en vain.

When I reflect on loves of long ago, and how Pygmalion's prayer performed a miracle and at last the statue changed from stone to flesh at his entreaty, his example gives me great hope that by my constant prayer I may be sure of grace; and for so noble a reward God grant my prayer is not in vain.

Like a man in a dream who does not know what he is doing, but seems to himself to be going about and acting and talking, so, when I am alone, I put to myself many a question, and state my case, and then reply to my own argument; I cannot tell whether I am a creature of enchantment or a human being, so lost I am in love's contemplation. God grant my prayer is not in vain.

You only, after God, have me in subjection and are my sovereign; to you I send this supplication: God grant my prayer is not in vain.

EUSTACHE DESCHAMPS

Ballade

Charogne à vers, povre fragilité,
Qui peus estre comparee à la rose
Qui est bouton et naist ou temps d'esté,
Enmi le jour s'espanit, lors desclose
Odoure un peu et plaist, mais, la nuit close,
Flour et bouton et rose est amatie:
En moins d'un jour est sa beauté perie.
Certes autel est il d'homme et de femme:
En un moment perdons corps, ame et vie.
Dieu nous veuille garder et Nostre Dame!

Ne meurt enfant en sa plus grant beauté,
Femme en jouvent, hom aussi? Comment ose
Orgueil avoir, fors que simplicité
Et craindre Dieu? Comme tres peu de chose
De fer, de fust ou de fievre l'enosse!

Ballade

Carrion for worms, poor fragile thing, that can be likened to
the rose, a bud that is born in summertime, blooming at midday,
then full-blown, giving a little scent, a little pleasure but, when
night has fallen, flower, bud, and rose, all come to nothing, its
beauty perished in less than a day. Thus indeed it is with man and
woman: in a moment we lose body, soul, and life. May God and
Our Lady protect us!

May not a child die in the height of its beauty? a woman in her
youth, a man too? How can he dare to harbour pride, or anything
except humility and fear of God? How small a thing of iron or

Un povre ver, iraigne ou orillie,
Le mors d'un chien, ou beste qui le lie,
Le fait mourir et mettre sous la lame
En moins de temps que fleur n'est espanie.
Dieu nous veuille garder et Nostre Dame!

Las! que nous vaut nostre grant parenté,
Nos grans palais, nostre grant cité close,
Nos grans tresors, le regne conquesté,
Force de corps, nostre sens et la glose?
Tout ce ne peut deffendre nostre fosse.
Sanson est mort, Alexandre et Urie,
Cresus, David, Salemon, Jeremie,
Et tous mourrons en paiant celle dragme.
Es biens mondains ne soit nul qui se fie.
Dieu nous veuille garder et Nostre Dame!

Prince et seigneur, ne vous confiez mie,
Ne hom mortel, en chose qui varie.
Le corps mourra; or pensons donc de l'ame,
De Dieu servir et la vierge Marie,
Ou autrement nostre gloire est perie.
Dieu nous veuille garder et Nostre Dame!

wood or fever creeps into his bones; a lowly worm, a spider, an earwig, bite of a dog or claw of a beast can make him die and lay him in his tomb in less time than the blooming of a flower. May God and Our Lady protect us!

Alas! what avails our noble ancestry, our great palaces, our great walled city, our great treasures, conquered kingdom, strength of body, skill of mind and tongue – all this cannot defend us from the grave. Samson is dead, Alexander and Uriah, Croesus, David, Solomon, Jeremiah, and we shall all die and pay our mortal debt. Let there be none to trust in worldly goods. May God and Our Lady protect us!

Princes and lords and mortal men, do not put your trust in perishable things. The body will die; therefore let us take thought for the soul, serving God and the Virgin Mary, for failing that our glory perishes. May God and Our Lady protect us!

234

Ballade

QUI aime bien, il a peu de repos;
De son amour toudis perdre se doute;
Il tremble, il frit; il n'a ne cuir ne os,
Cuer ne penser où paour ne se boute;
Il craint, il plaint, il ne repose goute.
Tel est amour entre ami et amie:
Toudis enquiert, cerche, oreille et escoute.
Onques Amour ne fut sans Jalousie.

Si n'en doit on pas dire vilains mos,
Ne l'appeler fausse, vieille ne gloute
Si comme on fait; qui la blame, il est fols;
Car s'elle fust desloial ne estoute,
Amour l'eüst pieça destruite toute;
Mais pour son bien l'a en sa compagnie:
C'est son escu, sa servant, son escoute.
Onques Amour ne fut sans Jalousie.

Ballade

HE who loves well has little peace; he is always afraid of losing his
love; he trembles, he quivers; dread invades his skin, his bones, his
heart, and his mind; he fears, he groans, he knows no rest. Such is
love between a lover and his mistress, always spying and probing,
alert, and listening. Love never existed without Jealousy.

And yet we should not say harsh things about Jealousy, nor call
her false, old, and greedy as people do; he who abuses her is
foolish, for if she was really treacherous and arrogant, Love would
long ago have destroyed her completely. It is for Love's own good
that he keeps company with her. She is his shield, his servant, and
his sentinel. Love never existed without Jealousy.

Qui n'aime à droit, il est d'elle forclos,
De ce qu'il het en tel cas ne fait doute;
Donc est Amour en Jalousie enclos;
Dame et ami l'un de l'autre fordoute,
Et bon signe est de suivre droite route
De vrai Amour: jaloux ne seroit mie
Cil qui harroit, pour ce ne la reboute.
Onques Amour ne fut sans Jalousie.

Ballade

SE tout le ciel estoit de feuilles d'or,
Et li airs fust estellés d'argent fin,
Et tous les vens fussent pleins de tresor,
Et les gouttes fussent toutes florin
D'eaue de mer, et pleust soir et matin
Richesses, biens, honeurs, joiaux, argent,
Tant que rempli en fust toute la gent,
La terre aussi en fust mouillee toute,
Et fusse nu, – de tel pluie et tel vent
Ja sur mon cors n'en cherroit une goutte.

He who does not love truly has no part in her, for then he is not anxious about what he hates; therefore Love is wrapped up in Jealousy. Mistress and lover, each one doubts the other, and that is a good sign that they are on the highroad of true love: for one who hated would never feel jealousy, and therefore let the lover not reject her. Love never existed without Jealousy.

Ballade

IF all the sky was made of gold leaf, and the air was starred with fine silver, and treasure borne on all the winds, and every drop of sea-water was a florin, and it rained down, morning and evening, riches, goods, honours, jewels, money, till all the people were filled with it, and I stood there naked in such rain and wind, never a drop of it would fall on me.

Et qui pis est, vous puis bien dire encor
Que qui dorroit trestout l'avoir du Rin,
Et fusse là, – vaillant un harenc sor
N'en vendroit pas vers moi vif un frelin;
Onques ne fui de nul donneur afin;
Biens me defaut, tout mal me vient souvent;
Se j'ai mestier de rien, on le me vent
Plus qu'il ne vaut, de ce ne faites doute.
Se beneurté plouvoit du firmament,
Ja sur mon cors n'en cherroit une goutte.

Et se je perds, ja n'en avrai restor;
Quant rien requier, on chante de Basin;
Se je fais bien, neant plus que d'un tor
N'est conneü; tousjours sui je Martin,
Qui cote avoit, chaperon et roucin,
Pain et paine, connoissance ensement,
Son tems usa, mais trop dolentement,
Car plus povre de lui n'ot en sa route.
Je sui celui que s'il plouvoit piment,
Ja sur mon cors n'en cherroit une goutte.

And what is worse, I can assure you too that if someone were giving away all the wealth of the Rhineland and I was there, not the price of a red herring, not even a farthingsworth would come my way. I was never yet acquainted with a giver; goods flee from me, ills often seek me out; if I need anything, it is sold to me for more than it is worth, make no doubt about that. If good fortune were raining from the firmament, never a drop of it would fall on me.

And if I lose a thing, I shall never get it back; when I ask for anything, I am put off with an old song. If I do a good deed, I get no more recognition than if it was a crime. I am always poor Martin, who had a gown, a hood, and a nag, bread and the sweat of his brow, and knew it too. He wore away his days, but very cheerlessly, for none more poor than he in all his band. I am such a man that if it rained spiced wine, never a drop of it would fall on me.

Princes, deux poins font ou riche ou meschant:
Eur et meseur; l'un aime et l'autre doute;
Car, s'il pouoit plouvoir mondainement,
Ja sur mon cors n'en cherroit une goutte.

Ballade

Moult se vantoit li cerfs d'estre legiers
Et de courir dix lieues d'une alaine,
Et li sengliers se vantoit d'estre fiers,
Et la brebis se louoit pour sa laine,
Et li chevreaux de sauter en la plaine
Se vantoit fort, li chevaux estre beaux,
Et de force se vantoit li toreaux,
L'ermine aussi d'avoir beau peliçon;
Adonc respont en sa coquille à ceaux:
«Aussi tost vient à Pasques limaçon.»

Princes, two things determine wealth or poverty: good luck and
bad; I love the one and dread the other, for if all the good things of
the earth could fall as rain, never a drop of it would fall on me.

Ballade

The stag took great pride in his swiftness and in being able to run
ten leagues without stopping for breath, and the wild boar was
proud of his ferocity, and the sheep extolled her wool, and the roebuck was very proud of his ability to bound over the plain; the
horse took pride in his beauty and the bull in his strength, and the
ermine in the beauty of its fur; then to all these replied he from his
shell: 'The snail will get to Easter just as soon.'

Les lions voy, ours et liepars premiers,
Loups et tigres, courir par la champaigne,
Estre chaciés de mastins et levriers
A cris de gens, et s'il est qu'on les preigne
Tant sont haïs que chascun les mehaigne,
Pour ce qu'ils font destruction de peaux;
Ravissables sont, fels et desloyaulx
Sans espargner, et pour ce les het on.
Courent ils bien? Sont ils fors et isneaux?
Aussi tost vient à Pasques limaçon.

Celui voient pluseurs par les sentiers;
Enclos se tient en la cruise qu'il maine,
Sans faire mal le laisse on volontiers,
Tousjours s'en va de semaine en semaine;
Si font pluseurs en leur povre domaine
Qui vivent bien sous leurs povres drapeaux,
Et, s'ils ne font au monde leurs aveaux,
Si courent ils par gracieus renom.
Quant desliés sont aux champs beufs et veaux,
Aussi tost vient à Pasques limaçon.

I see first lions, bears, and leopards, then wolves and tigers running through the countryside, pursued by mastiffs and hounds, and by the shouts of men; and if they are caught, they are so much detested that everyone maims them because of the harm they cause among the fleeces. They are wicked and treacherous thieves, and merciless, and so they are hated. Do they run well? Are they both strong and swift? The snail will get to Easter just as soon.

Many people see him on the path, housed in the shell he carries with him; they do not harm him, but gladly let him be, and on he goes from week to week; thus many men go on in their own poor sphere, who live their lives well under their poor attire; and if they do not get all they want from the world, yet they go on their way with men's good will. When oxen and calves run free in the field, the snail will get to Easter just as soon.

Prince, les gens fors, grans, riches, entr'eaulx
Ne tiennent pas toudis une leçon;
Pour eux haster n'approche temps nouveaux:
Aussi tost vient à Pasques limaçon.

Ballade

EN Hainaut et en Brabant ai
Apris à sauces ordonner:
Es hostels où je me logeai
Me fist on tousdis apporter
A rost, à mouton, à sangler,
A lievre, à connin, à ostarde,
A poisson d'eaue douce et mer,
Tousjours, sans demander, moustarde.

Harens frais quis, et demandai
Carpe au cabaret pour diner,
Bequet en l'eaue y ordonnay,
Et grosses soles au souper;
A Brusselles fis demander
Sauce vert; le clerc me regarde,
Par un varlet me fist donner
Tousjours, sans demander, moustarde.

Prince, among the strong, the great, the rich, there is one thing
that is not always kept in mind; not all their haste can bring spring
any nearer. The snail will get to Easter just as soon.

Ballade

IN Hainaut and in Brabant I used to order sauces: in the inns where
I stayed they always brought me, with roast, with mutton, with
boar, with hare, with rabbit, with bustard, with fresh-water fish and
with salt-water fish, always – without asking – mustard.

I asked for fresh herring, and I ordered carp for dinner at the
tavern; I ordered pike cooked in water and large soles for supper;
in Brussels I asked for green sauce; the head waiter gave me a look,
then sent a servant to bring, as always – without asking – mustard.

Sans li ne bu ne ne mangeai.
Avec l'eaue la font mesler
Du poisson, et encore sai
Que la graisse du rost jeter
Font en la moustarde et bouter.
D'en servir nul d'eux ne retarde:
Là avrez vous, pour vostre user,
Tousjours, sans demander, moustarde.

Prince, gingembre, c'est tout cler,
Clos, safran, graine n'ont d'eux garde,
Mais à chascun font destremper
Tousjours, sans demander, moustarde.

Rondeau

Poux, puces, puor et pourceaux
Est de Behaigne la nature,
Pain, poisson salé et froidure,

Poivre noir, choux pourris, poreaux,
Char enfumee, noire et dure;
Poux, puces, puor et pourceaux.

I never ate or drank without it. They mix it with the water they boil the fish in, and I know that they have the dripping from the roast thrown into the mustard and mixed up with it. Not one of them is slow to serve it. There you will have for your use, always – without asking – mustard.

Prince, it is clear that ginger, cloves, saffran, and cardamom have nothing to fear from these people. For everyone they have prepared, always – without asking – mustard.

Rondeau

Lice and fleas and stink and pigs, that's the essence of Bohemia, bread and salt fish and bitter cold,

Black pepper, rotten cabbages and leeks, smoked meat, both black and hard; lice and fleas and stink and pigs.

Vint gens mangier en deux plateaux,
Boire cervoise amere et sure,
Mal couchier, noir, paille et ordure,
Poux, puces, puor et pourceaux
Est de Behaigne la nature,
Pain, poisson salé et froidure.

Ballade

QUANT j'ai la terre et mer avironnee,
Et visité en chascune partie
Jerusalem, Egipte et Galilee,
Alixandre, Damas et la Surie,
Babiloine, le Caire et Tartarie,
　　　Et tous les pors qui y sont,
Les espices et sucres qui s'y font,
Les fins draps d'or et soie du pays,
Valent trop mieux ce que les François ont:
Rien ne se peut comparer à Paris.

Twenty people eating from two dishes, sour and bitter beer to drink, hard sleeping in dark rooms on straw and filth, lice and fleas and stink and pigs, that's the essence of Bohemia, bread and salt fish and bitter cold.

Ballade

WHEN I have encircled all the earth and the sea, and visited every part of Jerusalem, Egypt and Galilee, Alexandria, Damascus and Syria, Babylon, Cairo and Tartary, and seen all their ports, the spices and sugars that they make, the fine golden and silken cloths of each country, much better worth is what the French possess: Paris is quite beyond compare.

C'est la cité sur toutes couronnee,
Fontaine et puis de sens et de clergie,
Sur le fleuve de Seine situee,
Vignes, bois a, terres et praerie.
De tous les biens de ceste mortel vie
    A plus qu'autres cités n'ont;
Tous estrangiers l'aiment et ameront,
Car, pour deduit et pour estre jolis,
Jamais cité telle ne trouveront:
Rien ne se peut comparer à Paris.

Mais elle est bien mieux que ville fermee,
Et de chasteaux de grant anceserie,
De gens d'honneur et de marchans peuplee,
De tous ouvriers d'armes, d'orfeverie;
De tous les ars c'est la fleur, quoi qu'on die;
    Tous ouvrages à droit font;
Subtil engin, entendement parfont
Verrez avoir aux habitans toudis,
Et loyauté aux euvres qu'ils feront:
Rien ne se peut comparer à Paris.

She is the city crowned above all others, fountain and well of wisdom and of learning, established on the River Seine; vineyards and woods she has, ploughlands and meadows. Of all the good things of this earthly life she has more than other cities; all strangers love her and will always do so; for pleasure and elegance they will never find such a city: Paris is quite beyond compare.

But she is much better fortified than any town – and with castles of great antiquity – peopled with noblemen, merchants, with all kinds of makers of armour and of goldsmiths' work. She is the flower of all the arts, whatever anyone may say: her workmen excel in all crafts; subtle skill and deep understanding you will always find among her citizens, and true value in all their works: Paris is quite beyond compare.

Ballade

Sı comme on dit, chascuns sert quatre mois
Des serviteurs qui sont en ordonnance,
Entre lesquels en a quatre trop frais,
Où je ne sers nul temps à court de France,
Car il m'ont trop refroidi dès m'enfance:
Novembre y est, puis Decembre et Janvier,
Fevrier après qui tous reumes avance:
En ce froit temps s'en fait bon estrangier.

Car adonc sont et gelees et nois,
Pluies et vens, en grant desordonnance;
Lors aux sengliers s'en va chassier li rois,
Et officiers qui sont sur la despence
Soufflent leurs mains; chascun gare sa pance,
Batent leurs corps pour eux du froit vengier,
Page à cheval font nice contenance.
En ce froit temps s'en fait bon estrangier.

Ballade

THEY say that every one of the king's servants who is attached to
the Household is on duty for four months every year; but there are
four very chilly ones when I never serve at the Court of France, for
they have been too cold for me ever since my childhood: Novem-
ber is one of them, then December and January, and after that
February, the great promoter of colds. In this cold weather it is
best to keep away.

For then come frosts and snows and rains and winds in great
confusion; then the king goes off to hunt the boar, and the officers
in attendance blow on their hands; each one keeps his belly well
wrapped up, and they swing their arms to drive out the cold. Pages
on horseback cut a sorry figure. In this cold weather it is best to
keep away.

Petis pages pleurent de froit aux bois,
Qui de tenir leur bride n'ont puissance;
Quant au logis, Dieu set comme il est frois,
Et à dangier se fait la delivrance
De busche avoir; en sale on est en trance,
Deffublés sont servant et escuier.
Qui ne veut lors à court dancer tel dance,
En ce froit temps s'en fait bon estrangier.

Prince, qui a argent, gage ou creance,
Ces quatre mois s'en traie l'on arrier,
Ne voist à court pour oster sa grevance:
En ce froit temps s'en fait bon estrangier.

Ballade

J E deviens courbes et bossus,
J'oi tres dur, ma vie decline,
Je pers mes cheveux par dessus,
Je flue en chascune narine,
J'ai grant douleur en la poitrine,
Mes membres sens ja tous trembler,

Young page-boys out in the woods weep for cold and cannot
hold the horses' bridles. As for the courtiers' lodgings, God knows
how cold they are and how grudgingly the fuel is doled out; in hall,
everyone shivers, servants and squires are not permitted to wear
cloaks. If you don't want to dance this sort of dance, in this cold
weather it is best to stay away.

Prince, anyone who has enough money, or pledges, or credit,
should go back home for these four months; let him not go to
Court even to seek justice; in this cold weather it is best to stay
away.

Ballade

I AM growing bent and hunchbacked, hard of hearing and short of
vigour; my hair is getting thin on top; and both my nostrils run;
I have a bad pain in my chest; I find my limbs beginning to tremble;

Je suis tres hastif à parler,
Impatient; Desdain me mort;
Sans conduit ne sai mais aler:
Ce sont les signes de la mort.

Couvoiteus suis, blans et chanus,
Eschars, courrouceux; j'adevine
Ce qui n'est pas, et loe plus
Le temps passé que la doctrine
Du temps present; mon corps se mine;
Je voi envis rire et jouer,
J'ai grant plaisir à grumeler,
Car le temps passé me remort;
Tousjours veuil jeunesse blamer:
Ce sont les signes de la mort.

Mes dens sont longs, foibles, agus,
Jaunes, flairans comme sentine;
Tous mes corps est frois devenus,
Maigres et secs; par medecine
Vivre me faut; char ne cuisine
Ne puis qu'à grant peine avaler;

I am hasty in speech and lacking in patience; I feel the tooth of
Scorn; I can no longer walk without assistance: these are the signs
of Death.

I am greedy, and my hair is white and hoary; I am miserly and
irritable, suspicious without cause, more full of praise for old times
than for present-day opinions; my body is wasting away. I hate to
see other people laughing and enjoying themselves; I take great
pleasure in grumbling, for I look back with envy on the past; I am
always finding fault with youth: these are the signs of Death.

My teeth are long and weak and sharp, yellow and smelling like
bilge-water; all my body has become cold and thin and dried up;
I have to live on a diet; it is only with great difficulty that I can

Des jeusnes me faut baler,
Mes corps toudis sommeille ou dort,
Et ne veuil que boire et humer:
Ce sont les signes de la mort.

Prince, encor veuil ci ajouster
Soixante ans, pour mieux confermer
Ma vieillesse qui me nuit fort,
Quant ceux qui me doivent amer
Me souhaitent ja outre mer:
Ce sont les signes de la mort.

CHRISTINE DE PISAN

Rondeau

Source de plour, riviere de tristesse,
Flun de douleur, mer d'amertume pleine
M'avironnent, et noyent en grant peine
Mon povre cuer qui trop sent de destresse.

Si m'affondent et plongent en aspresse;
Car parmi moi courent plus fort que Seine
Source de plour, riviere de tristesse.

swallow meat or roast; I have to make my feasts of fasting; I am always dozing or asleep and can only manage drinks and slops; all these are signs of Death.

Prince, to all this I yet would wish to add sixty years more, to put the seal upon this old age which bears hard on me, when those who ought to love me already wish me over the sea: these are the signs of Death.

Rondeau

A spring of tears, a river of sorrow, a stream of grief, a sea full of bitterness surround me and drown in deep sadness my poor heart overburdened with distress.

And I am sunk and plunged in trouble, for over me there flows, stronger than the Seine, a spring of tears, a river of sorrow.

Et leurs grans flos cheent à grant largesse,
Si com le vent de Fortune les meine,
Tous dessus moi, dont si bas suis qu'à peine
Releverai, tant durement m'oppresse
Source de plour, riviere de tristesse.

Ballade

NE trop ne peu au cuer me sens frappee
Des dars d'Amour qu'on dit qui font grant guerre
A mainte gent, mais ne suis atrappee,
La Dieu merci! es las ne en la serre
      Du dieu d'Amours.
Je ne lui fais requestes ne clamours,
Je vif sans lui en plaisance et en joie:
Par amour n'aim, ne amer ne voudroie.

Ne n'ai paour que je soie happee
Ne par regars, par dons ne par long erre,
Ne par parler mignot enveloppee,

And their great waves break over me again and again, as the wind of Fortune blows them, bringing me so low that I shall hardly rise again, so heavily they press upon me, a spring of tears, a river of sorrow.

Ballade

MY heart has felt no wound, severe or slight, from Love's arrows, which, they say, make grievous war on many; but I have not been caught, thank God! in the snares or in the prison of the god of love. I make him no petition nor entreaty, I live without him in happiness and joy: I have no lover and I do not want one.

  And I am not afraid of being caught either by looks or gifts or long pursuit, nor entrapped by blandishment of words, for there is

Car il n'est hom qui mon cuer peust acquerre;
      Ne à secours
N'y viegne nul, car escondit le cours
De moi seroit, et tantost lui diroie:
Par amour n'aim, ne amer ne voudroie.

Et beau moquer m'ai de femme atrappee
En tel danger où mieux lui vausist querre
Pour soi tuer ou coustel ou espee,
Car perdu a du tout honneur sur terre.
        Pour ce à toujours
En cest estat je pense user mes jours;
A tous dirai, s'il avient qu'on m'en proie:
Par amour n'aim, ne amer ne voudroie.

Prince d'Amour, à vo court que feroie?
Par amour n'aim, ne amer ne voudroie.

Rondeau

Se souvent vais au moustier,
C'est tout pour veoir la belle
Fresche com rose nouvelle.

no man who can win my heart; and let none call to me for help, for I should promptly reject his suit, and say to him at once, 'I have no lover and I do not want one.'

And I can fairly laugh at any woman caught in such peril that she would have done better to take a knife or sword to kill herself, for she has lost all honour in the world. And therefore I intend to live my life still in this state, and say to all, if anyone should seek my love: 'I have no lover and I do not want one.'

Prince of Love, what should I do at your Court? I have no lover, and I do not want one.

Rondeau

IF I often go to church it is all to see the lovely girl, fresh as a new-blown rose.

D'en parler n'est nul mestier;
Pour quoi fait on tel nouvelle
Se souvent vais au moustier?

Il n'est voie ne sentier
Où je voise que pour elle;
Fols est qui fol m'en appelle
Se souvent vais au moustier.

Ballade

Ha! le plus doulz qui jamais soit formé!
Le plus plaisant qu'onques nulle acointast!
Le plus parfait pour estre bon clamé!
Le mieuz amé qu'onques mais femme amast!
De mon vrai cuer le savoreux repast!
Tout quanque j'aim, mon savoreux desir!
Mon seul amé, mon paradis en terre
Et de mes yeuz le tres parfait plaisir!
Vostre douceur me meine dure guerre.

There is no need to talk about it. Why does it give rise to so
much gossip if I often go to church?

There is no way nor path I ever take but for her sake. He is a
fool who calls me a fool if I often go to church.

Ballade

Gentlest of all men ever made, most charming lover any
woman ever knew, most perfect ever to be acclaimed for his worth,
best beloved ever loved by woman, sweet food of my true heart,
sum of all I love, my dearest desire, my only love, my Heaven on
earth, the very perfect delight of my eyes, the thought of your
sweetness works havoc in me.

Vostre douceur voirement entamé
A le mien cuer, qui jamais ne pensast
Estre en ce point, mais si l'a enflammé
Ardent desir qu'en vie ne durast
Se Doulz Penser ne le reconfortast;
Mais Souvenir vient avec lui gesir,
Lors en pensant vous embrace et vous serre,
Mais quant ne puis le doulz baisier saisir
Vostre douceur me meine dure guerre.

Mon doulz ami de tout mon cuer amé,
Il n'est penser qui de mon cuer jetast
Le doulz regard que vos yeuz enfermé
Ont dedans lui; rien n'est qui l'en ostast, —
Ne le parler et le gracieux tast
Des douces mains qui, sans lait desplaisir,
Veulent partout encerchier et enquerre;
Mais quant ne puis de mes yeuz vous choisir
Vostre douceur me meine dure guerre.

In very truth, your sweetness has broken into my heart, which never thought to be in this state; but burning desire has so inflamed it that it could never keep alive if Musing did not bring it consolation. But then comes Memory to lie down with my heart, then in my thoughts I hold you and embrace you; but when I cannot savour your sweet kiss, the thought of your sweetness works havoc in me.

My dear love, beloved of my whole heart, that thought does not exist which could drive from my heart that sweet look which your eyes have enclosed within it. Nothing could drive it out or make me forget your voice or the gentle touch of those dear hands, never resented, ever eager to search and to explore. But when I cannot see you with my eyes, the thought of your sweetness works havoc in me.

Tres bel et bon, qui mon cuer vient saisir,
Ne m'oubliez, ce vous vueil je requerre;
Car quant veoir ne vous puis à loisir
Vostre douceur me meine dure guerre.

Ballade

Tel douleur ai, ami, pour ton allee,
Que je ne sai se la pourrai porter.
Hélas! comment, ma douce amour celee,
Serai sans toi? car un jour deporter
      Sans te veoir
M'estoit si grief que ne pouoie avoir
Bien ne repos; comment endurerai
Un an ou plus, peut estre, ainz que te voie?
Je ne sai pas si tant y durerai,
Car bien n'avrai jusque je te revoie.

Est il besoin adès que mer salee
Passes, ami, pour ma joie emporter?
C'est ton honneur, n'en doi estre adoulee;

Fairest and best, oh! captor of my heart, do not forget me, this I
will beg of you, for when I cannot see you as often as I wish, the
thought of your sweetness works havoc in me.

Ballade

I feel such grief, my love, at your departure, that I do not know
how I shall be able to bear it. Alas! how can I live without you, my
sweet secret love, when to pass a single day without seeing you was
so hard for me that I could find neither ease nor rest? How shall I
endure a year, or more perhaps, before I see you? I do not know if
I can hold out so long, for nothing will please me until I see you
again.

Must it be so soon, my love, that you must cross the salt sea and
take away my happiness with you? It is for your honour, I ought

Mais nepourtant ne me puis conforter,
      Pour nul avoir,
De ce que tant serai sans reveoir
Toi, dont confort, je le te jurerai,
Tant que seras en ceste longue voie,
Je ne prendrai. Dieu set se pleurerai!
Car bien n'avrai jusque je te revoie.

Et simplement en atour affulee
Et en habit serai, ne deporter
Ne me verra nului; en recelee
Menrai mon dueil, ne homme reconforter,
      A dire voir,
Ne m'en pourroit, ainsi dolent et noir
Avrai le cuer; et ne procurerai
Chose que soit qui à soulas m'avoie;
En ce dolent ennui me murerai,
Car bien n'avrai jusque je te revoie.

Mon douz ami, et si t'assenerai
D'estre en ce point toudis, où que je soie,
Dont annee grieve et trop dure avrai,
Car bien n'avrai jusque je te revoie.

not to let it grieve me; but still nothing in the world will console me for being so long without you; and I swear I shall seek no consolation for your absence as long as you are on this distant journey. God knows how I shall weep! for nothing will please me until I see you again.

I shall go plainly dressed and unadorned, and none shall see me taking any pleasure. In secret I shall nurse my grief, and truly no man will be able to comfort me, so sorrowful and dark my heart will be; and I shall not seek for anything to give me solace, but I shall shut myself up in this sad melancholy; for nothing will please me until I see you again.

And I will promise you, dear love, to be always of this mind, wherever I may be; thus I shall have a cheerless and most weary year; for nothing will please me until I see you again.

Ballade

Ce mois de mai tout se resjoie,
Ce me semble, fors moi, lassette!
Qui n'ai pas cil qu'avoir souloie,
Dont je souspire à voix bassette.
C'estoit ma belle amour doucette
Qui ores est si loin de mi.
Helas! reviens tost, mon ami,

En ce douz mois où tout verdoie,
Si irons jouer sus l'herbette
Où orrons chanter à grant joie
Rossignols et mainte alouette,
Tu sais bien où. A voix simplette
Encor te pri disant: «Aimi!
Helas! reviens tost, mon ami.»

Ballade

In this May month it seems to me that everything rejoices except for me, alas! when I lack him I used to have with me; and therefore I lament with smothered sighs; he was my dearest, sweetest love, who is now so far away from me. Alas! come back soon, my love.

In this sweet month, when everything grows green, let us go and take our pleasure on the fresh young grass, where we shall hear the nightingale and many a lark, you well know where. In truest tones I beg you once again, ah! me, alas! come back soon, my love.

Car en ce mois, où Amour proie
Prent souvent, m'est vis que c'est dette
A tout amant qu'il se resjoie
Avec sa dame et s'amiette:
Ne la doit pas laissier seulette,
Ce me semble, jour ne demi.
Helas! reviens tost, mon ami.

Pour t'amour mon cuer fent par mi;
Helas! reviens tost, mon ami.

Ballade

Tu soies le tres bien venu,
M'amour! Or m'embrace et me baise.
Et comment t'es tu maintenu
Puis ton depart? Sain et bien aise
As tu esté toujours? Ça vien,
Coste moi te sié et me conte
Comment t'a esté, mal ou bien;
Car de ce vueil savoir le compte.

For in this month, when Love claims many a victim, I think that it is every lover's duty to make merry with the one who is his lady and his darling. He ought not to leave her all alone, it seems to me, even a day or even half a day. Alas! come back soon, my love.

For love of you my heart is breaking. Alas! come back soon, my love.

Ballade

'Welcome back, my darling! Now put your arms round me and kiss me. How have you been since you went away? Have you been well and happy all the time? Come here, sit down beside me, and tell me how things have been with you, both ill and well, for I must know the full account of that.'

— Ma dame, à qui je suis tenu
Plus qu'autre, (à nul n'en desplaise!)
Sachez que desir m'a tenu
Si court qu'onques n'oz tel mesaise,
Ne plaisir ne prenoie en rien
Loin de vous: Amour, qui cuers dompte,
Me disoit: «Loyauté me tien,
Car de ce vueil savoir le compte.»

— Dont m'as tu ton serment tenu;
Bon gré t'en sai, par saint Nicaise.
Et puis que sain es revenu,
Joie avrons assez; or t'apaise
Et me dis se ses de combien
Le mal qu'en as eu à plus monte
Que cil qu'a souffert le cuer mien;
Car de ce vueil savoir le compte.

— Plus mal que vous, si com retien,
Ai eu; mais dites sans mescompte
Quans baisiers en avrai je bien?
Car de ce vueil savoir le compte.

'My Lady, whom I love more than any other (be it said without offence) know that my longing kept me so tight-reined that I was never so unhappy before, and I could not take pleasure in anything, parted from you. Love, who tames all hearts, said to me: 'Keep faith with me, for I must know the full account of that.'

'Then you have kept your word to me; I thank you for it, by St Nicaise; and since you have come back safely, we shall have joy enough; now be at peace, and tell me if you know by how much your pain has surpassed what my heart has suffered; for I must know the full account of that.'

'More pain than you, as I maintain, I have had; but now tell me exactly how many kisses I shall have for it; for I must know the full account of that.'

Ballade

QUANT je voi ces amoureux
Tant de si doux semblans faire
L'un à l'autre, et savoureux
Et doux regars entretraire,
Liement rire et eux traire
A part, et les tours qu'ils font,
A peu que mon cuer ne font.

Car lors me souvient, pour eux,
De cil dont ne puis retraire
Mon cuer qui est desireux
Qu'ainsi le peüsse attraire;
Mais le doux et debonnaire
Est loing, dont en dueil parfont
A peu que mon cuer ne font.

Ainsi sera langoureux
Mon cuer en ce grief contraire,
Plein de souspirs douloureux,
Jusques par deça repaire
Cil qu'Amour me fait tant plaire;
Mais du mal qui me confont
A peu que mon cuer ne font.

Ballade

WHEN I see these lovers looking so fondly at each other, and ex-
changing sweet soft glances and turning aside with happy laughter,
and all their ways with one another, my heart is fit to break.

For then they bring back to my mind the one I cannot tear my
heart away from, my heart that longs to draw him close; but he, so
dear, so courteous, is far away, and that is why for bitter grief my
heart is fit to break.

My heart will languish in this heavy sorrow, full of sad sighs,
until he comes back across the sea, the one whom Love has made
so pleasing to me; but with all the pain I suffer my heart is fit to
break.

Princes, je ne me puis taire:
Quant je voi gent paire à paire
Qui en joie se refont,
A peu que mon cuer ne font.

Ballade

HELAS! au moins se aucune nouvelle
Pëusse ouir, par quoi seusse comment
Le fait celui qui mes maux renouvelle,
Et qui tenu l'a ja si longuement
De moi lointain, ce feist aucunement
Moi resjouir, mais nul n'en fait raport,
Ne plus ne moins ne que s'il estoit mort.

Ne sai s'en nef, en barge ou en nacelle
Passa la mer ou s'il va autrement;
S'en Aragon, en Espagne, en Castelle,
Ou autre part soit alé où briefment
Ne puist venir, ou si prochainement;
Car je ne sai où il est, n'a quel port,
Ne plus ne moins ne que s'il estoit mort.

Princes, I cannot keep silence: when I see people meeting pair by pair, each making the other's joy, my heart is fit to break.

Ballade

ALAS! if only I could hear some news to tell me how he is, the cause of all my sorrow, and what has kept him so long away from me, that would give me some slight comfort; but no one ever mentions him, neither more nor less than if he were dead.

I do not know if he has crossed the sea in ship or barge or skiff, or if he travels by other means; if he has gone to Aragon, to Spain, to Castile, or to some other place which he could not reach quickly, or whether his journey was short; for I do not know where he is, or in what port, neither more nor less than if he were dead.

Ou peut estre qu'il aime autre plus belle
Que je ne suis, si ne lui chaut granment
De revenir; mais il n'est damoiselle
Ne nulle autre, ce sai certainement,
Qui jamais jour l'aime plus loiaument;
Mais que me vaut, quant je n'en ai confort
Ne plus ne moins ne que s'il estoit mort?

Ballade

JAMAIS à moi plus ne s'attende,
Celui à qui plus ne m'attens,
Puis que vers moi ne vient ne mande.
Attendu l'ai deux ans par temps,
Plus ne m'en quier donner mal temps;
Folie m'en feroit douloir,
Puis qu'il m'a mise en nonchaloir.

Au vrai corps Dieu le recommande,
Qui le gard de mauvais contens,
Et de tout peril le defende,

Or perhaps he loves another woman more beautiful than I am,
and so cares little about coming back; but there is no girl, whatever
be her rank, I surely know, who could ever love him more truly
than I do. But how does that help me, when I have no solace from
him, neither more nor less than if he were dead?

Ballade

LET him expect no more of me, the man I no longer hope to see,
since he neither comes to me nor sends a message. I have waited
for him almost two years; I will not suffer further pain for him. It
would be madness if I were to grieve, since he no longer cares for
me.

I commend him to the true God Himself, that He may keep him
from evil strife, and protect him from all peril, although I am no

Combien que plus je ne l'attens
Et à m'en retraire je tens;
Et de ce fais je mon devoir,
Puis qu'il m'a mise en nonchaloir.

Mespris a vers moi, mais l'amende
N'affiert pas de deniers contans,
Mais du devoir qu'Amour commande
A ceux qui sont entremettans
D'amour servir; mais malcontens
S'en tient mon cuer, à dire voir,
Puis qu'il m'a mise en nonchaloir.

Lai Mortel

... LE mal que j'ai, et tu le ses, Amours,
Me vient d'amer un desloyal ami
Qui me promist qu'il seroit à tousjours
Mon vrai amant; lasse! dolent, aimi!
Je m'i fiai, dont mon cuer fent par mi;
Car son parler attrayant, decevable,
Et son maintien courtois et amiable,

longer waiting for him, and am trying to forget him: and this is
what I ought to do, since he no longer cares for me.

He has wronged me, but the fine he owes cannot be paid in coin,
but in the duty which Love enjoins on those who undertake his
service; and truth to tell, my heart is comfortless, since he no longer
cares for me.

Lay of Death

... MY sickness comes, oh! Love, you know it, from loving a false
friend who promised me that he would always be my true lover;
alas for me, poor wretch, I trusted him, and so my heart is breaking;
for his falsely charming words and his courteous, loving manner

Me disoient qu'il disoit verité,
Et non faisoit, c'est bien chose prouvable,
Dont de joie a mon cuer desherité.

Car plus a veu que mon cuer estoit mis
En sienne amour et que bien sienne estoie,
Adont s'est il de moi amer remis
Du tout en tout, ne plus n'a quise voie
De moi veoir, et je pleure et larmoie,
Pleine de dueil et de desir ensemble,
Pour ce que voi que son cuer se dessemble
De mon amour et qu'il est faux et faint,
Et ne m'en puis retraire, ce me semble,
Car tout y mis mon las cuer qui s'en plaint ...

Et quel conseil a ce martire,
        Se Dieu te gart,
Y pourrai je, Amour, donc eslire?
        Car mon cuer art
De s'amour, et adès m'empire,
        Ne n'ai regart
Ailleurs, lasse! dont je souspire
        Seullette à part

made me believe that he was speaking the truth; and he was not:
the thing is fully proved; and thus he robbed my heart of all its joy.

For no sooner did he see that my heart was set on loving him,
and I was fully his, than he withdrew his love from me entirely, and
never since has tried to find a way of seeing me; and I lament and
weep, full of both grief and longing, because I see that he is casting
out my love from his heart, and that he is false and faithless. And
yet it seems I cannot free myself, for I gave him all my poor suffering heart. ...

And what remedy for this torment, as God may save you, oh!
Love, can I then choose? For my heart burns ever more and more
for love of him, and I care for nothing else; and so alas I sigh alone,
apart, when I cannot see him who grudges me his presence, and

Quant ne voi celui qui à tart
Me voit et qui me fait maudire
Ma vie, car il m'est si tart
Que le voie; et ne fais que dire:
   «Le cuer me part;
Venez vers moi, mon tres doux mire,
    Ou main ou tart.»
Mais tout n'i vaut rien, car il tire
   En autre part.
Si ne me doit mie souffire
   D'avoir tel part
De celui que je tant desire.

Mais, se pour mon mal alegier
Et moi oster de ce dangier,
Pouoie prendre aucun plaisir
Autre part, et lui estrangier,
Ce me pourroit assouagier;
Mais nenil: tout m'est desplaisir,
Quanqu'autre fait ne puis saisir,
Autre vouloir n'autre desir
Ne se peut en moi hebergier;
Car tout li mis sans deslogier,
Et, en deusse vive enragier,
En ce point me convient gesir.

who makes me curse my life because I long to see him so; and I can only say, 'My heart is breaking. Come to me, my sweet physician, early or late.' But it is all in vain, for now his steps are bent towards another; and how can it suffice me to have so poor a share in him I so desire?

If only, to ease my pain and save myself from this peril, I could take any pleasure in another, and banish him from my thoughts, that might heal me; but no, nothing can please me, other men's deeds mean nothing to me; no other wish, no other desire can find a home in me; for all my hopes were set immutably on him and, though it drive me mad, there they must stay.

Si le me faut ainsi porter
    Jusqu'au mourir,
Bien le voi, puis que deporter,
    Pour moi garir,
Ne te veux de moi tourmenter,
    Ne acourir
Pour mon bien; mais ma grief complainte
Au moins il te plaise aporter
    Et tost courir
A celui qui me fait perir
    Sans arrester,
Combien qu'il n'a nul vueil d'oster
    Ne secourir
Mon mal, dont j'ai la couleur tainte.

    Ainsi finerai mon age
    Assez jeune, en ce malage
    Qui m'est rente et heritage,
    Dont ma lasse vie est mendre.
    Et se je te fusse ombrage
    Jadis, plus que au feur l'emplage
    Le me rens de ton paage.
    Nul n'est qui se peust defendre,
    Bien le voi, c'est le rivage
    De durté où douleur nage;

So I must bear it thus until I die, as well I see, since you, oh! Love, will not spare me your torments in order to heal me, nor will you come to my aid. But at least be pleased to take my sad lament and hasten with it to the man who is causing my death. Do not delay: although he has no wish to cure or to allay the sickness which has made my face so pale.

Thus shall I end my days, still young, from this malady which is my revenue and my inheritance and cuts short my weary life. And if in former times, oh! Love, I shunned your service, more than due measure you have paid me back. None could save himself, I see it well, on these bitter shores where grief sails. Thither you have

La tu adreças ma barge,
Fortune m'y fist descendre,
Ouquel lieu ne truis suffrage
Ne nul bien, fors le message
De mort qui corps et visage
Me fera tourner en cendre.

ALAIN CHARTIER

La Belle Dame sans Merci

NAGUERE, chevauchant, pensoie,
Comme homme triste et doulereux,
Au dueil où il faut que je soie
Le plus dolent des amoureux,
Puis que, par son dart rigoureux,
La Mort me tolit ma maistresse,
Et me laissa seul, langoureux,
En la conduite de Tristesse.

Si disoie: «Il faut que je cesse
De ditter et de rimoyer,
Et que j'abandonne et delaisse
Le rire pour le lermoyer.

steered my boat and there has Fortune made me land, in a place
where I can find no help nor comfort, but the sentence of death
which will turn my body and my face to ashes.

La Belle Dame sans Merci

THE other day I was riding along, sadly and sorrowfully reflecting
on the mourning that makes me the most grief-stricken of lovers,
since Death with his dreadful dart has robbed me of my mistress
and left me lonely and forlorn with no guide but Sorrow.

And I said: 'I must desist from writing and making verses, and
I must abandon laughter and forsake it for weeping. That is how

Là me faut le temps employer,
Car plus n'ai sentement ne aise,
Soit d'escrire, soit d'envoyer
Chose qu'à moi n'à autre plaise.

«Qui voudroit mon vouloir contraindre
A joyeuses choses escrire,
Ma plume n'y savròit attaindre,
Non feroit ma langue à les dire.
Je n'ai bouche qui puisse rire
Que les yeux ne l'en desmentissent,
Car le cuer l'envoiroit desdire
Par les larmes qui des yeux issent.

«Je laisse aux amoureux malades
Qui ont espoir d'alegement
Faire chançons, dis et balades,
Chascun à son entendement.
Car ma dame en son testament
Prist, à la Mort, Dieu en ait l'ame!
Et emporta mon sentement
Qui gist o elle sous la lame.

I must spend my time, for I have no longer heart or inclination either to write or send anything which might please myself or anyone else.

'If anyone should wish to constrain my will to write of happy things, they would prove beyond the reach of my pen or the power of my tongue. There could be no laughter on my lips but my eyes would belie it, for my heart would send a denial by the tears that would fall from my eyes.

'I leave it to those lovers whose sickness can still hope for healing to make songs and poems and ballades, each according to his skill. For, by her will, my lady, when she died (God save her soul!) carried away with her all my power of feeling, which lies with her beneath the stone.

«Desormais est temps de moi taire,
Car de dire je suis lassé.
Je vueil laisser aux autres faire.
Leur temps est, le mien est passé.
Fortune a le forcier cassé
Où j'espargnoie ma richesse
Et le bien que j'ai amassé
Ou meilleur temps de ma jeunesse.

«Amour a gouverné mon sens;
Se faute y a, Dieu me pardonne.
Se j'ai bien fait, plus ne m'en sens,
Cela ne me toult ne me donne.
Car au trespas de la tres bonne
Tout mon bienfait se trespassa.
La Mort m'assist illec la bonne
Qu'onques puis mon cuer ne passa.» ...

'Henceforth it is time for me to keep silence, for I am weary of rhyming. I will leave the task to others; it is their hour now, mine is over. Fate has broken open the strong-box where I laid up my riches and all the wealth I gathered in the best days of my youth.

'Love has ruled my mind: if that was wrong, may God forgive me! If I did right, I am no better for it now; I have neither loss nor gain, for on the death of the best of women all my well-being died. And there Death set a limit for my heart that it could never pass again.' ...

L'AMANT

... Vous direz ce que vous voudrez,
Et du povoir avez assez,
Mais ja espoir ne m'en toudrez,
Par qui j'ai tant de maux passés.
Car quant Nature a enchacés
En vous des biens à tel effors,
El ne les a pas amassés
Pour en mettre pitié dehors.

LA DAME

Pitié doit estre raisonnable
Et à nul desavantageuse,
Aux besogneux tres proffitable,
Et aux piteux non dommageuse.
Se dame est à autrui piteuse
Pour estre à soi mesme cruelle,
Sa pitié devient despiteuse
Et son amour haine mortelle.

THE LOVER

Say what you will, despite all your power over me, you cannot
rob me of hope, which has brought me through so many troubles.
For since Nature has striven so hard to enshrine all excellences
within you, she never heaped all these together to shut out Pity
from their midst.

THE LADY

Pity must be reasonable and not work to anyone's disadvantage;
profitable to those in need, without being hurtful to those who
show compassion. If a lady is pitiful towards someone else at the
cost of being cruel to herself, her pity becomes pitiless and her love
deadly hatred.

L'AMANT

Conforter les desconfortés
N'est pas cruauté, ainz est los.
Mais vous qui si dur cuer portez
En si beau corps, se dire l'os,
Gagnez le blasme et le deslos
De cruauté qui mal y siet,
Se Pitié qui depart les los
En vostre haut cuer ne s'assiet.

LA DAME

Qui me dit que je suis amee,
Se bien croire je l'en vouloie,
Me doit il tenir pour blasmee
S'à son voloir je ne foloie?
Se de tels confors me mesloie,
Ce seroit pitié sans maniere,
Et depuis, se je me douloie,
C'en est la soudee derniere.

THE LOVER

Comforting the comfortless is not cruelty: it is a deed deserving
praise. But you who bear so hard a heart within so fair a body – if
I may dare to say so – will earn the blame and reproach of cruelty
which suits you very ill, if bountiful Pity does not take her seat
within your noble heart.

THE LADY

If a man tells me I am loved, even if I were willing to believe
him, is he to hold me worthy of blame if I do not stoop to folly at
his will? If I were to involve myself in giving that kind of comfort,
that would be pity out of all measure; and afterwards, if I was left
lamenting, that would be my final reward.

L'AMANT

Ha! cuer plus dur que le noir marbre,
En qui merci ne peut entrer,
Plus fort à ploier qu'un gros arbre,
Que vous vaut tel rigueur moustrer?
Vous plaist il mieulx me veoir outrer
Mort devant vous pour vostre esbat
Que, pour un confort remoustrer,
Respiter la mort qui m'abat?

LA DAME

De vos maux guerir vous pourrez,
Car des miens ne vous requerrai;
Ne pour mon plaisir ne mourrez
Ne pour vous guerir n'en gerrai.
Mon cuer pour autrui ne herrai,
Pleure, crie, rie ou chante.
Mais, se je puis, j'y pourverrai
Que vous ne autre ne s'en vante. ...

THE LOVER

Oh! heart harder than blackest marble, where mercy cannot enter, harder to bend than a great tree, what does it profit you to show such rigour? Would you rather see me meet my death before you for your sport than put off the death that is assailing me, by showing me a little comfort?

THE LADY

You may heal your own ills, for I shall never trouble you with mine; it is not for my pleasure that you will die, nor shall I take to my bed to heal your sickness. I will not make war on my own heart for the sake of another, whether he weeps or cries or laughs or sings, but as far as I can I shall take care that neither you nor any other man can boast its conquest. ...

Ballade

J' AI un arbre de la plante d'amours
Enraciné en mon cuer proprement
Qui ne porte fruit sinon de doulours,
Feuilles d'ennui et flours d'encombrement.
Mais, puis qu'il fut planté premierement,
Il est creü de racine et de branche,
Que son ombre qui me porte nuisance
Fait au dessous toute joie sechier,
Et si ne puis, pour toute ma puissance,
Autre y planter ne celui arrachier.

Dès long temps a, l'ai arrosé de plours
Et de lermes tant douloureusement,
Et si n'en sont les fruis de rien meillours
Ne je n'y truis gaires d'amendement.
Je les recueil neantmoins soigneusement.
C'est pour mon cuer amere soustenance
Qui trop mieux fust en friche ou en souffrance
Que porter fruit qui le deüst blecier.
Mais pas ne veut l'amoureuse ordonnance
Autre y planter ne celui arrachier.

Ballade

I HAVE a tree of the plant of love firmly rooted in my heart; it bears no fruit but fruit of grief, leaves of sorrow, and flowers of unhappiness. But since first it was planted it has grown in root and branch until its unprofitable shade makes every joy beneath it wither. And yet all my strength is not enough to plant another there or root up this.

For long years I have watered it with weeping and with tears so sorrowfully shed, and yet its fruits are in no way better, nor do I find any improvement in them. But none the less I gather them carefully. They are bitter sustenance for my heart, which would be far better lying fallow or vacant than bearing fruit only to harm itself. But Love's order will not allow me to plant another there or root up this.

S'en ce printemps, que les feuilles et flours
Es arbrisseaux percent nouvellement,
Amour vouloit moi faire ce secours
Que les branches qui font empeschement
Il retrenchast du tout entierement
Pour y enter un rainseau de plaisance,
Il jeteroit bourgeons à suffisance,
Joie en istroit, dont il n'est rien plus chier,
Et ne faudroit ja par desesperance
Autre y planter ne celui arrachier.

Ma princesse, ma premiere esperance,
Mon cuer vous sert en dure penitance.
Faites le mal qui l'assaut retrenchier
Et ne souffrez en vostre souvenance
Autre y planter ne celui arrachier.

If in this springtime, when the leaves and flowers are newly budding on the bushes, Love would give me so much help as to cut
clean away the encumbering branches and graft instead a sprig of
happiness, it would make buds in plenty and such joy would grow
from it as cannot be surpassed. Then I should not be driven by
despair to plant another there or root up this.
My Princess, my first hope, for you my heart endures a heavy
penance. Cut away the evil that attacks it, and suffer no one in your
memory to plant another there or root up this.

CHARLES D'ORLÉANS

Ballade

BIEN moustrez, printemps gracieux,
De quel mestier savez servir,
Car hiver fait cuers ennuieux
Et vous les faites resjouir;
Si tost comme il vous voit venir,
Lui et sa meschant retenue
Sont contrains et prestz de fuir
A vostre joyeuse venue.

Hiver fait champs et arbres vieux,
Leurs barbes de neige blanchir,
Et est si froit, ort et pluieux
Qu'emprés le feu couvient croupir.
On ne peut hors des huis issir,
Comme un oiseau qui est en mue;
Mais vous faites tout rajeunir
A vostre joyeuse venue.

Hiver fait le soleil, es cieux,
Du manteau des nues couvrir;
Or maintenant, loué soit Dieux,

Ballade

GRACIOUS Springtime, well you show what trade you can ply,
for Winter makes hearts heavy and you make them rejoice. As soon
as he sees you on your way, he and his evil retinue are forced to
flee in haste at your joyous coming.

Winter makes fields and trees grow old, their beards grow white
with snow. He is so cold, so muddy and rainy that we must crouch
over the fire. A man cannot go out of doors; he is like a bird in the
moult. But you make all things young again at your joyous coming.

Winter hides the sun in the heavens behind the mantle of the
clouds; but now, praised be God, you are come to shine on

Vous estes venue esclercir
Toutes choses et embellir;
Hiver a sa peine perdue,
Car l'an nouveau l'a fait bannir
A vostre joyeuse venue.

Ballade

QUANT je suis couchié en mon lit,
Je ne puis en paix reposer;
Car toute la nuit mon cuer lit
Ou roman de Plaisant Penser,
Et me prie de l'escouter;
Si ne l'ose desobeir
Pour doute de le courroucer:
Ainsi je laisse le dormir.

Ce livre ci est tout escrit
Des fais de ma Dame sans per;
Souvent mon cuer de joie rit,
Quant il les lit ou oit conter;
Car certes tant sont à louer
Qu'il y prent souverain plaisir;
Moi mesme ne m'en puis lasser:
Ainsi je laisse le dormir.

everything and make it beautiful. Winter's work is all in vain,
for the new year has banished him at your joyous coming.

Ballade

WHEN I am lying in my bed I cannot sleep in peace, for all night
long my heart reads from the Romance of Pleasant Thoughts, and
begs me to listen; and I dare not disobey, for fear of angering him:
and so I let sleep go by.

This book is all written about the deeds of my peerless Lady.
Often my heart laughs for joy when he reads them or hears them
recounted; for indeed they are so much to be praised that he takes
the utmost pleasure in them, and I myself can never weary of them:
and so I let sleep go by.

Se mes yeux demandent respit
Par Sommeil qui les vient grever,
Il les tense par grant despit,
Et si ne les peut surmonter;
Il ne cesse de soupirer
A part soi; j'ai lors, sans mentir,
Grant paine de le rapaiser:
Ainsi je laisse le dormir.

Amour, je ne puis gouverner
Mon cuer; car tant vous veut servir
Qu'il ne set jour ne nuit cesser:
Ainsi je laisse le dormir.

Ballade

Se Dieu plaist, briefment la nuee
De ma tristesse passera,
Belle tres loyaument amee,
Et le beau temps se moustrera;
Mais savez vous quant ce sera?
Quant le doux soleil gracieux
De vostre beauté entrera
Par les fenestres de mes yeux.

If my eyes seek a respite because of drowsiness which weighs upon them, my heart reproves them with great scorn, and yet he cannot master them; he sighs to himself unceasingly; then I have in truth the greatest trouble to soothe him again: and so I let sleep go by.

Oh! Love, I cannot rule my heart, for he is so eager to serve you that he can never cease either by day or night: and so I let sleep go by.

Ballade

Please God, soon the cloud of my sadness will pass, my lovely one, so dearly loved, and fine weather will show itself; but do you know when that will be? When the sweet, gracious sunlight of your beauty shines through the windows of my eyes.

Lors la chambre de ma pensee
De grant plaisance reluira
Et sera de joie paree;
Adonc mon cuer s'esveillera,
Qui en dueil dormi long temps a.
Plus ne dormira, se m'aid Dieu,
Quant ceste clarté le ferra
Par les fenestres de mes yeux.

Helas! quant vendra la journee
Qu'ainsi avenir me pourra?
Ma maistresse tres desiree,
Pensez vous que brief avendra?
Car mon cuer tousjours languira
En ennui, sans point avoir mieux,
Jusqu'à tant que ceci verra
Par les fenestres de mes yeux.

De reconfort mon cuer aura
Autant que nul dessous les cieux,
Belle, quant vous regardera
Par les fenestres de mes yeux.

Then the chamber of my thought with great delight will shine, and will be decked with joy; then my heart will awake, which has long slept in grief. It will sleep no longer, so may God help me, when this brightness strikes it through the windows of my eyes.

Alas! when will the day come that this will come to pass for me? My longed-for love, do you think it will be soon? For my heart will always languish in grief, without a sign of recovery, until it sees this [light] through the windows of my eyes.

Solace my heart will have, as much as any heart under the heavens, my love, when it looks out at you through the windows of my eyes.

Ballade

Le premier jour du mois de mai
S'aquitte vers moi grandement;
Car, ainsi qu'à present je n'ai
En mon cuer que dueil et tourment,
Il est aussi pareillement
Troublé, plein de vent et de pluie;
Estre souloit tout autrement
Ou temps qu'ai conneu en ma vie.

Je croi qu'il se met en essai
De m'accompaignier loyaument;
Content m'en tiens, pour dire vrai,
Car meschans, en leur pensement,
Reçoivent grant allegement
Quant en leurs maux ont compaignie;
Essayé l'ai certainement
Ou temps qu'ai conneu en ma vie.

Las! j'ai veu mai joyeux et gai
Et si plaisant à toute gent
Que raconter au long ne sai
Le plaisir et esbatement
Qu'avoit en son commandement;

Ballade

May Day is treating me with great generosity; for just as I have
now nothing in my heart but grief and torment, he too is stormy,
full of wind and rain. How different he used to be in days that I
have known!

I think that he is doing all he can to keep me loyal company, and
I am glad of it, to tell the truth; for the unfortunate find that their
thoughts are greatly lightened when they have a companion in their
ills; I have made certain proof of this in days that I have known.

Alas! I have seen May joyful and gay, and so delightful to everyone that I could not tell all the sport and pleasure that he had at his

Car Amour en son abbaye
Le tenoit chief de son couvent,
Ou temps qu'ai conneu en ma vie.

Le temps va je ne sai comment,
Dieu l'amende prochainement!
Car Plaisance s'est endormie,
Qui souloit vivre liement,
Ou temps qu'ai conneu en ma vie.

Ballade

LE beau soleil, le jour saint Valentin,
Qui aportoit sa chandelle allumee,
N'a pas long temps, entra un bien matin
Priveement en ma chambre fermee.
Celle clarté qu'il avoit aportee
Si m'esveilla du somme de Souci
Où j'avoie toute la nuit dormi
Sur le dur lit d'Ennuieuse Pensee.

bidding; for in the Abbey of Love he was appointed head in days
that I have known.

The world has come to such a pass, may God amend it soon!
For Pleasure is fast asleep, who used to lead a merry life in days
that I have known.

Ballade

NOT long ago, on St Valentine's day, the beauteous sun bearing
his lighted candle stole early in the morning into my closed chamber. The brightness he brought with him roused me from the sleep
of Care, where I had slept all night on the hard bed of Woeful
Thoughts.

Ce jour aussi, pour partir leur butin
Des biens d'Amours, faisoient assemblee
Tous les oiseaux, qui parlant leur latin
Crioient fort, demandant la livree
Que Nature leur avoit ordonnee:
C'estoit d'un per, comme chascun choisi.
Si ne me peu rendormir, pour leur cri,
Sur le dur lit d'Ennuieuse Pensee.

Lors en mouillant de larmes mon coissin
Je regrettai ma dure destinee,
Disant: «Oiseaux, je vous voi en chemin
De tout plaisir et joie desiree;
Chascun de vous a per qui lui agree,
Et point n'en ai, car Mort, qui m'a trahi,
A pris mon per, dont en dueil je langui
Sur le dur lit d'Ennuieuse Pensee.»

Saint Valentin choisissent ceste annee
Ceux et celles de l'amoureux parti;
Seul me tendrai, de confort desgarni,
Sur le dur lit d'Ennuieuse Pensee.

On that day too, all the birds had assembled to share their booty
of Love's treasures; and all were calling out in their own language
for Nature to deliver what she had prescribed for them: that is, a
mate for each as each should choose. And I could not go to sleep
again, for their clamour, on the hard bed of Woeful Thoughts.

Then wetting my pillow with my tears I lamented my hard fate,
saying 'Oh! birds, I see you on the way to every pleasure and joy
you long for. Each of you has a mate to suit his fancy, and I have
none, for Death, who has betrayed me, has borne my mate away,
and so I languish in sorrow, on the hard bed of Woeful Thoughts.'

This year let all those men and women in the ranks of Love
choose each his Valentine; I shall stay alone, bereft of comfort, on
the hard bed of Woeful Thoughts.

Ballade

EN la forest d'Ennuyeuse Tristesse,
Un jour m'avint qu'à par moi cheminoie,
Si encontrai l'Amoureuse Deesse
Qui m'appela, demandant où j'aloie.
Je respondi que par Fortune estoie
Mis en exil en ce bois, long temps a,
Et qu'à bon droit appeler me povoie
L'homme esgaré qui ne set où il va.

En sousriant, par sa tres grant humblesse,
Me respondi: «Ami, se je savoie
Pourquoi tu es mis en ceste destresse,
A mon povoir volentiers t'aideroie;
Car, ja pieça, je mis ton cuer en voie
De tout plaisir, ne sai qui l'en osta;
Or me desplaist qu'à present je te voie
L'homme esgaré qui ne set où il va.»

«Helas! dis je, souveraine Princesse,
Mon fait savez, pourquoi le vous diroie?
C'est par la Mort, qui fait à tous rudesse,

Ballade

IN the forest of Grievous Sadness, one day it chanced I was
journeying alone and I met the Goddess of Love, who called to me,
asking where I was going. I replied that Fortune had long ago
banished me to this wood, and that with good right I could call
myself the Wanderer who does not know his way.

Smiling, in her great humility, she answered me: 'Friend, if I
knew why you are cast into this sorrow, I would willingly do all
I could to help you; for some time ago I set your heart on the road
to all delight; I do not know who has led it astray; now it distresses
me to see that you are the Wanderer who does not know his way.'

'Alas!' I said, 'sovereign Princess, you know my story, why
should I tell it to you? It is the fault of Death, who injures all men,

Qui m'a tollu celle que tant amoie,
En qui estoit tout l'espoir que j'avoie,
Qui me guidoit; si bien m'acompagna
En son vivant que point ne me trouvoie
L'homme esgaré qui ne set où il va.

«Aveugle suis, ne sai où aler doie;
De mon baston, afin que ne forvoie,
Je vais tastant mon chemin ça et là;
C'est grant pitié qu'il couvient que je soie
L'homme esgaré qui ne set où il va.»

Ballade

TROP long temps vous voi sommeillier,
Mon cuer, en dueil et desplaisir;
Vueilliez vous, ce jour, esveillier:
Alons au bois le mai cueillir,
Pour la coustume maintenir.
Nous orrons des oiseaux le glai
Dont ils font les bois retentir,
Ce premier jour du mois de Mai.

who has taken from me the one I loved so much, in whom was all the hope I had, who guided me; she travelled by my side as long as she lived, so that I never found myself the Wanderer who does not know his way.

'I am a blind man, I do not know which way to go; I go here and there, feeling my way with my stick lest I go quite astray. How sad it is that I should have to be the Wanderer who does not know his way.'

Ballade

TOO long I see you slumbering, my heart, in grief and sadness; awake, I beg of you, today, and let us go to the woods to gather the may, to keep the custom. We shall hear the warbling of the birds, making the woods resound, on this first day of May.

Le Dieu d'Amours est coustumier,
A ce jour, de feste tenir,
Pour amoureux cuers festier
Qui desirent de le servir;
Pour ce, fait les arbres couvrir
De fleurs, et les champs de vert gay,
Pour la feste plus embellir,
Ce premier jour du mois de Mai.

Bien sai, mon cuer, que faux Dangier
Vous fait mainte paine souffrir;
Car il vous fait trop esloignier
Celle qui est vostre desir.
Pour tant vous faut esbat querir;
Mieux conseillier je ne vous sai
Pour vostre douleur amendrir,
Ce premier jour du mois de Mai.

Ma dame, mon seul souvenir,
En cent jours n'auroie loisir
De vous raconter, tout au vrai,
Le mal qui tient mon cuer martir,
Ce premier jour du mois de Mai.

The God of Love is accustomed on this day to hold his feast to entertain the hearts of lovers who desire to serve him. For this he has the trees covered with blossom, and the fields with gay green, the more to decorate his festival on this first day of May.

I know well, my heart, that false Disdain makes you suffer many a torment, for he has too far removed from you her who is your desire; and therefore you should seek some pastime. I cannot give you better counsel, to lessen your grief on this first day of May.

My lady, my only memory, in a hundred days I should not have time enough to tell you truly all the ill that keeps my heart in torment on this first day of May.

Ballade

Je fu en fleur ou temps passé d'enfance,
Et puis après devins fruit en jeunesse;
Lors m'abati de l'arbre de Plaisance,
Vert et non meur, Folie, ma maistresse.
Et pour cela Raison, qui tout redresse
A son plaisir, sans tort ou mesprison,
M'a à bon droit, par sa tres grant sagesse,
Mis pour meurir ou feurre de prison.

En ce j'ai fait longue continuance,
Sans estre mis à l'essor de largesse;
J'en suis content et tiens que, sans doutance,
C'est pour le mieux, combien que par paresse
Deviens fletri et tire vers vieillesse.
Assez esteint est en moi le tison
De sot desir, puis qu'ai esté en presse
Mis pour meurir ou feurre de prison.

Ballade

I was in blossom in the long-past days of childhood, then afterwards I became fruit in my youth; then from the tree of Delight,
green and unripe, my mistress Folly shook me down. And therefore Reason, who amends all things at her pleasure, without any
wrong or injury, rightly, in her great wisdom, laid me to ripen in
the straw of prison.

There I have made a long sojourn, without being put in the
fresh air of liberty; I am glad of it, and I hold that without a doubt
it is for the best, although through idleness I am becoming withered
and tending towards old age. The spark of foolish desire is almost
quenched in me since I have been shut away and laid to ripen on the
straw of prison.

Dieu nous doint paix, car c'est ma desirance!
Adonc serai en l'eaue de Liesse
Tost refreschi, et au soleil de France
Bien nettié du moisi de Tristesse;
J'attens bon temps, endurant en humblesse,
Car j'ai espoir que Dieu ma guerison
Ordonnera; pour ce m'a sa hautesse
Mis pour meurir ou feurre de prison.

Fruit suis d'hiver qui a meins de tendresse
Que fruit d'esté; si suis en garnison,
Pour amolir ma trop verde duresse,
Mis pour meurir ou feurre de prison.

Ballade

BALLADES, chançons et complaintes
Sont pour moi mises en oubli,
Car ennui et pensees maintes
M'ont tenu long temps endormi.
Nonpourtant, pour passer souci,
Essaier vueil se je sauroie
Rimer, ainsi que je souloie.

God give us peace, for that is all my wish. Then I shall soon be refreshed in the water of happiness, and in the sunshine of France well cleansed of the mildew of sorrow. I wait for fair weather with humble endurance, for I hope that God will ordain my recovery; it was for this that the Almighty laid me to ripen on the straw of prison.

I am a winter fruit, less soft than fruits of summer, and I am stored away to mellow my too-green hardness, and laid to ripen on the straw of prison.

Ballade

BALLADES, songs, and complaints have been long out of my mind, for sorrow and many cares have kept me long benumbed. Nevertheless, to chase my cares away, I will try if I am able to rhyme as

Au moins j'en ferai mon povoir,
Combien que je connois et sai
Que mon langage trouverai
Tout enrouillié de Nonchaloir.

Plaisans paroles sont estaintes
En moi qui deviens rassoti;
Au fort, je vendrai aux attaintes
Quant beau parler m'aura failli.
Pour quoi pri ceux qui m'ont ouï
Langagier, quant pieça j'estoie
Jeune, nouvel et plein de joie,
Que vueillent excusé m'avoir.
Onques mais je ne me trouvai
Si rude, car je suis, pour vrai,
Tout enrouillié de Nonchaloir.

Amoureux ont paroles paintes
Et langage frois et joli:
Plaisance, dont ils sont acointes,
Parle pour eux; en ce parti
J'ai esté, or n'est plus ainsi;
Alors de beau parler trouvoie
A bon marchié tant que vouloie;
Si ai despendu mon savoir,

I used to do. At least I will do my best, although I know and
acknowledge that I shall find my words all rusted by Indifference.
   Delightful words are all dried up in me as I become old and
foolish, but at least I will achieve my end, even if the gift of speech
proves to have failed me. Therefore I beg all those who heard me
spinning words, long ago when I was young, fresh, and full of joy,
that they will excuse my shortcomings. Never before have I known
myself so rough of speech, for in truth I am all rusted by Indifference.
   Lovers have painted words and fresh and lively language; the
pleasures they frequent speak for them; of this company I have
been, but now it is no longer so. Then I found fair words with
greatest ease at will; and so I have squandered all my skill, and if I

Et s'un peu espargnié en ai,
Il est, quant vendra à l'essai,
Tout enrouillié de Nonchaloir.

Mon jubilé faire devroie,
Mais on diroit que me rendroie
Sans coup ferir, car Bon Espoir
M'a dit que renouvellerai;
Pour ce, mon cuer fourbir ferai
Tout enrouillié de Nonchaloir.

Ballade

EN tirant d'Orleans à Blois,
L'autre jour par eaue venoie.
Si rencontrai, par plusieurs fois,
Vaisseaux, ainsi que je passoie,
Qui cingloient leur droite voie
Et alloient legierement,
Pour ce qu'eurent, comme veoie,
A plaisir et à gré le vent.

have saved a little of it, when it is put to the test it will prove all rusted by Indifference.

I ought to be celebrating my jubilee [age 50: immunity from love], but people would say I was surrendering without striking a blow; for Good Hope has told me that I shall renew my youth. Therefore I will burnish up my heart all rusted by Indifference.

Ballade

MAKING from Orleans to Blois the other day, I was travelling by river, and I met, time after time, vessels, as I passed, sailing straight before the wind and scudding lightly along, because they had, as I saw, a favourable wind at will.

Mon cuer, Penser et moi, nous trois,
Les regardames à grant joie;
Et dit mon cuer à basse vois:
«Volentiers en ce point feroie:
De Confort la voile tendroie,
Se je cuidoie seurement
Avoir, ainsi que je voudroie,
A plaisir et à gré le vent.

«Mais je treuve, le plus des mois,
L'eaue de Fortune si quoie
Quant ou bateau du monde vois
Que, s'avirons d'Espoir n'avoie,
Souvent ou chemin demouroie
En trop grant ennui longuement;
Pour neant en vain attendroie
A plaisir et à gré le vent.»

Les nefs dont ci devant parloie
Montoient, et je descendoie
Contre les vagues de Tourment;
Quant il lui plaira, Dieu m'envoie
A plaisir et à gré le vent.

My heart, my thought, and I, we three, watched them with great
joy, and my heart murmured: 'I should like to do like that: I would
spread the sail of comfort if I could only be sure of having at my
command a favourable wind at will.

'But I find, most months of the year, Fortune's waters so
motionless as I voyage in the ship of the world that, if I had not
Hope for oars, often I should be quite becalmed, lingering in the
midst of troubles; and all for nothing I should await in vain a
favourable wind at will.'

The ships I spoke of just now were going upstream, and I was
coming down against the waves of Trouble. When it shall please
Him, may God send me a favourable wind at will.

Ballade

Par les fenestres de mes yeux
Le chaut d'Amour souloit passer;
Mais maintenant que deviens vieux,
Pour la chambre de mon penser
En esté freschement garder,
Fermees les ferai tenir,
Laissant le chaut du jour aler
Avant que je les face ouvrir.

Aussi en hiver le pluieux,
Qui vens et brouillars fait lever,
L'air d'Amour epidimieux
Souvent par mi se vient bouter;
Si faut les pertuis estouper
Par où pourroit mon cuer ferir;
Le temps verrai plus net et cler
Avant que je les face ouvrir.

Desormais en sains et seurs lieux
Ordonne mon cuer demourer,
Et par Nonchaloir, pour le mieux,
Mon medecin, soi gouverner;

Ballade

Through the windows of my eyes the heat of Love was wont to pass; but now that I am growing old, in order to keep the chamber of my thought cool in summer, I shall have them kept closed, letting the heat of the day go by before I have them opened.

In rainy winter, too, which gives rise to winds and fog, the contagious air of Love often forces its way indoors; so I must stop all the cracks through which it could strike at my heart; I'll wait to see the weather bright and clear before I have them opened.

Henceforth I command my heart to dwell in safe and healthy places, and to follow for his good the advice of my doctor,

S'Amour à mes huis vient hurter,
Pour vouloir vers mon cuer venir,
Seurté lui faudra me donner
Avant que je les face ouvrir.

Amour, vous venistes frapper
Pieça mon cuer sans menacer;
Or ai fait mes logis batir
Si fors que n'i pourrez entrer
Avant que je les face ouvrir.

Ballade

PRIEZ pour paix, douce Vierge Marie,
Roine des cieux et du monde Maistresse,
Faites prier, par vostre courtoisie,
Saints et saintes, et prenez vostre adresse
Vers vostre fils, requerant sa hautesse
Qu'il lui plaise son peuple regarder,
Que de son sang a voulu racheter,
En deboutant guerre qui tout desvoie;
De prieres ne vous veuilliez lasser:
Priez pour paix, le vrai tresor de joie!

Indifference; if Love comes knocking at my doors, wishing to enter and approach my heart, he will have to give me some security before I have them opened.

Love, long ago you came and struck my heart without a warning. Now I have had my houses made so strong that you will not be able to get into them until I have them opened.

Ballade

PRAY for peace, sweet Virgin Mary, Queen of the skies and Mistress of the world, and of your courtesy beg all the saints to pray, and take your way towards your Son, beseeching his high majesty to deign to look down on his people whom he has wished to ransom with his blood, and drive away war, which leads all things astray. Pray without wearying, we beg of you; oh! pray for peace, the true treasure of joy.

Priez, prelas et gens de sainte vie,
Religieux ne dormez en paresse,
Priez, maistres et tous suivans clergie,
Car par guerre faut que l'estude cesse;
Moustiers destruis sont sans qu'on les redresse,
Le service de Dieu vous faut laissier.
Quant ne povez en repos demourer,
Priez si fort que briefment Dieu vous oie;
L'Eglise voult à ce vous ordonner:
Priez pour paix, le vrai tresor de joie!

Priez, princes qui avez seigneurie,
Rois, ducs, contes, barons pleins de noblesse,
Gentils hommes avec chevalerie,
Car meschans gens surmontent gentillesse;
En leurs mains ont toute vostre richesse,
Debats les font en haut estat monter,
Vous le povez chascun jour veoir au cler,
Et sont riches de vos biens et monnoie
Dont vous deussiez le peuple supporter:
Priez pour paix, le vrai tresor de joie!

Pray, you prelates and men of holy life; monks, do not slumber in idleness; pray, you scholars and all who follow learning, for because of war study must cease; churches are ruined and never rebuilt; you have to abandon the service of God. Since you cannot live undisturbed, pray so hard that God will hear you quickly; it was for this that the Church ordained you. Oh! pray for peace, the true treasure of joy.

Pray, you princes who have lordship, kings, dukes, counts, barons, full of nobility, men of gentle birth and chivalry; for evil men are triumphing over gentility. They hold in their hands all your riches; strife sets them up in high estate, as you can clearly see every day, and they are rich with your goods and money, with which you should be giving support to the people. Oh! pray for peace, the true treasure of joy.

Priez, peuple qui souffrez tirannie;
Car vos seigneurs sont en telle foiblesse
Qu'ils ne peuent vous garder par maistrie,
Ne vous aidier en vostre grant destresse;
Loyaux marchans, la selle si vous blesse
Fort sur le dos; chascun vous vient presser
Et ne povez marchandise mener,
Car vous n'avez seur passage ne voie,
Et maint peril vous couvient il passer:
Priez pour paix, le vrai tresor de joie!

Priez, galans joyeux en compaignie,
Qui despendre desirez à largesse,
Guerre vous tient la bourse desgarnie;
Priez, amans, qui voulez en liesse
Servir Amour, car guerre, par rudesse,
Vous destourbe de vos dames hanter,
Qui maintes fois fait leurs vouloirs tourner;
Et quant tenez le bout de la courroie,
Un estrangier si le vous vient oster:
Priez pour paix, le vrai tresor de joie!

Pray, humble folk who suffer tyranny, for your lords are so en-
feebled that they cannot protect you by their authority or help you
in your great distress. Honest merchants, the saddle galls your
backs so cruelly; you are the victims of everyone's extortions, and
you cannot convey your goods because you have no sure passage
or road, and many a peril do you have to brave. Oh! pray for peace,
the true treasure of joy.

Pray, gallants who rejoice in company and wish to spend your
money freely: war keeps your purses thin. Pray, lovers who want
to serve Love in gladness, for rough war snatches you from your
ladies' company and often makes them change their fancy, and
when you have almost made a conquest a stranger comes and robs
you of it. Oh! pray for peace, the true treasure of joy.

Dieu tout puissant nous vueille conforter!
Toutes choses en terre, ciel et mer,
Priez vers lui que brief en tout pourvoie;
En lui seul est de tous maux amender:
Priez pour paix, le vrai tresor de joie!

Rondeau

LE temps a laissié son manteau
De vent, de froidure et de pluie,
Et s'est vestu de broderie,
De soleil luyant, cler et beau.

Il n'y a beste ne oiseau
Qu'en son jargon ne chante ou crie:
«Le temps a laissié son manteau.»

Riviere, fontaine et ruisseau
Portent, en livree jolie,
Gouttes d'argent d'orfeverie;
Chascun s'abille de nouveau:
Le temps a laissié son manteau.

May the all-powerful God be pleased to comfort us! Let everything that is in earth or sky or sea pray to Him that soon He may put all things right; in Him alone is the power to amend all ills. Oh! pray for peace, the true treasure of joy.

Rondeau

NATURE has cast her winter cloak of wind and cold and rain, and dressed herself in embroidery of clear and lovely sunshine.

There is not a single bird or beast but sings or shouts in his own tongue, 'Nature has cast her winter cloak.'

Every river, spring, and stream puts on a splendid livery of silver drops of jewellery, and everyone is freshly clad: Nature has cast her winter cloak.

Rondeau

LES fourriers d'Esté sont venus
Pour appareillier son logis,
Et ont fait tendre ses tapis
De fleurs et verdure tissus.

En estendant tapis velus
De vert herbe par le pays,
Les fourriers d'Esté sont venus.

Cuers d'ennui pieça morfondus,
Dieu merci, sont sains et jolis.
Allez vous en, prenez pays,
Hiver; vous ne demourrez plus:
Les fourriers d'Esté sont venus.

Rondeau

EN regardant ces belles fleurs
Que le temps nouveau d'amours prie,
Chascune d'elles s'ajolie
Et farde de plaisans couleurs.

Rondeau

SUMMER's harbingers have come to make his dwelling ready, and they have had his carpets laid, woven of flowers and greenery.

Spreading velvet carpets of green grass through the land, Summer's harbingers have come.

Hearts that but now were moping in dullness, thanks be to God, are sound and gay. Be off with you, begone elsewhere, Winter; you shall stay no longer: Summer's harbingers have come.

Rondeau

WHILE looking at these lovely flowers to whom the Spring pays court, [we see] each one adorn herself and paint herself with splendid colours.

Tant embasmees sont d'odeurs
Qu'il n'est cuer qui ne rajeunie
En regardant ces belles fleurs.

Les oiseaus deviennent danseurs
Dessus mainte branche flourie,
Et font joyeuse chanterie
De contres, deschans et teneurs,
En regardant ces belles fleurs.

Rondeau

ALLEZ vous en, allez, allez,
Soussy, Soing et Merencolie!
Me cuidez vous, toute ma vie,
Gouverner, comme fait avez?

Je vous promets que non ferez:
Raison aura sur vous maistrie.
Allez vous en, allez, allez,
Soussy, Soing et Merencolie!

They are so fragrant with perfume that every heart grows younger while looking at these lovely flowers.

The birds turn dancers on many a flowery branch and make a joyful carolling – altos, descants, and tenors – while looking at these lovely flowers.

Rondeau

AWAY with you, begone, begone, Grief, Care, and Melancholy! Do you think to rule me all your life, as you have done?

I promise you, you shall not do it: Reason shall have the upper hand of you. Away with you, begone, begone, Grief, Care, and Melancholy!

Se jamais plus vous retournez
Avecques vostre compaignie,
Je pri à Dieu qu'il vous maudie,
Et ce par qui vous revendrez:
Allez vous en, allez, allez,
Soussy, Soing et Merencolie!

Rondeau

DEDANS mon Livre de Pensee,
J'ai trouvé escrivant mon cuer
La vraie histoire de douleur,
De larmes toute enluminee,

En defassant la tres amee
Image de plaisant douceur,
Dedans mon Livre de Pensee.

Helas! où l'a mon cuer trouvee?
Les grosses gouttes de sueur
Lui saillent, de peine et labeur
Qu'il y prent, et nuit et journee,
Dedans mon Livre de Pensee.

If ever you come back again, you and your wretched crew, I
pray to God that he will curse both you and whatever brings you
back. Away with you, begone, begone, Grief, Care, and Melancholy!

Rondeau

IN my Book of Thoughts I found my heart writing the true story
of grief, all illuminated with tears.

Quite effacing the beloved picture of pleasant sweetness in my
Book of Thoughts.

Alas! where can my heart have found this story? Great drops of
sweat pour from him, for the toil and labour that he spends both
night and day on my Book of Thoughts.

Rondeau

QUANT j'ai ouy le tabourin
Sonner pour s'en aller au mai,
En mon lit fait n'en ai effrai
Ne levé mon chef du coissin,

En disant: il est trop matin,
Un peu je me rendormirai,
Quant j'ai ouy le tabourin.

Jeunes gens partent leur butin:
De Nonchaloir m'acointerai,
A lui je m'abutinerai;
Trouvé l'ai plus prochain voisin
Quant j'ai ouy le tabourin.

Rondeau

NE hurtez plus à l'uis de ma Pensee,
Soing et Souci, sans tant vous traveiller,
Car elle dort et ne veut s'esveiller;
Toute la nuit en peine a despensee.

Rondeau

WHEN I heard the drum sounding a call to go and fetch the may,
I did not start up out of bed nor lift my head up from the pillow,
  Saying: it is still too early, I shall sleep a little longer – when I
heard the drum.
  Let the young folk share their spoils: I shall make friends with
Indifference; he is the one who shall share mine; for him I found
my nearest neighbour when I heard the drum.

Rondeau

KNOCK no more at the door of my Thought, Care and Trouble,
cease your turmoil. For he is asleep and does not wish to wake;
he has spent all the night in pain.

En dangier est, s'elle n'est bien pensee:
Cessez, cessez, laissez la sommeiller.
Ne hurtez plus à l'uis de ma Pensee,
Soing et Souci, sans tant vous traveiller.

Pour la guerir Bon Espoir a pensee
Medecine qu'a fait appareiller;
Lever ne peut son chief de l'oreiller,
Tant qu'en repos se soit recompensee.
Ne hurtez plus à l'uis de ma Pensee.

Rondeau

LES en voulez vous garder
Ces rivieres de courir
Et grues prendre et tenir
Quant haut les veez voler?

A telles choses muser
Voit on fols souvent servir:
Les en voulez vous garder
Ces rivieres de courir?

He is in danger if he is not well tended. Stop! stop! and let him sleep. Knock no more on the door of my Thought, Care and Trouble, cease your turmoil.

To cure him, Good Hope has thought of a medicine which she has had prepared. He cannot lift his head up from his pillow until he has refreshed himself with sleep. Knock no more on the door of my Thought.

Rondeau

WOULD you stop them, these running rivers, or catch and hold cranes when you see them flying high in the air?

To dream of such things is a pastime for fools; would you stop them, these running rivers?

Laissez le temps tel passer
Que Fortune veut souffrir,
Et les choses avenir
Que l'on ne set destourber.
Les en voulez vous garder?

Chanson

N'est elle de tous biens garnie,
Celle que j'aime loyaument?
Il m'est advis, par mon serment,
Que sa pareille n'a en vie.

Qu'en dites vous? je vous en prie,
Que vous en semble vraiement?
N'est elle de tous biens garnie,
Celle que j'aime loyaument?

Soit qu'elle dance, chante ou rie,
Ou face quelque esbatement,
Faites-en loyal jugement
Sans faveur et sans flaterie:
N'est elle de tous biens garnie?

Let time pass by just as Fortune wills it, and let things happen that you cannot prevent. Would you stop them?

Song

Is she not adorned with every virtue, she that I truly love? It's my belief, upon my oath, that she has not her match on earth.

What do you say? pray tell me, what do you really think of her? Is she not adorned with every virtue, she that I truly love?

Whether she's dancing, singing, laughing, however she disports herself, judge of her fairly, without favour or flattery: is she not adorned with every virtue?

Chanson

JE ne prise point tels baisiers
Qui sont donnés par contenance,
Ou par maniere d'acointance:
Trop de gens en sont parçonniers.

On en peut avoir par milliers,
A bon marchié grant abondance.
Je ne prise point tels baisiers
Qui sont donnés par contenance.

Mais savez vous lesquels sont chiers?
Les privés, venans par plaisance;
Tous autres ne sont, sans doutance,
Que pour festier estrangiers.
Je ne prise point tels baisiers.

Song

I THINK nothing of such kisses as are given by convention, as a matter of politeness: far too many people share them.

You can have them by the thousand, cheap enough and in abundance. I think nothing of such kisses as are given by convention.

Do you know the ones I value? Secret ones, bestowed in pleasure; all the rest are doubtless nothing but a way of greeting strangers. I think nothing of such kisses!

VAILLANT

Rondeau

Bonnes gens, j'ai perdu ma dame:
Qui la trouvera, sur mon ame,
Combien qu'elle soit belle et bonne,
De tres bon cuer je la lui donne,
Sans en prendre debat à ame.

La belle sait tres bien sa gamme,
Dieu sait comme loyaument ame.
Pour Dieu, qui l'avra mot ne sonne.
Bonnes gens, j'ai perdu ma dame.

Gardez la bien, la gentifame,
Que nul ne la blesse ou entame;
Car, par Dieu, la gente mignonne
Est à chascun douce personne.
Helas! povre et desert me clame!
Bonnes gens, j'ai perdu ma dame.

Rondeau

Good people, I have lost my lady. To him who finds her, on my soul, although she is both fair and kind, I give her up with all my heart, without raising any dispute with anyone.

The lady has all her graces at command; God knows how loyally she loves! For Heaven's sake, let him who has her never breathe a word. Good people, I have lost my lady.

Look after her well, the gentle lady, let no one hurt or wound her, for by Heaven! the pretty darling is sweetness itself to all men. Now 'woe is me' must be my cry: good people I have lost my lady.

ANONYMOUS RONDEAUX

Depuis deux ou trois jours en ça
S'en est allé mon bel ami,
Sans ce qu'il ait parlé à mi.
Helas! qui me confortera?

Ne sai se brief retournera,
Mais il m'a mis en grant souci
Depuis deux ou trois jours en ça.

Demander le me conviendra
A ceux qui sont allez o lui;
Car par ma foi je vous affi
Qu'onques mieux mon cuer ne l'ama
Depuis deux ou trois jours en ça.

Ne me mettez en oubli,
Mon seul bien et reconfort,
Qu'estes de moy le plus fort
Amé de ce monde ci.

Mon tant gent loyal ami,
Se vous ne voulez ma mort,
Ne me mettez en oubli.

These last few days my handsome lover has been away, and he left without a word to me. Alas! who will console me?

I do not know if he will come back soon, but he has put me into great distress these last few days.

I must ask news of him from those who went with him; for by my faith I assure you that my heart never loved him so much as these last few days.

Do not forget me, my only wealth and comfort, for I love you the best of all the world.

My most noble, loyal lover, if you do not wish to kill me, do not forget me.

Mais d'une chose vous pri:
Tous dis soions d'un accort,
Sans plus croire nul raport;
Puis que seul vous ai choisi,
Ne me mettez en oubli.

LA fiance que j'ai en vous,
Mon ami seul, sans autre eslire,
Me fait oublier le martire
Que j'ai, et tout mon grant courroux.

Car une fois nous verrons nous;
Mais qu'est ce qui le me fait dire?
La fiance que j'ai en vous.

Eh! par Dieu, voire, et malgré tous
Ceux qui l'ont voulu contredire;
Autre que Dieu ne nous peut nuire.
C'est de tout mon bien le recours,
La fiance que j'ai en vous.

But one thing I beg of you: let us always be agreed, and let us never again believe any rumour; since you only are my choice, do not forget me.

THE trust I have in you, my only love, chosen above all others, makes me forget my suffering and all my great sorrow.

For some day we shall meet again; but what makes me say so? The trust I have in you.

I swear by God we shall, and despite all those who have wished to prevent it; no one else but God can hurt us. This is the source of all my comfort: the trust I have in you.

FRANÇOIS VILLON

LE TESTAMENT

... Pour ce que foible je me sens
Trop plus de biens que de santé,
Tant que je suis en mon plein sens,
Si peu que Dieu m'en a presté,
(Car d'autre ne l'ai emprunté!)
J'ai ce testament tres estable
Fait, de derniere volonté,
Seul pour tout et irrevocable.

Escrit l'ai l'an soixante et un,
Lors que le roi me delivra
De la dure prison de Meung,
Et que vie me recouvra,
Dont suis, tant que mon cuer vivra,
Tenu vers lui m'humilier,
Ce que ferai tant qu'il movra:
Bienfait ne se doit oublier.

Or est vrai qu'après plains et pleurs
Et angoisseux gemissemens,
Après tristesses et douleurs,
Labeurs et griefs cheminemens,

LAST WILL AND TESTAMENT

... Since I feel myself to be weak (and even weaker in goods than in health), while I am still in my right mind – such little mind as God has lent me (for I have borrowed it from none other!) – I have made this firm testament of my last will, irrevocably, once for all.

I have written it in the year 'sixty-one, when the king delivered me from the cruel prison of Meung and gave me life again, for which, as long as my heart lives, I am bound to bow down before him, as I shall as long as it beats. Benefits should not be forgotten.

Now it is true that after lamentations, tears, and groans of anguish, after griefs and sorrows, toils, and weary journeyings,

Travail mes lubres sentemens,
Aiguisiés comme une pelote,
M'ouvrit plus que tous les Commens
D'Averroÿs sur Aristote.

Combien, au plus fort de mes maux,
En cheminant sans croix ne pile,
Dieu, qui les pelerins d'Emmaus
Conforta, ce dit l'Evangile,
Me monstra une bonne ville
Et pourveue du don d'esperance;
Combien que pecheur soie vile,
Rien ne hait que perseverance.

Je suis pecheur, je le sai bien;
Pourtant ne veut pas Dieu ma mort,
Mais convertisse et vive en bien,
Et tout autre que pechié mort.
Combien qu'en pechié soie mort,
Dieu vit, et sa misericorde,
Se conscience me remort,
Par sa grace pardon m'accorde.

Suffering gave life to my shifting thoughts, till then no sharper than a ball, much more than all the Commentaries of Averroes on Aristotle.

Nevertheless, in the depths of my misfortunes, as I was journeying without a penny, God who comforted the pilgrims at Emmaus, as the Gospel says, showed me a good town provided with the gift of hope; although I am a vile sinner, God hates nothing but obduracy.

I am a sinner, well I know it; nevertheless, God does not desire my death, but that I should repent and live virtuously, and every other man that Sin has his teeth into. And though I am dead in sin, God lives, and His mercy – if conscience pricks me – grants me forgiveness through His grace.

Et, comme le noble Rommant
De la Rose dit et confesse
En son premier commencement
Qu'on doit jeune cuer en jeunesse,
Quant on le voit vieil en vieillesse,
Excuser, helas! il dit voir;
Ceux donc qui me font telle presse
En meurté ne me voudroient veoir.

Se, pour ma mort, le bien publique
D'aucune chose vausist mieux,
A mourir comme un homme inique
Je me jugeasse, ainsi m'aid Dieux!
Griefs ne fais à jeunes n'à vieux,
Soie sur piés ou soie en biere:
Les mons ne bougent de leurs lieux
Pour un povre, n'avant n'arriere.

Ou temps qu'Alixandre regna,
Un hom nommé Diomedès
Devant lui on lui amena,

And as the noble Romance of the Rose states and admits at its
first beginning that we should overlook the sins a man has committed in his youth when we see him in old age, alas! it speaks the
truth, and that is why those that are so hard on me do not wish to
see me reach ripeness.

If by my death the public good would benefit in any way I
should condemn myself to die like a criminal, so may God help
me! But I do no harm to young or old, whether I am alive or in my
grave. The mountains do not move from their places, backwards or
forwards, for a poor man.

In the days when Alexander reigned, a man called Diomedes was
brought before him, thumbs and fingers fettered like a thief, for he

Engrillonné pouces et dès
Comme un larron, car il fut des
Escumeurs que voions courir;
Si fut mis devant ce cadès,
Pour estre jugié à mourir.

L'empereur si l'araisonna:
«Pourquoi es tu larron en mer?»
L'autre response lui donna:
«Pourquoi larron me fais nommer?
Pour ce qu'on me voit escumer
En une petiote fuste?
Se comme toi me peusse armer,
Comme toi empereur je feusse.

«Mais que veux tu? De ma fortune,
Contre qui ne puis bonnement,
Qui si faussement me fortune,
Me vient tout ce gouvernement.
Excuse moi aucunement
Et sache qu'en grant povreté
(Ce mot se dit communement)
Ne gist pas grande loyauté.»

was one of those pirates that we see ranging the seas and was brought before this captain to be condemned to death.

The emperor addressed him thus: 'Why are you a robber on the high seas?' and the other replied: 'Why do you call me a robber? Because you see me scouring the seas in my little skiff? If I could arm myself like you, I should be an emperor like you.

'But what can you expect? This way of life comes to me from my fate, against which I am helpless, since it endows me with so poor a fortune. Hold me somewhat excused, and know that great poverty, as people say, does not make for great honesty.'

Quant l'empereur eut remiré
De Diomedès tout le dit:
«Ta fortune te muerai
Mauvaise en bonne» si lui dit.
Si fist il. Onc puis ne mesdit
A personne, mais fut vrai homme;
Valere pour vrai le baudit,
Qui fut nommé le Grant à Rome.

Se Dieu m'eust donné rencontrer
Un autre piteux Alixandre
Qui m'eust fait en bon eur entrer,
Et lors qui m'eust veu condescendre
A mal, estre ars et mis en cendre
Jugié me feusse de ma vois.
Necessité fait gens mesprendre
Et faim saillir le loup du bois.

Je plains le temps de ma jeunesse,
Ouquel j'ai plus qu'autre gallé
Jusqu'à l'entree de vieillesse,
Qui son partement m'a celé.

When the emperor had considered all that Diomedes had to say, he said to him: 'I will change your fortune from bad to good.' And so he did. Never more did Diomedes [so much as] speak ill of anyone, but was a true man. Valerius gives it out as true, he who was called 'the Great' in Rome.

If God had permitted me to meet another merciful Alexander to set me on the road to good fortune, and if anyone after that had seen me stoop to wrongdoing, I should with my own voice have condemned myself to be burnt to ashes. Necessity makes men take to evil ways, and hunger brings the wolf out of the forest.

I regret the days of my youth, when I enjoyed myself more than another man, right up to the threshold of old age, while youth was slipping away. He did not leave on foot, nor yet on horseback;

Il ne s'en est à pié allé
N'a cheval: helas! comment don?
Soudainement s'en est volé
Et ne m'a laissié quelque don.

Allé s'en est, et je demeure,
Povre de sens et de savoir,
Triste, failli, plus noir que meure,
Qui n'ai ne cens, rente, n'avoir;
Des miens le mendre, je dis voir,
De me desavouer s'avance,
Oubliant naturel devoir
Par faute d'un peu de chevance.

Si ne crains avoir despendu
Par friander ne par leschier;
Par trop amer n'ai rien vendu
Qu'amis me puissent reprochier,
Au moins qui leur couste moult chier.
Je le dis et ne croi mesdire;
De ce me puis je revenchier:
Qui n'a mesfait ne le doit dire.

alas! how then? He suddenly flew away, and left no gift for me behind him.

He is gone, and I am left, poor in wisdom and in knowledge, sad, worn out, blacker than a mulberry, with neither property, income, nor money. The least of my relations, I can truly say, hastens to disown me, forgetting his natural obligations because I lack a few worldly goods.

And I need have no regrets for having spent money on feasting and dissipation; and too much loving has not made me sell anything that my friends could reproach me with, nothing at least that cost them very dear. I think I can say that without lying; from that accusation I can defend myself; he who has done no wrong need not confess.

Bien est verté que j'ai amé
Et ameroie volentiers;
Mais triste cuer, ventre affamé
Qui n'est rassasié au tiers
M'oste des amoureux sentiers.
Au fort, quelqu'un s'en recompense
Qui est rempli sur les chantiers!
Car la dance vient de la pance.

Hé! Dieu, se j'eusse estudié
Ou temps de ma jeunesse folle
Et à bonnes meurs dedié,
J'eusse maison et couche molle.
Mais quoi? Je fuyoie l'escole
Comme fait le mauvais enfant.
En escrivant ceste parole,
A peu que le cuer ne me fent.

Le dit du Sage trop lui fis
Favorable (bien en puis mais!)
Qui dit: «Esjouis toi, mon fils,
En ton adolescence»; mais

It is very true that I have loved, and would willingly love again, but a sad heart and a famished stomach, not a third part filled, keep me from the paths of love. Ah! well, let someone with a well-filled belly profit from my absence, for a man can't dance on an empty stomach.

Oh! God, if only I had studied in the days of my foolish youth, and taken up good habits, I should now have a home and a soft bed. But alas! I ran away from school like a naughty child. As I write these words my heart is fit to break.

I gave the Sage too much credit (much good did it do me!) when he says, 'Rejoice, oh! young man in thy youth'; but elsewhere he

Ailleurs sert bien d'un autre mes,
Car «Jeunesse et adolescence»
C'est son parler, ne moins ne mais,
«Ne sont qu'abus et ignorance.»

Mes jours s'en sont allés errant
Comme, dit Job, d'une touaille
Font les filets, quant tisserant
En son poing tient ardente paille:
Lors, s'il y a nul bout qui saille,
Soudainement il le ravit.
Si ne crains plus que rien m'assaille,
Car à la mort tout s'assouvit.

Où sont les gracieux gallans
Que je suivoie ou temps jadis,
Si bien chantans, si bien parlans,
Si plaisans en fais et en dis?
Les aucuns sont morts et roidis,
D'eux n'est il plus rien maintenant:
Repos aient en Paradis,
Et Dieu sauve le remenant!

serves up a very different dish, for 'Childhood and youth are vanity', these are his words, neither more nor less.

My days have flown by, as Job says, like the threads of the weaver's cloth, when he holds in his hand a burning straw: then if any end of thread projects he has it off in a moment. And I have no fear now of anything that may assail me, for Death pays all scores.

Where are those handsome gallants whose company I used to keep in the old days, singing so true, speaking so fair, pleasant in all they did and said? Some of them are dead and stiff, nothing now is left of them; may they have rest in Paradise, and God save those that are left!

Et les autres sont devenus,
Dieu merci! grans seigneurs et maistres;
Les autres mendient tous nus
Et pain ne voient qu'aux fenestres;
Les autres sont entrés en cloistres
De Celestins et de Chartreux,
Botés, housés, com pescheurs d'oistres.
Voyez l'estat divers d'entre eux.

Aux grans maistres Dieu doint bien faire,
Vivans en paix et en requoi;
En eux il n'y a que refaire,
Si s'en fait bon taire tout quoy.
Mais aux povres qui n'ont de quoi,
Comme moi, Dieu donne patience!
Aux autres ne faut qui ne quoi,
Car assez ont pain et pitance.

Bons vins ont, souvent embrochiés,
Sauces, brouets, et gros poissons,
Tartes, flans, oefs frits et pochiés,
Perdus et en toutes façons.

And others have become, thanks be to God, great lords and masters; other go naked, begging, and never see bread except in shop windows; others have gone into monasteries of Celestines or of Carthusians, booted and gaitered like oyster-fishers: see to what varying estates they have come!

As for those in high estate, may God grant them to do good, living in peace and quiet; in them there is nothing to amend, and it is best to say no more about them. But to the poor who have nothing to live on, like me, may God give patience; as for the rest, they want for nothing, they have bread and they have their monk's ration.

Good wines they have, often freshly broached, sauces, broth and fine fish, tarts, flans, eggs fried, poached, scrambled, and cooked in every kind of way. They are not like the masons, who have to be

Pas ne ressemblent les maçons,
Que servir faut à si grant peine:
Ils ne veulent nuls eschançons,
De soi verser chascun se peine.

En cest incident me suis mis
Qui de rien ne sert à mon fait;
Je ne suis juge, ne commis
Pour punir n'absoudre mesfait:
De tous suis le plus imparfait,
Loué soit le doux Jhesu Crist!
Que par moi leur soit satisfait!
Ce que j'ai escrit est escrit.

Laissons le moustier où il est;
Parlons de chose plus plaisante:
Ceste matiere à tous ne plaist,
Ennuyeuse est et desplaisante.
Povreté, chagrine, dolente,
Tousjours, despiteuse et rebelle,
Dit quelque parolle cuisante;
S'elle n'ose, si la pense elle.

served with so much trouble; they do not need any butlers, each one takes the trouble to pour out for himself.

I have embarked on this digression, which in no way serves my purpose; for I am neither judge nor appointed to punish or absolve crime. I am the most imperfect of all men, praise be to the sweet Jesus Christ. Let them be satisfied as far as I am concerned: what I have written is written.

So much for that! Now let us speak of something more attractive; for that subject does not please everyone, it is tiresome and unpleasant. Vexed and grieving Poverty, spiteful and rebellious, is ever apt to speak the wounding word – and if she does not speak it, still she thinks it.

Povre je suis de ma jeunesse,
De povre et de petite extrace;
Mon pere n'eut onc grant richesse,
Ne son aieul nommé Horace;
Povreté tous nous suit et trace.
Sur les tombeaux de mes ancestres,
Les ames desquels Dieu embrasse!
On n'y voit couronnes ne sceptres.

De povreté me guementant,
Souventesfois me dit le cuer:
«Homme, ne te doulouse tant
Et ne demaine tel douleur:
Se tu n'as tant qu'eut Jacques Cuer,
Mieux vaut vivre sous gros bureau
Povre, qu'avoir esté seigneur
Et pourrir sous riche tombeau.»

Qu'avoir esté seigneur! ... Que dis?
Seigneur, las! et ne l'est il mais?
Selon les davitiques dis
Son lieu ne connoistras jamais.

I have been poor from my childhood, of poor and humble origins; my father never had great riches, nor his father, who was called Horace. Poverty follows us all, and tracks us down: on the tombs of my ancestors, whose souls may God take to himself, you will see no crowns or sceptres.

When I lament my poverty, my heart often tells me: 'Do not grieve like that, man, and bewail yourself so much: if you are not so well provided as Jacques Cœur, it is better to be a poor man alive under the coarsest woollen garment than to have been a lord and lie rotting in a rich tomb.'

Than to have been a lord? What am I saying? A lord – alas! is he that no longer? According to the words of David, 'Thou shalt not find his place.' Further than that I will not venture; it would ill

Quant du surplus, je m'en desmets:
Il n'appartient à moi, pecheur;
Aux theologiens le remets,
Car c'est office de prescheur.

Si ne suis, bien le considere,
Fils d'ange portant diademe
D'estoile ne d'autre sidere.
Mon pere est mort, Dieu en ait l'ame!
Quant est du corps, il gist sous lame.
J'entens que la mere mourra,
El le set bien, la povre femme,
Et le fils pas ne demourra.

Je connois que povres et riches,
Sages et fols, prestres et lais,
Nobles, vilains, larges et chiches,
Petiz et grans, et beaux et lais,
Dames à rebrassés collets,
De quelconque condicion,
Portans atours et bourrelets,
Mort saisit sans excepcion.

become me, a sinner. I leave it to the theologians, for it is the province of a preacher.

And I am well aware that I am not the son of an angel crowned with a star or any other heavenly body. My father is dead, God save his soul. As for his body, it lies beneath the tombstone. I realize that my mother is going to die, and she, poor woman, knows it well; and her son will not stay long behind.

I know that poor and rich, wise and foolish, priests and laymen, nobles, peasants, the open-handed and the miserly, the small, the great, the handsome, and the ugly, ladies in their upturned collars, whatever their rank, whether they wear *atours** or *bourrelets*,† death takes them all without exception.

---

* Head-dress of noble women.
† Head-dress of citizens' wives.

Et meure Paris ou Helaine,
Quiconques meurt, meurt à douleur
Telle qu'il pert vent et alaine;
Son fiel se creve sur son cuer,
Puis sue, Dieu set quelle sueur!
Et n'est qui de ses maux l'alege:
Car enfant n'a, frere ne seur,
Qui lors voulsist estre son plege.

La mort le fait fremir, pallir,
Le nez courber, les veines tendre,
Le col enfler, la chair mollir,
Jointes et nerfs croistre et estendre.
Corps femenin, qui tant es tendre,
Poli, souef, si precieux,
Te faudra il ces maux attendre?
Oui, ou tout vif aller es cieux.

And even if it be Paris or Helen who is dying, whoever dies, dies in such pain that he loses air and breath; his gall bursts over his heart, and then he sweats, God knows with what a sweat, and none can relieve him of his ills, for he has neither child nor brother nor sister who would take his place.

Death makes him shiver and turn pale, curves his nose and draws tight his veins, swells out his neck and makes his flesh go limp, stretches and extends his joints and muscles. Body of woman, so tender, polished, smooth, so precious, must you, too, expect these ills? Yes, or go straight to Heaven alive.

Ballade des Dames du Temps jadis

DITES moi où, n'en quel pays
Est Flora la belle Romaine,
Archipiades, ne Thaïs,
Qui fut sa cousine germaine,
Echo, parlant quant bruit on maine
Dessus riviere ou sus estan,
Qui beauté eut trop plus qu'humaine.
Mais où sont les neiges d'antan?

Où est la tres sage Heloïs
Pour qui chastré fut et puis moine
Pierre Esbaillart à Saint Denis?
Pour son amour eut ceste essoine.
Semblablement, où est la roine
Qui commanda que Buridan
Fust jeté en un sac en Seine?
Mais où sont les neiges d'antan?

La roine Blanche comme lis
Qui chantoit à vois de seraine,
Berte au grant pié, Bietris, Alis,
Haremburgis qui tint le Maine,

Ballade of the Ladies of Days Gone by

TELL me where, or in what country, is Flora the fair Roman girl,
or Archipiades, or Thais, who was her counterpart, or Echo, reply-
ing whenever sound is made over river or pool, who had more than
human beauty. But where are last year's snows?

Where is that wisest lady Heloise, for whose sake Pierre Abelard
was first castrated, then became a monk at Saint-Denis? It was
through love that he suffered this misfortune. And where, too, is
the queen who ordered Buridan to be thrown into the Seine in a
sack? But where are last year's snows?

Queen Blanche, white as a lily, who sang with a siren's voice,
Berte of the big foot, Beatrice, Alice, Haremburgis, who ruled over

Et Jehanne la bonne Lorraine
Qu'Anglois brulerent à Rouan;
Où sont ils, où, Vierge souvraine?
Mais où sont les neiges d'antan?

Prince, n'enquerez de semaine
Où elles sont, ne de cest an,
Qu'à ce refrain ne vous remaine:
«Mais où sont les neiges d'antan?» ...

Puis que papes, rois, fils de rois
Et conceus en ventres de roines,
Sont ensevelis morts et frois,
(En autrui mains passent leurs regnes)
Moi, povre mercerot de Rennes,
Mourrai je pas? Oui, se Dieu plaist;
Mais que j'aie fait mes estrennes,
Honneste mort ne me desplaist.

Ce monde n'est perpetuel,
Quoi que pense riche pillart:
Tous sommes sous mortel coutel.
Ce confort prent povre vieillart,
Lequel d'estre plaisant raillart

Maine, and Joan the good maid of Lorraine, who was burnt by the
English at Rouen, where are they, where, oh! sovereign Virgin?
But where are last year's snows?

Prince, do not ask within the week where they are, nor within
this year, or I shall quote you this refrain: 'But where are last year's
snows?' ...

Since popes, kings, and sons of kings conceived in the womb of
queens are buried, dead and cold, and their kingdoms pass into the
hands of others, I, a poor pedlar of Rennes, shall I not die? Yes, if
it please God; provided that I have had my fling, an honourable
death is not displeasing to me.

This world is not eternal, whatever the rich extortioner may
think. Above us all is the fatal knife. That thought comforts the

Eut le bruit, lors que jeune estoit,
Qu'on tendroit à fol et paillart,
Se, vieil, à railler se mettoit.

Or lui convient il mendier,
Car à ce force le contraint.
Regrete hui sa mort et hier,
Tristesse son cuer si estraint;
Se, souvent, n'estoit Dieu qu'il craint,
Il feroit un horrible fait;
Et advient qu'en ce Dieu enfraint
Et que lui mesme se desfait.

Car s'en jeunesse il fut plaisant,
Ore plus rien ne dit qui plaise:
(Toujours vieil singe est desplaisant,
Moue ne fait qui ne desplaise).
S'il se taist, afin qu'il complaise,
Il est tenu pour fol recreu;
S'il parle, on lui dit qu'il se taise
Et qu'en son prunier n'a pas creu.

poor old man, who was renowned as a gay jester in his youth, and who would be considered both a fool and a libertine if he took to joking in his old age.

Now he must beg, for he is brought to it by necessity; he longs for death today and yesterday, sorrow so weighs upon his heart. Often, were it not for his fear of God, he would do a horrible deed, and it may happen that in this matter he trespasses against God and does away with himself.

For if he was amusing in his youth, now he can never say anything that pleases (an old monkey is always ugly, he cannot make any but an ugly face). If he hopes to win favour by keeping silent, he is considered a poor, weak fool; if he speaks, he is told to be quiet and not to behave like an idiot.

FRANÇOIS VILLON

Aussi ces povres femmelettes
Qui vieilles sont et n'ont de quoi,
Quant ils voient ces pucelettes
Emprunter elles, à requoi
Ils demandent à Dieu pourquoi
Si tost naquirent, n'à quel droit.
Nostre Seigneur se taist tout quoi,
Car au tancer il le perdroit.

La Vieille en Regrettant le Temps de sa Jeunesse
(Les Regrets de la Belle Hëaumiere)

Avis m'est que j'oi regreter
La belle qui fut hëaumiere,
Soi jeune fille souhaiter
Et parler en telle maniere:
«Ha! vieillesse felonne et fiere,
Pourquoi m'as si tost abatue?
Qui me tient, qui, que ne me fiere,
Et qu'à ce coup je ne me tue?

And these poor little women who are old and have nothing to live on, when they see the young girls supplanting them, within their hearts they ask God why they were born so soon, and by what right. Our Lord is silent and gives no reply, for if it came to a dispute He would lose.

The Old Woman's Lament for the Days of her Youth
(The Lament of the Fair Armouress)

I SEEM to hear the lamentations of the once-lovely Armouress, wishing herself a girl again, and speaking thus: 'Ah! wicked and cruel Old Age, why have you struck me down so soon? What is it, what indeed, that holds me back from striking myself and killing myself with the blow?

«Tollu m'as la haute franchise
Que beauté m'avoit ordonné
Sur clercs, marchans et gens d'Eglise:
Car lors il n'estoit homme né
Qui tout le sien ne m'eust donné,
Quoi qu'il en fust des repentailles,
Mais que lui eusse abandonné
Ce que refusent truandailles.

«A maint homme l'ai refusé,
Qui n'estoit à moi grant sagesse,
Pour l'amour d'un garçon rusé,
Auquel j'en fis grande largesse.
A qui que je feisse finesse,
Par m'ame je l'amoie bien!
Or ne me faisoit que rudesse,
Et ne m'amoit que pour le mien.

«Si ne me sut tant detrainer,
Fouler aux piez, que ne l'aimasse;
Et m'eust il fait les reins trainer,
S'il m'eust dit que je le baisasse,
Que tous mes maux je n'oubliasse.

'You have bereft me of the high command that Beauty had ordained for me over clerks, merchants, and churchmen, for in those days there was not a man born who would not have given me all that he possessed, however much he might have repented later, if only I would have yielded to him what now the very beggars refuse.

'To many a man I have refused it – and this was not great wisdom on my part – for the sake of one crafty lad to whom I gave it with the greatest freedom. Whoever else I may have cheated, upon my soul I loved him dearly, while he did nothing but ill-treat me and only loved me for my money.

'Yet however much he bullied me and trampled me underfoot, I loved him still; and if he had dragged me about on the ground, if only he asked me to kiss him, I would forget all my ills. The

Le glouton, de mal entechié,
M'embrassoit. ... J'en suis bien plus grasse!
Que m'en reste il? Honte et pechié.

«Or est il mort, passé trente ans,
Et je remains, vieille, chenue.
Quant je pense, lasse! au bon temps,
Quelle fus, quelle devenue!
Quant me regarde toute nue,
Et je me voi si tres changiee,
Povre, seche, megre, menue,
Je suis presque toute enragiee.

«Qu'est devenu ce front poli,
Cheveux blons, ces sourcils voutiz,
Grant entr'oeil, ce regart joli
Dont prenoie les plus soubtilz;
Ce beau nez droit grant ne petiz,
Ces petites jointes oreilles,
Menton fourchu, cler vis traitiz,
Et ces belles levres vermeilles?

black-hearted scoundrel would take me in his arms – and little good
it did me! What now remains for me? Only shame and sin.
 'Now he is dead – more than thirty years ago – and I am left old
and grey. Alas, when I think of the good time that was, what I was
then, and what I have become! When I look at myself all naked,
and see myself so very changed, wretched, dried up, thin, and
withered, I almost go out of my mind.
 'What has become of that smooth forehead, that fair hair, those
arched eyebrows, those well-spaced eyes, that merry glance with
which I would entrap even the most wary, that fine straight nose,
neither large nor small, those dainty little ears, that dimpled chin,
the curve of those bright cheeks, and those beautiful red lips?

«Ces gentes espaulles menues,
Ces bras longs et ces mains traitisses,
Petis tetins, hanches charnues,
Elevees, propres, faitisses
A tenir amoureuses lisses;
Ces larges reins, ce sadinet
Assis sur grosses fermes cuisses,
Dedans son petit jardinet?

«Le front ridé, les cheveux gris,
Les sourcils cheus, les yeux estains
Qui faisoient regars et ris
Dont mains marchans furent attains;
Nez courbe de beauté lointains,
Oreilles pendantes, moussues,
Le vis pali, mort et destains,
Menton froncé, levres peaussues:

«C'est d'humaine beauté l'issue!
Les bras cours et les mains contraites,
Les espaulles toutes bossues;
Mamelles, quoi? toutes retraites;

'Those lovely slender shoulders, those long arms, and those
shapely hands, small breasts, high and rounded hips, perfectly
shaped for holding jousts of love, those wide loins, that precious
treasure set over full, firm thighs within its little garden?

'Lined brow, grey hair, eyebrows all fallen out; those eyes
grown dull that used to cast glances and smiles that were the un-
doing of many a merchant, nose hooked and far from beauty, ears
pendulous and hairy, cheeks pale, lifeless, and dull, wrinkled chin,
and skinny lips:

'This is the end that human beauty comes to! Short arms,
gnarled hands, shoulders all humped. What of the breasts? all

Telles les hanches que les tetes;
Du sadinet, fi! Quant des cuisses
Cuises ne sont plus, mais cuissetes
Grivelees comme saucisses.

«Ainsi le bon temps regretons
Entre nous, povre vieilles sotes,
Assises bas, à crouppetons,
Tout en un tas comme pelotes,
A petit feu de chenevotes
Tost allumees, tost estaintes;
Et jadis fumes si mignotes!
– Ainsi en prent à mains et maintes.» …

Premier, je donne ma povre ame
A la benoite Trinité,
Et la commande à Nostre Dame,
Chambre de la Divinité,
Priant toute la charité
Des dignes neuf Ordres des cieux
Que par eux soit ce don porté
Devant le trosne precieux.

shrunk away, and the hips no better than the dugs. The treasure? ugh! As for the thighs, they are no longer worth the name, poor shrivelled things speckled like sausages.

'So we lament the good old days among ourselves, poor, silly old women, squatting on our haunches, each one hunched up like a ball, around a wretched fire of hemp-twigs, soon lit, soon dying down; and in our time we were so lovely. … But that's the way it goes with many men and women.'

First, I give my soul to the Blessed Trinity, and commend it to Our Lady, the dwelling-place of God, beseeching all the charity of the worthy nine Orders of Heaven, that this gift may be carried by them before the precious throne.

Item, mon corps j'ordonne et laisse
A nostre grant mere la terre;
Les vers n'y trouveront grant gresse,
Trop lui a fait faim dure guerre.
Or lui soit delivré grant erre:
De terre vint, en terre tourne;
Toute chose, se par trop n'erre,
Volentiers en son lieu retourne.

Item, et à mon plus que pere,
Maistre Guillaume de Villon,
Qui esté m'a plus doux que mere
A enfant levé de maillon:
Degeté m'a de maint bouillon,
Et de cestui pas ne s'esjoie,
Si lui requier à genouillon
Qu'il m'en laisse toute la joie;

Je lui donne ma librairie,
Et le Rommant du Pet au Diable,
Lequel maistre Guy Tabarie
Grossa, qui est hom veritable.

Item, I give and bequeath my body to our great mother the
earth; the worms won't find much fat on it, hunger has waged too
fierce a war against it. And let it be delivered speedily: from earth
it came, to earth let it return; everything, unless I am much mis-
taken, goes back gladly to its own place.

Item, to my more than father, Master Guillaume de Villon, who
has been more tender to me than a mother to a child just out of
swaddling-clothes; he has got me out of many a tight corner, and
is not happy about the one I am in now, and I beg him on my knees
that he will leave all the joy of it to me.

I give him my library, and the Romance of the Pet au Diable,*
which was copied by Master Guy Tabarie, who is a trustworthy

* This refers to a students' rag in which a huge stone was removed from the Hôtel du Pet au Diable.

Par cahiers est sous une table;
Combien qu'il soit rudement fait,
La matiere est si tres notable
Qu'elle amende tout le mesfait.

Item, donne à ma povre mere
Pour saluer nostre Maistresse,
(Qui pour moi eut douleur amere,
Dieu le set, et mainte tristesse),
Autre chastel n'ai, ne fortresse,
Où me retraie corps et ame,
Quant sur moi court male destresse,
Ne ma mere, la povre femme!

Ballade pour prier Nostre Dame

DAME du ciel, regente terrienne,
Emperiere des infernaux palus,
Recevez moi, vostre humble chrestienne,
Que comprise soie entre vos esleus,
Ce non obstant qu'onques rien ne valus.
Les biens de vous, ma Dame et ma Maistresse,

man. It is in quires under a table. Although it is roughly written,
the matter is so notable that it makes up for all defects.

Item, I give to my poor mother, who suffered for my sake bitter
grief, God knows, and many a sorrow, [this ballad] to offer in
praise of Our Lady; I have no other stronghold nor fortress where
I can take refuge, body and soul, when evil fortune falls upon me,
nor has my mother, poor woman.

Ballade of Prayer to Our Lady

LADY of Heaven, Sovereign over earth, empress of the infernal
swamps, receive me, your humble Christian woman, let me be
counted among your elect, for all my unworthiness. For your
goodness, my Lady and my Mistress, is far greater than all my sin-

Sont trop plus grans que ne suis pecheresse,
Sans lesquels biens ame ne peut merir
N'avoir les cieux. Je n'en suis jangleresse:
En ceste foi je vueil vivre et mourir.

A vostre Fils dites que je suis sienne;
De lui soient mes pechiés abolus;
Pardonne moi comme à l'Egipcienne,
Ou comme il fist au clerc Theophilus,
Lequel par vous fut quitte et absolus,
Combien qu'il eust au diable fait promesse.
Preservez moi de faire jamais ce,
Vierge portant, sans rompure encourir,
Le sacrement qu'on celebre à la messe:
En ceste foi je vueil vivre et mourir.

Femme je suis povrette et ancienne,
Qui rien de sai; onques lettre ne lus.
Au moustier voi dont suis paroissienne
Paradis peint, où sont harpes et lus,
Et un enfer où damnez sont boullus;
L'un me fait peur, l'autre joie et liesse.

fulness, that goodness without whose help no soul can merit
Heaven nor win it. This is no idle chatter: in this faith I desire to
live and die.

Say to your Son that I am His; by Him may my sins be swept
away; may He forgive me as He did the Egyptian woman or as He
did the clerk Theophilus, who through you was acquitted and
absolved, although he had made a compact with the Devil. Preserve me from ever doing that, oh! Virgin who bore without defile-
ment the Sacrament we celebrate at Mass. In this faith I desire to
live and die.

I am only a poor old woman, quite unlearned and unlettered. On
the walls of my parish church I see a picture of Heaven with harps
and lutes, and one of Hell where the damned are boiled. One fills
me with terror, the other with joy and gladness. Make that joy be

La joie avoir me fai, haute Deesse,
A qui pecheurs doivent tous recourir,
Comblés de foi, sans feinte ne paresse:
En ceste foi je vueil vivre et mourir.

Vous portastes, digne Vierge, princesse,
Iesus regnant qui n'a ne fin ne cesse.
Le Tout puissant, prenant nostre foiblesse,
Laissa les cieux et nous vint secourir,
Offrit à mort sa tres chiere jeunesse;
Nostre Seigneur tel est, tel le confesse:
En ceste foi je vueil vivre et mourir. ...

Item, à maistre Andry Courault,
«Les Contredis Franc Gontier» mande;
Quant du tirant seant en hault,
A cestuy la rien ne demande.
Le Sage ne veut que contende
Contre puissant povre homme las,
A fin que ses filets ne tende
Et qu'il ne trebuche en ses las.

mine, oh! high Goddess, to whom all sinners must resort, brimming with faith in all sincerity and zeal. In this faith I desire to live and die.

You bore, oh! worthy Virgin Princess, Jesus, who reigns for ever without end. The Almighty, taking on our frailty, left the Heavens and came to succour us, gave up to death His dear young life; such is Our Lord and such I acknowledge Him. In this faith I desire to live and die....

Item, to Master Andry Courault, I send 'The Reply to Honest Gontier'. As to the tyrant seated on high, of him I ask nothing: the Sage says that the poor and weary should not contend with the mighty, lest he should stretch his nets for him and the poor man should fall into his snare.

Gontier ne crains: il n'a nuls hommes,
Et mieux que moi n'est herité;
Mais en ce debat ci nous sommes
Car il loue sa povreté –
Estre povre hiver et esté;
Et à felicité repute
Ce que tiens à maleureté.
Lequel a tort? Or en dispute:

Les Contredis Franc Gontier

Sur mol duvet assis, un gras chanoine,
Lès un brasier, en chambre bien nattee,
A son costé gisant dame Sidoine,
Blanche, tendre, polie et attintee,
Boire ypocras, à jour et à nuitee,
Rire, jouer, mignonner et baisier,
Et nu à nu, pour mieux des corps s'aisier,
Les vi tous deux, par un trou de mortaise:
Lors je connus que, pour dueil appaisier,
Il n'est tresor que de vivre à son aise.

I am not afraid of Gontier: he has no men, and no better share of worldly goods than I; but we are in disagreement about one thing, for he extols his poverty – poverty winter and summer alike; and holds as happiness what I consider misfortune. Which of us is in the wrong? Now I argue thus:

The Reply to Honest Gontier

On soft down seated [I saw] a plump canon, beside a stove in a well-carpeted room, with Dame Sidoine lying by his side, white, soft, smooth, and elegant; with hippocras to drink, both day and night, laughing and playing, toying and kissing, naked together for their bodies' pleasure – I watched them through a keyhole. Then I understood that to banish sorrow there's no delight like living at your ease.

Se Franc Gontier et sa compagne Helaine
Eussent ceste douce vie hantee,
D'oignons, civots, qui causent forte alaine,
N'aconçassent une bise tostee.
Tout leur matton, ne toute leur potee,
Ne prise un ail, je le di sans noisier.
S'ils se vantent couchier sous le rosier,
Lequel vaut mieux? Lit costoyé de chaise?
Qu'en dites vous? Faut il à ce musier?
Il n'est tresor que de vivre à son aise.

De gros pain bis vivent, d'orge, d'avoine,
Et boivent eaue tout au long de l'annee.
Tous les oiseaux d'ici en Babiloine
A tel escot une seule journee
Ne me tendroient, non une matinee.
Or s'esbate, de par Dieu, Franc Gontier,
Helaine o lui, sous le bel eglantier:
Se bien leur est, cause n'ai qu'il me poise;
Mais, quoi que soit du laboureux mestier,
Il n'est tresor que de vivre à son aise.

If Honest Gontier and his mate Helen had been accustomed to
this pleasant way of life they would never have spread on their
toasted black bread onions and chives that taint the breath. For all
their curds and all their stew I would not give a straw, be it said
without offence. Though they may boast of the pleasure of lying
beneath the rose-trees, which is the better, that or a bed with a chair
beside it? What do you think? No need to hesitate: there's no delight like living at your ease.

Let them live on coarse black bread made with barley and oats,
and drink water the whole year round. All the birds from here to
Babylon would not make me accept such a diet for a single day –
no, not for a single morning! Now let Honest Gontier, for God's
sake, disport himself beneath the lovely briar, and Helen with him:
if it suits them, why should I worry? But whatever may be said for
the laborious life, there's no delight like living at your ease.

Prince, jugiez, pour tous nous accorder.
Quant est de moi, mais qu'à nul ne desplaise,
Petit enfant, j'ai ouï recorder:
Il n'est tresor que de vivre à son aise.

Épistre

Ayez pitié, ayez pitié de moi,
A tout le moins, si vous plaist, mes amis!
En fosse gis, non pas sous houx ne mai,
En cest exil ouquel je suis transmis
Par Fortune, comme Dieu l'a permis.
Filles, amans, jeunes gens et nouveaux,
Danceurs, sauteurs, faisans les piez de veaux,
Vifs comme dars, agus comme aguillon,
Gosiers tintans cler comme cascaveaux,
Le laisserez là, le povre Villon?

Chantres chantans à plaisance, sans loi,
Galans, rians, plaisans en fais et dis,
Courans, alans, francs de faux or, d'aloi,

Prince, judge between us, to bring all to agreement. As for myself, let no one take it ill, from childhood up I've always heard it
said: there's no delight like living at your ease.

Epistle

Have pity on me, I beg, have pity, you at least, my friends. I lie
in a dungeon, not beneath the holly or the may-bush, in this exile
where Fate has carried me, by God's good leave. You girls and
lovers, young men in your first freshness, dancers and jugglers
turning somersaults, as quick as darts, as sharp as a goad, with
throats that chime as clear as little bells, will you leave him there,
poor Villon?

You singers singing what you like without compulsion, ribald
and laughing, joyous in deed and word, always in movement, free
of false gold or alloy, nimble-witted if rather scatter-brained, you

Gens d'esperit, un petit estourdis,
Trop demourez, car il meurt en tandis.
Faiseurs de lais, de motets et rondeaux,
Quant mort sera, vous lui ferez chaudeaux!
Où gist, il n'entre escler ne tourbillon:
De murs espois on lui a fait bandeaux.
Le laisserez là, le povre Villon?

Venez le veoir en ce piteux arroy,
Nobles hommes, francs de quart et de dix,
Qui ne tenez d'empereur ne de roi,
Mais seulement de Dieu de Paradis:
Jeuner lui faut dimanches et mardis,
Dont les dens a plus longues que rateaux;
Après pain sec, non pas après gasteaux,
En ses boyaux verse eaue à gros bouillon;
Bas en terre, table n'a ne tresteaux.
Le laisserez là, le povre Villon?

Princes nommés, anciens, jouvenceaux,
Impetrez moi graces et royaux seaux,
Et me montez en quelque corbillon.

wait too long, for meanwhile he is dying. You makers of lays, motets, and rondeaux, he will be dead before you bring his gruel. He lies where neither lightning nor whirlwind can reach him, blindfolded by thick walls; and will you leave him there, poor Villon?

Come and see him in this piteous state, you noble men who pay neither wine-tax nor tithe, who hold your fiefs from neither king nor emperor, but only from the God of Heaven. Even Sundays and Tuesdays are fast-days for him, till his teeth have grown longer than rakes. To wash down his dry bread (not cakes!) he fills his belly with bubbling water, deep in the earth with neither table nor bench. Will you leave him there, poor Villon?

Princes aforementioned, both old and young, procure for me pardons and royal seals, and find some basket that will draw me up.

Ainsi le font, l'un à l'autre, pourceaux,
Car, où l'un brait, ils fuyent à monceaux.
Le laisserez là, le povre Villon?

L'Épitaphe Villon (*La Ballade des Pendus*)

FRERES humains qui après nous vivez,
N'ayez les cuers contre nous endurcis,
Car, se pitié de nous povres avez,
Dieu en aura plus tost de vous mercis.
Vous nous voyez ci attachés cinq, six;
Quant de la chair, que trop avons nourrie,
Elle est pieça devoree et pourrie,
Et nous, les os, devenons cendre et poudre.
De nostre mal personne ne s'en rie,
Mais priez Dieu que tous nous veuille absoudre.

Se freres vous clamons, pas n'en devez
Avoir desdain, quoi que fusmes occis
Par justice. Toutesfois, vous savez
Que tous hommes n'ont pas bon sens rassis;

Even the swine will do as much to help each other, for where one squeals they rush in crowds towards him. And will you leave him there, poor Villon?

Villon's Epitaph (*The Ballade of the Hanged*)

BROTHERS, fellow-men, you who live on after we are dead, do not harden your hearts against us. For if you feel pity for us poor wretches God will the sooner have mercy on you. You see us hanging here, five or six of us. As to the flesh we fed so well, it has long ago been devoured or rotted away, and we, the bones, are turning to dust and ashes. Let no one laugh at our sufferings, but pray God to forgive us all.

If we call you brothers, you must not be offended, although we died at the hands of the hangman; after all, you know that all men are not endowed with good judgement. Now that we are gone,

Excusez nous, puis que sommes transis,
Envers le fils de la Vierge Marie,
Que sa grace ne soit pour nous tarie,
Nous preservant de l'infernale foudre.
Nous sommes morts, ame ne nous harie;
Mais priez Dieu que tous nous veuille absoudre.

La pluie nous a debués et lavés,
Et le soleil dessechiés et noircis;
Pies, corbeaux, nous ont les yeux cavés,
Et arrachié la barbe et les sourcis.
Jamais nul temps nous ne sommes assis;
Puis ça, puis là, comme le vent varie,
A son plaisir sans cesser nous charie,
Plus becquetés d'oiseaux que dés à coudre.
Ne soiez donc de nostre confrerie;
Mais priez Dieu que tous nous veuille absoudre.

Prince Jesus, qui sur tous a maistrie,
Garde qu'Enfer n'ait de nous seigneurie;
A lui n'ayons que faire ne que soudre.
Hommes, ici n'a point de moquerie;
Mais priez Dieu que tous nous veuille absoudre.

intercede for us with the Son of the Virgin Mary, that for us the
spring of His grace may not run dry but may preserve us from the
thunderbolt of Hell. We are dead, let no one molest us, but pray
God to forgive us all.

The rain has washed and scoured us; the sun has dried and
blackened us. Magpies and crows have pecked out our eyes and
plucked our beards and eyebrows. We are never left at peace for a
moment, driven endlessly this way and that at the whim of every
changing wind. The birds have pecked at us until we are more
pitted than a thimble. Take care, then, that you never join our company, but pray God to forgive us all.

May Prince Jesus, who rules over all men, save us from the
power of Hell; may we have no dealings there and no account to
pay there. Men, here is no subject for your mirth; but pray God to
forgive us all.

CHANSONS POPULAIRES

NE renvoyez plus, mon ami,
A moi parler: venez y vous,
Car messagiers sont dangeroux.

Vostre homme fut asoir ici,
N'y renvoyez plus, mon ami:
Onques ne me parla de vous,
Mais toujours m'y pria d'amours.

Il est si beau et si joli,
N'y renvoyez plus, mon ami,
Il est vestu de cramoisi,
Et satin broché par dessous;

Si le renvoyez plus vers mi, —
N'y renvoyez plus, mon ami, —
Je prendrai lui et lairrai vous;
Car toujours m'y prie d'amours.

Si vous estiez malade au lit,
N'y renvoyez plus, mon ami,
Volentiers iroie devers vous
Pour vous montrer signe d'amours.

SEND no more, my love, to speak to me, but come yourself, for messengers are dangerous.

Your man was here last night – send no more, my love – he never mentioned you, but kept begging for my love.

He is so handsome and so gay – send no more, my love – he is clothed in crimson, with brocaded satin beneath.

If you send him to me again – send no more, my love – I shall take him and forsake you, for he keeps begging me to love him.

If you were ill in your bed – send no more, my love – I would willingly go to visit you, to give you a proof of my love.

Qui belles amours a, souvent si les remue.
L'autrier quant chevauchoie à Paris la grant rue,
Sur mon cheval moreau qui souvent saut et rue, –
(Qui belles amours a, souvent si les remue!)

Les quatre fers qu'il a font la poudre menue;
La dame du chasteau est aux creneaux venue.
«Qui est ce garçon là qui point ne me salue?»
Qui belles amours a, souvent si les remue.

«Tel garçon que je suis, ailleurs vous ai tenue,
Et dessus vostre lit ai laissé ma ceinture,
Et à vostre chevet mon espee esmoulue.»
Qui belles amours a, souvent si les remue.

If a man is in love, let him change his love often. The other day as
I rode down the high road in Paris, on my black horse which keeps
curvetting and bucking (he who is in love, let him change his love
often!), the four shoes on his feet kicked up a fine dust. The lady of
the castle came out on the battlements. 'Who is that fellow there
who gives me no greeting?' – If a man is in love, let him change his
love often.

'Fellow though I may be, I have held you elsewhere, and left my
belt on your bed and my sharp sword at your bed head.' If a man is
in love, let him change his love often.

Vrai Dieu, qu'amoureux ont de peine!
Je sai bien à quoi m'en tenir:
Au cuer me vient un souvenir
De la belle que mon cuer aime.

Je la fus veoir l'autre semaine:
«Belle, comment vous portez vous?»
«Je me porte tres bien sans vous;
A bref parler, point ne vous aime.»

Tous les bateaux qui sont sur Seine
Ne sont pas tous à un seigneur;
Aussi ne suis je pas à vous:
Qui bien vous aime y pert sa peine.

Adieu la blanche marjolaine,
Aussi la fleur de romarin,
Que j'ai cueuilli soir et matin
En attendant celle que j'aime.

Dear God! what lovers have to suffer! I know what I am saying:
a memory comes to my heart of the fair lady that I love.

I went to see her the other week: 'My lovely one, how do you
do?' 'I do very well without you; to put it shortly, I care nothing
for you.'

All the boats on the Seine are not owned by one master, nor do
I belong to you: a man who loves you truly is wasting his trouble.

Farewell to the white marjoram and to the rosemary that I have
picked both night and morning waiting for her I love.

INDEX OF FIRST LINES

INDEX OF POETS AND
ANONYMOUS WORKS

MORE ABOUT PENGUINS

Penguin Book News, which appears every month, contains details of all the new books issued by Penguins as they are published. From time to time it is supplemented by *Penguins in Print*, which is a complete list of all books published by Penguins which are in print. (There are nearly three thousand of these.)

A specimen copy of *Penguin Book News* will be sent to you free on request, and you can become a subscriber for the price of the postage – 3s. for a year's issues (including the complete lists). Just write to Dept EP, Penguin Books Ltd, Harmondsworth, Middlesex, enclosing a cheque or postal order, and your name will be added to the mailing list.

Some other books published by Penguins are described on the following pages.

Note: *Penguin Book News* and *Penguins in Print* are not available in the U.S.A. or Canada

The New Poetry

Selected and introduced by

A. ALVAREZ

'This is a personal anthology. It makes no claims to give a sample of
every kind of verse now being written in Great Britain. I am, however, trying to represent what I think is the most significant work of
the British poets who began to come into their own in the fifties. I
have also included the work of four American writers who, although
established before then, seem, as I try to explain in the Introduction,
to be concerned with problems that some of the new generation of
poets over here are beginning to face.

This is not, in short, an anthology for the reader who wants a
complete guide to the contemporary poetic scene; but then, anyone
who wants that already has a large number of excellent collections
from which to choose. In this book I am, instead, simply attempting
to give my idea of what, that really matters, has happened to poetry
in England during the last decade.' – A. Alvarez

NOT FOR SALE IN THE U.S.A.

A Short History of French Literature

GEOFFREY BRERETON

This compact history deals in outline with the whole of French literature, from the *chansons de geste* to the theatre today. While the chief works of the Middle Ages are described briefly, the great writers since the beginnings of the Renaissance receive fuller treatment, and almost half the book is devoted to the nineteenth and twentieth centuries. Over eight hundred years of rich and varied writing are treated on a scale which makes clear the great general movements of thought and taste without neglecting the characteristic qualities of individual authors and their works. These are approached primarily as literature, to be read as the personal expressions of particularly interesting minds, but they are related to the social history of their time and, on occasion, to the literature of countries other than France. The book is intended for the general reader and for the student who wishes to take his bearings before specializing in any one particular field. Based on modern scholarship and reflecting modern critical opinion, it is a concisely informative as well as a companionable work.

A Short History of Italian Literature

J. H. WHITFIELD

It is over sixty years since Richard Garnett published in 1898 the last History of Italian Literature to be written by an Englishman. The time is therefore more than ripe for this first-hand account of the whole field, from the origins and from the first great figure, Dante, through Petrarch, Machiavelli, and the Renaissance, Tasso, Leopardi, and Manzoni, down to Pirandello in our own day. In this book, synopsis and biography have been kept at bay, to give place to a reasoned and a personal account of the major authors and the major trends of Italian culture. The strength of this new *History of Italian Literature* lies especially in the fact that its author has never been afraid to tackle in his criticism the greatest authors, and the greatest problems, of the Italian tradition, and is in consequence one of the few whose views on certain major authors have made their impact in Italy itself. In this book the whole field of Italian Literature, with its unrivalled contribution to the general culture of Europe, is seen from a new standpoint. This is not only a useful and reliable manual for reference, but also a book to be read.

Penguin Modern European Poets

CAVAFY; ELYTIS; GATSOS; SEFERIS:
Selected Poems

Penguin Modern European Poets is designed to present, in verse translations, the work of significant European poets of this century for readers unfamiliar with the original languages. The series already includes Yevtushenko, Rilke, Apollinaire, Prévert, and Quasimodo.

This volume contains translations of a selection of modern Greek poetry. Of the four authors, two are established poets with international reputations, one is already well known in Greece, and one, the youngest, shows promise of achieving an international standing in time.

Yevtushenko: Selected Poems

Yevgeny Yevtushenko is the fearless spokesman of his generation in Russia. In verse that is young, fresh, and outspoken he frets at restraint and injustice, as in his now famous protest over the Jewish pogrom at Kiev.

Rilke: Selected Poems

Few writers of German poetry have exercised so great an influence on modern European literature as Rainer Maria Rilke, who died in 1926.

This edition contains J. B. Leishman's verse translations, which for so many readers in England and America were the first introduction to a European poet of acute sensitivity.

NOT FOR SALE IN THE U.S.A.

Apollinaire: Selected Poems

Guillaume Apollinaire was a friend and supporter of the Cubists. His own experimental poetic forms employ rhythms which dispense with punctuation and a style of typography derived from exercises on postcards sent from the front in the First World War. Yet he is also in France the last of the poets whose lines young people know by heart.

The Penguin Modern Poets

* NOT FOR SALE IN THE U.S.A.
† NOT FOR SALE IN THE U.S.A. OR CANADA

Penguin Modern European Poets

MIROSLAV HOLUB
SELECTED POEMS

'Miroslav Holub would like people to read poems as naturally as they read the papers, or go to a football match. Not to consider it as anything more difficult, or effeminate, or praiseworthy.' Holub, an internationally distinguished scientist, is Czechoslovakia's most lively and experimental poet. The scientist in him is always creatively present in his poems, lurking behind his restless experiments in free verse and his constant probing below the obvious surface of things. Above all he shows an unwavering sense of the realities of life.

Penguin Modern European Poets is designed to present, in verse translations, the work of significant European poets of this century for readers unfamiliar with the original languages. The series already includes Yevtushenko, Rilke, Apollinaire, Prévert, Quasimodo, and four Greek poets.